FROM
WONDER
TO
WISDOM

FROM
WONDER
TO
WISDOM

USING STORIES TO
HELP CHILDREN GROW

CHARLES A. SMITH, Ph.D.

NAL BOOKS

NEW AMERICAN LIBRARY

A DIVISION OF PENGUIN BOOKS USA INC., NEW YORK
PUBLISHED IN CANADA BY
PENGUIN BOOKS CANADA LIMITED, MARKHAM, ONTARIO

Published simultaneously in Canada by Penguin Books Canada Limited.

 NAL TRADEMARK REG. U.S. PAT. OFF. AND FOREIGN COUNTRIES
REGISTERED TRADEMARK—MARCA REGISTRADA
HECHO EN DRESDEN, TN, U.S.A.

SIGNET, SIGNET CLASSIC, MENTOR, ONYX, PLUME, MERIDIAN and
NAL BOOKS are published *in the United States* by New American Library,
a division of Penguin Books USA Inc.,
1633 Broadway, New York, New York 10019,
in Canada by Penguin Books Canada Limited,
2801 John Street, Markham, Ontario L3R 1B4

Designed by Leonard Telesca

Library of Congress Cataloging-in-Publication Data

Smith, Charles A.
  From wonder to wisdom : using stories to help children grow /
Charles A. Smith.
      p.   cm.
  Includes bibliographies and index.
  ISBN 0-453-00697-3
  1. Storytelling. 2. Children—Books and reading. I. Title.
Z718.3.S65 1989
027.62'51—dc20   89-12513
                                                              CIP

First Printing, November, 1989

1 2 3 4 5 6 7 8 9

PRINTED IN THE UNITED STATES OF AMERICA

To William Sandborn, my grandfather

Contents

CHAPTER SEVEN

From Saint George and the Dragon to The Changing Maze: Offering Kindness to Others   140

CHAPTER EIGHT

From The Emperor's New Clothes to Crow Boy: Preserving An Openness to the World   173

FROM
WONDER
TO
WISDOM

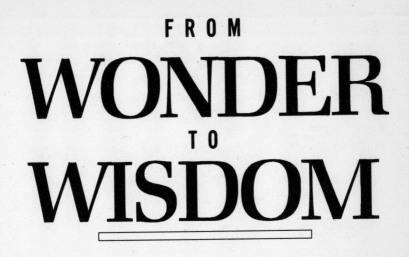

Preface

My grandpa was a storyteller. When I was about four years old he took me aside one winter evening and entertained me with a story about the "saddest" experience of his childhood. It began, he said, during an all-night vigil to spy on Santa Claus through a crack in the living room door. Wonder of wonders! Shortly after midnight, Santa emerged from the sooty fireplace carrying a large sack of gifts over his shoulder.

As he placed the presents under the gaily decorated Christmas tree, Santa noticed the little boy peeking at him from behind the door. He dropped his bag and walked to my grandpa's hiding place, probably to give him a good scolding for being up so late. Unfortunately, grandpa panicked and slammed the door on Santa's long white beard. As I listened with wide-eyed amazement he sadly described the gifts Santa left for him under the Christmas tree that morning—a rotten banana and a few cold lumps of coal. Poor grandpa!

Grandpa's stories were more than entertaining words. Storytime also consisted of bright smiles, dark frowns, and sorrowful expressions. His stories were a concert of sensory

1

images: the rhythm of a deeply resonant voice, the gestures of rough, gnarled hands, and the smell of pipe to-
bacco clinging about him like marsh mist to water. Every
story was a gift of both his presence and his imagination.
Our storytimes together were precious moments that allowed me to draw closer to a fascinating, kind man.

My grandfather's love for telling stories was more than a
simple pastime. As a young man he acquired a special
affection for nature while carrying mail and freighting
furs for the Hudson Bay Company in the Canadian north-
west. Later, after settling down in the 1930s to raise four
daughters with my grandmother, he drew from this experience when he wrote a half-hour radio program called "White
Wolf" for WMBC in Detroit. But he never saw one of his
greatest dreams come true—to have his stories published.

I have picked up the threads of my grandfather's love of
drama and woven them into the fabric of my own personal
and professional life. As a preschool teacher at Texas Tech
University I made reading aloud an important part of my
educational program for young children. To promote family storytime I invited parents of my students to check out
picture books directly from our school. To encourage greater
dialogue about the ideas in these books, I also provided
parents with a handbook for using the check-out library.
This material included topics for discussion and family
activities centered on the themes in each of these books.

Because of the success of this small-scale effort, I later
expanded the potential audience in 1978 when I joined the
Cooperative Extension Service at Kansas State University.
My colleague Carolyn Foat and I rewrote the handbook,
and I prepared leader guides for the program, now called
"Once Upon a Mind." Librarians, teachers, and parent
educators used "Once Upon a Mind" materials to introduce
parents to the idea of using stories to talk with their
children about the important things in life.

After examining thousands of children's books over the
past seventeen years, I have concluded that the messages
or concepts found in stories that affect children's self-worth

and their relationship with others can be organized into
eight primary themes:

• Becoming a goal-seeker
• Confronting challenges courageously
• Growing closer to others
• Coming to terms with loss and grief
• Offering kindness to others
• Preserving an openness to the world
• Becoming a social problem-solver
• Forming a positive self-image

From Wonder to Wisdom examines each of these themes
for their importance to young children and includes re-
views of over 250 picture books appropriate for children
from about two to eight years of age. Age ranges for each
of these books are provided in the Bibliography of Children's
Books.

Each theme chapter also includes "Butterberry Hill" stories suitable for retelling to children. For two years my
colleague Zoe Slinkman and I wrote and served as puppe-
teers for "Butterberry Hill," a monthly children's television program we created for Topeka's NBC affiliate,
KTSB-TV. "Butterberry Hill" combined elements of "Mis-
ter Roger's Neighborhood," "Kukla, Fran and Ollie," and
"Howdy Doody." It had its own "peanut gallery" of children
and grandparents who responded to the actions of puppet
characters. Butterberry Hill stories emphasized elder-child
relationships and focused on such issues as competition,
violence, love, and friendship. The short "Butterberry Hill"
stories included in *From Wonder to Wisdom* are completely
new tales based on the characters in the original television
program and the puppet "family" I used with my preschool
classes.

Family storytime is important because reading aloud
and storytelling are powerful forms of communication. Children learn from stories. If actions speak louder than words
then stories speak louder than lectures. Worthwhile stories
bring action to the imagination. Stories show characters

making choices, solving problems, and experiencing the consequences of what they do.

Stories make their points through drama. We don't have to tell children the "moral" of the story. The moral emerges through character action. Children draw from stories what they are ready to hear and understand, what is in synchrony with their hearts.

These dramatic images are more powerful in reaching a child's mind than a parent's explanations or demands. *Midnight Farm* by Susan Jeffers may calm a child's fears of the dark more effectively than direct appeals to relax and go to sleep. *The Man Who Could Call Down Owls* by Eve Bunting may impress a child more thoroughly with the consequences of the selfish abuse of power than a speech about the topic. Stories place ideas in a dramatic context that children can relate to their own experiences. The voice of the storyteller can be a whisper of encouragement, a declaration of tenderness and love, a friendly reassurance that calms a child's fears.

Young children deserve stories that are well written and beautifully illustrated. Stories written to "teach" obvious moral lessons may never find a special place on a child's bookshelf because they may be little more than disguised lectures that fail to delight and inspire their young listeners. For a story to work its magic in reaching a child's mind it must entertain, not through the front door of logic, but through the back door of intuition and feeling. *Little Red Riding Hood*'s themes of deception, honesty, and justice are more powerful than the mindless and shallow fluff that admonishes children to behave properly.

The quality books described in *From Wonder to Wisdom* were selected for review because they are good entertaining stories. But they also have something important to say to young children. They make their points with a subtle, soft touch. Like a visitor to someone's home, these stories wait to be invited into a child's mind. They do not bang loudly on the door to the child's heart and demand to be admitted.

Many people have contributed to the completion of this

work. I would like to thank Carolyn Foat and Bob Jackson for their contributions to "Once Upon a Mind." Don Reynolds, Marquita Boehnke and Marcia Ransom of the Central Kansas Library System were responsible for introducing the program in its early stages to parents and librarians throughout Kansas. Their confidence in my work has meant a lot to me. I would also like to thank all the librarians at the Manhattan, Kansas Public Library for their cheerful help with finding books over the last ten years. John Murray, head of the Department of Human Development and Family Studies at Kansas State University, has provided invaluable support. I have also benefitted from the children who listened to my stories over the years and from the many parents, teachers and librarians who attended my workshops. As Captain Kangaroo, Bob Keeshan nurtured my love of picture books and reading aloud during my early childhood. Thanks also to my agents Francesca Coltrera and Doe Coover at the Doe Coover Agency and to Alexia Dorszynski, Senior Editor at NAL, for their suggestions and encouragement. Finally, I would like to express appreciation to my family. First, to my mother for the stories she made a part of my childhood, especially those storytimes we shared in the middle of the night on the porch of our Detroit home. And second, to Betsy, Sarah, and Bill for their confidence and patience. Their support provided the encouragement I needed to complete this undertaking.

CHAPTER ONE

Stories: The Heart of Enchantment

A young girl snuggles close to her mother to hear a bedtime story. A nearby lamp casts a warm glow throughout the room, pushing away the darkness of the advancing night. Falling snow can be seen through the window, the bright white flakes illuminated by the soft glow of a corner street light. A well-worn book nestles in the thick quilt that covers the mother's and daughter's laps. Casual conversation about the day is over. Now there is only silence, a moment of anticipation before the enchantment begins.

Like a conductor of a symphony of the imagination the mother begins: "Once upon a time, in a kingdom far, far away, a young princess never laughed or sang or danced with joy. Her day was filled with frowns, her nights with tears, for she had lost what she loved the most . . ." The mother's words, uttered with deep emotion, breathe life into her story. The young girl cuddles closer. Soothed by the gentle rise and fall of her mother's voice, her mind drifts to the land of make-believe. The child listens intently now, her face transformed, her imagination given wings.

Storytime is a powerful opportunity for this mother and daughter to share a common adventure. Their minds, linked

6

by their imaginations, journey together across the dramatic landscape of the story. Together they witness a tragic loss and heart-breaking grief, a betrayal, a danger confronted, a successful rescue. For twenty minutes, time is suspended. Troubles at school, work, or home recede. While the magic of the moment rules, nothing matters but the story—will the princess ever be happy again?

We have always loved stories. From the beginning of human history, bards, wise elders, medicine men, tribal shamans and other visionaries have used stories to teach, heal, and entertain. Storytellers have often been our historians, chronicling great deeds for all to hear—a courageous stand against a terrible enemy, a victorious hunt, a journey of a thousand tears, a love rekindled. The first recorded stories were left by hunting races of the Paleolithic millennia, who created illustrations of their greatest adventures and triumphs on cave walls. Talented storytellers became important members of their cultures. African *griots,* German *minnesingers*, French *troubadours*, Norman *minstrels*, and chanting Moslem *rawis* recalled the events of their day and provided their listeners with guidance.

Many of our greatest storytellers are beloved historical figures. Aesop left us his fables, Jesus of Nazareth his parables, and Abraham Lincoln his homespun narratives. Jacob and Wilhelm Grimm collected stories told by their Hessian neighbors and gave us *Sleeping Beauty* and *Snow White*, two of our dearest fairy tales. Hans Christian Andersen created wonderful fairy stories for children, stories like *The Steadfast Tin Soldier* and *The Ugly Duckling*, that resonate with his personal longing, loneliness, and sense of injustice. Today, authors like Chris Van Allsburg carry on this tradition by creating stories like *The Polar Express* and *The Wreck of the Zephyr*, which appeal to the delightful side of our imaginations, inviting us to explore all the dimensions of our childlike sense of mystery and wonder.

Most storytellers, of course, are not so famous. The mother who eases her son's asthmatic struggle in the middle of the night with a story about a prince who wins his crown by overcoming terrible foes is an important storyteller; so is a grandmother who puts her frightened grandson to sleep with stories of kind and gentle fairies. A grandfather who delights his admiring granddaughter with mythical tales of King Arthur and Prince Valiant, a teacher who takes 15 minutes a day to read *Treasure Island* to her third-grade class, and a father who tells his daughter about his first "puppy love" are all powerful storytellers. They offer insights into life, show respect and sympathy to children's feelings, and strengthen children's sense of community and belonging. They use wonder to nurture wisdom.

We are drawn to stories because of our desire to give meaningful order to the world. We want to be more than insignificant dust motes drifting aimlessly across the face of the earth. Deep within ourselves we yearn to discover a purpose that will give a sense of direction to our lives. We want to understand the forces that affect us and find the strength to overcome the obstacles that confront us. Our lives are more like novels than dictionaries. Storytelling gives us our humanity.

Our Personal Stories

We love to hear others read or tell us stories. But we are more than just listeners. Each of us is a storyteller, too. Each of us creates a *personal story* for ourselves that dramatically redescribes our past, present, and future. Personal stories have three components: *experiences, concepts,* and *themes. Experiences* are the "facts" that happen to us. They are the people, places, and events that are a part of our history. The spanking from a second-grade teacher, a fight with a playground bully, and the adventures we had in a neighborhood park are experiences that could become part of our personal stories. Experiences are the "surface" features of stories.

Concepts are beliefs or ideas we have about ourselves and others that we use to screen and interpret experiences and to guide our behavior. "It's OK to feel angry or afraid," "Hitting hurts," and "Show affection toward others" are examples of concepts we might have for ourselves and our social world. Stories we read or tell can offer children concepts that enhance their self-esteem and strengthen their relationships with others. For example, some stories convey to children that nighttime and darkness can be peaceful (*The Midnight Farm*), that people can persevere in their efforts to reach a valued goal despite setbacks or handicaps (*The Steadfast Tin Soldier*), and that there can be tragic consequences to the abuse of power (*The Man Who Could Call Down Owls*). A participant in one of my story workshops described a newspaper report of a young grade-schooler who pulled his mother from their wrecked car and dragged her up a slight incline away from the vehicle. Unable to move herself, the mother recalled hearing her son say over and over again, as he struggled to pull her away from danger, "I think I can, I think I can, I think I can!" His experience of the accident and threat to his mother and his response to the danger were based on his interpretation of the situation, the options available to him for taking action, and how effectively he could respond. According to his mother, *The Little Engine that Could* was one of her son's favorite stories when he was a preschooler.

Themes are general, abstract principles that summarize and consolidate experiences and concepts. Themes give unity to personal stories. They are like templates that organize the concepts of a personal story into a coherent, meaningful whole. We may view our personal story as an unfolding panorama of thrilling adventures, bitter tragedies, slapstick comedies, and dangerous passages. As Shakespeare wrote in the *Merchant of Venice*: "I hold the world but as the world . . . a stage, where every man must play a part, and mine a sad one."

Eight themes in the stories we offer children are especially important for helping them grow personally and socially:

Becoming a Goal Seeker
Confronting Challenges Courageously
Growing Closer to Others

Coming to Terms with Loss and Grief
Offering Kindness to Others
Preserving an Openness to the World
Becoming a Social Problem Solver
Forming a Positive Self-Image

For young children, the dramatic concepts and themes found in stories exist everywhere and in everything. According to Swiss psychologist Jean Piaget, young children are significantly impressed by appearances, naturally investing consciousness, motivation, and personality to those things that appear to be living. Everything that seems alive has a personal story of its own. While on a walk with his father, Timothy notices leaves falling from a tree. "Look, daddy, the tree is crying! Why is he so sad?" the three-year-old asks. While strolling with her mother through the woods, three-year-old Jenny insists in a trembling voice that the bare, spindly branches swaying overhead in the wind are trying to grab her. For young children life is story.

Children often use their personal stories to communicate their impressions of the world to us. Adults, though, may consider these "stories" little more than exaggerations, distortions, or deliberate fabrications. "Don't you be telling me any *stories*, now!" a father insists to his young son. But lacking the ability to evaluate their experiences and describe them clearly to others, young children often use narrative, the language of the storyteller and poet, to convey what *feels* true to them.

After hearing a noise in his room, for example, Jamie becomes frightened, jumps out of bed, and runs crying to his mother. Between sobs he insists there is a tiger under his bed that is going to jump on him as soon as he closes his eyes. His mother knows there is no tiger. But the four-year-old's belief that a "tiger" lurks under his bed is his concept of reality at that moment. He is frightened and his words are a desperate plea for support. His story really says, "Mother, I am so scared. I hear things in my room that I can't explain. I think it sounds like scratching under my bed. Tigers scratch so maybe there is a tiger under my bed. Please protect me, Mommy!" The young boy translates his fear into a simple story that conveys his genuine interpretation of the situation. German folklorist Max Luthi would point out that though this child's story is *unreal*, it is not *untrue*.

In her book, *Children and Story: The Literary Connection*, Kay Vandergrift provides an impressive example of how children use story to express their honest perceptions of the world. A group of twenty-three third graders and two teachers stood on a street corner in New York City on a cold and rainy day, waiting for a city bus to take them on a field trip to the Museum of Natural History. An elderly lady in a black raincoat, black hat and scarf, and carrying a black umbrella approached the bus stop. She was obviously unhappy about having to wait with so many children.

She was first in line when the bus arrived and took a seat far in back. As the dripping wet and boisterous children edged around her, the old woman slowly and carefully used her umbrella to mark off a boundary around the front of her seat. "Woe be to the child who enters this space," her gesture seemed to say. The children heard the message, and no one dared to cross her imaginary boundary. Nothing else happened during the bus ride. The visit to the museum was completed without further incident.

When the children returned later that day and began to talk about the trip, a young boy interrupted the group's discussion about dinosaur bones and unusual cockroaches. He described in dramatic detail his encounter on the bus with a witch who drew a magic circle around her seat. He had almost been pushed into the circle but, knowing the terrible fate that would befall him, had just managed to save himself. When others tried to point out that the old woman was not really a witch the young boy insisted, "She was to me! I don't care what you think happened; that's what happened to me!" His story was an honest description of what he observed. He felt the woman's hostility and recognized the subtle threat of her gestures. He was frightened of her. His reference to a "witch" was the strongest and most accurate image he could think of to describe the woman.

Children use their personal stories not only to explain the past or describe the present but also to predict their future. They may, for example, tell themselves that their future is filled with happiness and success. Listen to pre-school or grade-school children talk about what they think they would like to be when they grow up. They may talk enthusiastically about becoming doctors, nurses, jet pilots, ballerinas, artists, engineers, policemen, or fire fighters. One of my kindergarten friends told me that she was going to grow up to be a "vegetarian." "Wow!" I responded, "what does a vegetarian do?" "You know," she insisted, "that's somebody who takes care of animals!" A vision for one's future, emphasizing hope and success or despair and failure, is an integral part of every person's story.

Surface and Deep Meaning in Stories

The impact of stories is easier to understand if we differentiate between surface and deep meaning. *Surface meaning* is the more obvious story line, the explicit message of the story. Surface meaning is conveyed through a literal interpretation of the story. At the surface level, for example, the child's story about a tiger under his bed is a fictional account of danger and rescue from an imaginary beast. At the surface level, the story *Sleeping Beauty* is about a knight seeking a princess who is in a deep magical sleep. To reach her he has to pass several guards and cut his way through a forest of thorns. The surface meaning of these two stories is primarily a factual description of experiences—what we first see when making a casual inspection of their content. But worthwhile stories offer much deeper pools of meaning and wisdom for our minds to explore.

Deep meaning is found in the core structure of the story—its implicit, or less obvious, messages. Deep meaning draws from the mythical dimensions of a story to touch the less conscious central concepts and themes of one's personal story. The child who tells his parents about the tiger under his bed may be conveying deep-seated fears of abandonment and making a desperate appeal for reassurance. *Sleeping Beauty* is more than a story about a beautiful princess and a gallant prince. Beneath this surface meaning the story urges its listeners to find the courage to persevere in their pursuit of valued goals. *Sleeping Beauty* is also a promise—an assurance that kind forces will help us during difficult times. At a deeper level of meaning, *Sleeping Beauty* is about life, courage, love, and sacrifice. Deep meaning is found at the story's center.

A four-year-old in my preschool class told a story that combined several familiar experiences in a wonderful blend of fantasy:

Once upon a time there was a bunny, and he wanted to be an Easter bunny. He said, "I don't know how!" But he cried, and cried, and cried. And then a mouse came, and the mouse didn't help him. And then a bee came [she makes buzz sounds], and then it flew away—he had so many things to do, and then the bees landed, and he said, "The bee flew right on!" [she yells] And then, and then, but he said, "But the bee has so many things he can do anytime." So the bunny started to cry again. [She laughs.]

And then, and then a bird stayed and it wasn't very busy so, so, the bunny went up and said . . . "I want to be an Easter Bunny!" And you know what? And then, and the bird said, "Yes, I will help you!" And then he said, first he said, "You'll have to go to the woods and find an oak tree and waltz around it three times." And next he has to put one ear up and the other ear down, then close his eyes and sing this song, "One, two, three— one, two, three, oh Easter Fairy come to me." And then you will see something.

And then he, and then he was ready. He hopped into the woods, and he hopped and ran, and ran and hopped until he bumped. . . . And then danced around it three times, and then he stopped. And then he put one ear up and the other one down and closed his eyes and sang, "One, two, three, one, two, three, oh Easter Fairy come to me." And then when he finished singing he opened his eyes and then there was the Easter Fairy. And then she said, "Baby," and then if he wouldn't cry any more, she, she'd make him an Easter Rabbit. The Easter Fairy gave him a green hat, blue coat, and a pair of red shoes. They looked very nice. That's the end!

At a deep level of meaning, Susan tells us a lot about herself in her story. At the core of her story are concepts of rejection and sadness, helping and persistence, shaped around a theme of personal transformation. Susan's story radiates hope and compassion. First the bird and then the delightful Easter Fairy come to the poor bunny's aid. With their help he reaches his dream to become the Easter Bunny. Susan's story is not just entertainment; at a deeper level it is a personal statement, revealing some of her innermost feelings and beliefs about herself and the world around her.

In *The Uses of Enchantment* psychiatrist Bruno Bettelheim examines deep meaning in fairy tales from the perspective of psychoanalytic theory.

Each fairy tale is a magic mirror which reflects some aspects of our inner world, and of the steps required by our evolution from immaturity to maturity. For those who immerse themselves in what the fairy tale has to communicate, it becomes a deep, quiet pool which at first seems to reflect only our own image, but behind it we discover the inner turmoils of our soul—its depths, and ways to gain peace within ourselves and with the world, which is the reward of our struggles (p. 309).

Deep meaning in stories touches a less conscious part of children's minds. Young children cannot discuss such abstractions as justice, honor, courage, or love. But they know what it means to be treated unfairly, to be disappointed, to be afraid, and to feel the warmth of another's affection.

Although they cannot always put these experiences into words, children long for stories that touch these deeper concerns that linger in their hearts.

Sometimes the messages conveyed by a story lie dormant in a child's mind, appearing only under the right conditions long after the story is over. During a workshop on family storytime, a parent described a conflict she had with her son, a college freshman. He wanted to come home on weekends to help with the farm work, but she wanted him to remain on campus over the weekend so he could make friends and participate in student government.

During one of their early Saturday morning arguments, her son pushed his chair from the breakfast table and declared, "But, Mother! I REMEMBER THE LITTLE RED HEN!" His sudden outburst startled her. When he was a young child *The Little Red Hen* was his favorite story. But, as far as she knew, he had not heard or talked about the story since that time.

The tale of a mother hen who insists that others share the work before benefitting from her labor had special meaning for this young man. Despite the intervening years, he could still remember its theme of fairness and responsibility. *The Little Red Hen* contributed to personal story concepts and themes that emphasized a strong work ethic and a sense of justice. These values influenced his decision to return to the farm on weekends.

What children see within the "deep, quiet pool" of a story depends on what they have experienced in their own personal struggles to make sense of the world. Children do not passively accept the deeper meaning we may see shimmering beneath the surface. The "moral" of the story from the adult's point of view may not be what a child draws from a story. We may read *Rosalie*, by Joan Hewett, for example, to emphasize the importance of recognizing the value of all living things, regardless of their age. A child who hears this story, though, might be more interested in talking about the pet dog he wants. Children recreate every story in their minds, reshaping what they see and hear into a form that makes sense to them. We cannot successfully impose story concepts and themes on children's minds. Children have to be ready and open to the idea we believe resides at our story's core.

Resonance in Stories

Children are drawn to stories that *resonate* to their own hopes and dreams, their loves and fears, their deepest emotional experiences. As children listen to such stories, the deep pool becomes a mirror bringing their own personal selves into sharper focus. Children who find themselves responding sympathetically to story characters do so because they see in them a reflection of themselves.

Jenny is four years old and afraid of the dark. When the lights are turned off at night and the sheets pulled up around her chin, Jenny listens and waits. Are those scratching sounds coming from behind the closet door? She begins to worry. Will the thing that makes those sounds leave the darkness of the closet to creep across the floor and up her bedspread? The more she thinks about it, the more frightened she becomes. Her fear is not just emotional. It is tangible . . . and it's hiding in the closet.

One evening, Jenny's dad reads Mercer Mayer's *There's Something in My Attic* to her just before bedtime. Jenny loves the story. Here is another young girl who overcomes her fear of monsters that lurk in darkness. Now Jenny thinks, "Maybe I can be brave too!" At this point in Jenny's life, *There's Something in My Attic* resonates to her needs.

Resonant stories have two special kinds of magic. In *Touch Magic: Fantasy, Faerie, and Folklore in the Literature of Childhood,* writer and critic Jane Yolen introduces the terms *Touch Magic* and *Tough Magic* to describe different types of intensity that can capture a child's imagination. Stories with *Touch Magic* gently touch a child's mind with insights about human experience. They convey important ideas without arousing intense emotions like apprehension, fear, sadness or anger. James Marshall's

"George and Martha" books, about two unusual hippo friends, are wonderful examples of stories that delight children while conveying important truths about relationships. In *The Mare on the Hill* Thomas Locker asks us to accept another's fear. In *Mother's Day Mice* Eve Bunting advises us to show love for a special person in our own unique way. Stories with Touch Magic are satisfying without being cute or cloying. They provide a relatively comfortable experience for listeners.

In contrast, stories with *Tough Magic* emphasize heroic action, risk, and sacrifice. In these stories, the hero or heroine confronts and overcomes a great obstacle or danger to reach a goal or restore order and peace. Jane Yolen believes that stories of Tough Magic

> . . . are never easy stories, nor should they be. . . . They force a confrontation with a harsher, deeper, truer reality. They ask heart—and give it in return. . . . Yet in the end, this borrowed cup of courage, this acting out in fantasy, frees the reader from the fear of failing, the fear of powerlessness, the fear of fearfulness and shame (pp. 72–73).

Young children love to hear stories of Touch Magic. They like simple and familiar stories. But sometime during their fourth year they also begin to yearn for stories that provide a greater sense of drama. Folklorist Andre Favat contends that an interest in fairy tales and other stories of great adventure emerges during the preschool years and peaks at about second or third grade. During this period of time children need stories with powerful models who deserve their admiration.

In her introduction to *Once Upon a Time*, by Max Luthi, Francis Lee Utley wrote,

> The fairy tale is a poetic vision of man and his relationship to the world—a vision that for centuries inspired the fairy tale's hearers with strength and confidence because they sensed the fundamental truth of this vision (p. 14).

Over and over again, these tales depict an upward development—rising to a great challenge, mastering mortal dangers, resolving complex problems.

Teachers and parents who shy away from stories with Tough Magic because their themes focus on danger and violence deprive children of inspirational heroes and heroines. Children experience failure and face danger so they want stories about someone who courageously perseveres despite all obstacles. They know what it means to be separated from someone or something they love, so they want to hear stories about those who have come to terms with their loss and grief.

Maurice Sendak knows that children are often frightened, that they often feel at the mercy of stronger, more dominant forces that surround them. So, in *Where the Wild Things Are*, Sendak has the young boy, Max, confront and tame the menacing Wild Things. Max takes charge and subdues the creatures to his will, just as each of us must confront the fears in our minds and, when necessary, demand that they "BE STILL!" Resonant stories tell children they are not alone.

Stories about these difficult experiences give words to children's deeper emotions. Deprived of such stories, children will look to television, movies, and comic books for the heroic figures and inspirational messages they need. Instead of Robin Hood, Prince Valiant, or Paul Bunyan, our children have Rambo, He-Man, and G.I. Joe—shallow substitutes who lack emotional depth and glorify violence.

Reading good books to children is like providing them with nutritious meals. Books with Tough Magic are high-protein stories, those with Touch Magic are vitamin-fortified. Other types of stories are like dessert. They are fun and light, without deep significance. What children need in storytime is a balanced diet with protein and vitamins and a little dessert. Each type of story has something special to offer children.

Resonant stories with Touch Magic and Tough Magic reaffirm children's experiences. But they can also draw children into the narrative, providing them with an opportunity to witness or experience for themselves what a fictional character feels and thinks. For a short while children leave the boundaries of the real world to live the events of a story.

Resonance is visible on our children's faces. We may see tears in their eyes when Hans Christian Andersen's Steadfast Tin Soldier is mistreated by his owner. They may smile and giggle when listening about friendship in James Marshall's "George and Martha" books. Or they may breathe a sigh of relief when hearing about the little boy who tames a monster in Mayer's *There's a Nightmare in My Closet*. Philosopher and storyteller C. S. Lewis wrote in *An Experiment in Criticism*, "We want to see with other eyes, to imagine with other imaginations, to feel with other hearts, as well as with our own" (p. 137).

For a few brief moments, the minds of the storyteller and listener join to create an imaginative, resonant story world suspended in time but not in space. Our children are there, next to Max when he tames the Wild Things. Their hearts beat with excitement as they flee with Peter Rabbit from Mr. McGregor's garden. They struggle with the prince through a forest of thorns to reach Sleeping Beauty. Here is the wonder-full power of enchantment—to grow rich in experience through participation in a shared story.

Storytellers are important figures in the lives of children. But who is now the most important storyteller in our children's lives? Is it a person who knows and cares about a child, who wants to share a story to enrich that child's life while growing closer to him or her? Some children are fortunate because they have a parent, grandparent, or teacher who share themselves through their stories.

Unfortunately, for many children in our high-tech society, the compassionate and responsive human storyteller has been replaced by television, the electronic storyteller. According to psychologist Jerome Singer, preschoolers watch an average of twenty-one hours of television each week; grade schoolers watch about thirty-five hours a week. So children are much more likely to sit passively in front of a television than participate in a satisfying storytime with a loving adult.

Regardless of the intentions of a program's creators, television can never respond personally to a child. A television set does not know what children hope for. It does not know about the fears that disturb their sleep or the hurt felt when the birthday invitation never arrives. A television cannot reassure children terrified of the images it thrusts before their eyes. A television cannot hug children who are on the verge of tears or calm them when they become anxious. A television gives but does not share, arouses without ever offering compassion.

Children react with strong emotions to many of the stories they see on television. But the constant stimulation of emotions by television, outside the context of a personal relationship, can gradually deaden children's feelings of tenderness toward real suffering. Exaggerations imposed by television can foster distorted concepts about life that may eventually lead to personal story themes emphasizing misery and hopelessness. Psychologists John Murray and Barbara Lonnborg report that children's television programs contain about twenty violent acts per hour. After reviewing the research, they concluded that children exposed to a steady diet of violent television programs during their elementary school years are likely to view the world as a cruel and dangerous place. They become less sensitive to the pain and suffering of others and are more likely to show a higher level of aggression as teenagers. Without a person who cares about how they feel and who can respond to them as individuals, children can become as mindless and emotionally lifeless as the technology that entertains them.

In *The Read-Aloud Handbook*, Jim Trelease points out the advantages of reading aloud over watching television. Reading encourages a longer attention span and is a social experience that encourages conversation. Much of children's television viewing is an addictive activity that stifles the imagination and provides no opportunity for asking questions. Trelease argues that television can have a pervasive, negative influence on children and family life. It can disrupt literacy and distort children's views of themselves and others.

If we are to regain our preeminence as children's storytellers, we must read and tell captivating and inspiring stories. Successful competition with television is possible only if we read and tell stories of Touch Magic and Tough Magic. Talented writers and illustrators have provided us with the tools to enrich our children's lives. But their stories are no more significant than dust if our children never hear them.

Stories are powerful tools because they confirm children's perception of the world, expand their awareness and knowledge of the human condition, involve them in experiences that deepen their sensitivity to others, and provide opportunities to express what they think and how they feel. Through storytime children also learn to expand their vocabulary and other language skills, to listen and track an idea across time, and to read.

Worthwhile stories also introduce children to life. Stories can be like windows to the world and inner experience. Through stories, children begin to make decisions about what is important and how they should behave. Storytime can be an important part of our relationship with children, one of the tools we can use to guide them to maturity.

Story Themes and Concepts

Stories that resonate to a child's moral imagination may include one or more of the following eight themes and related concepts:

Becoming a goal seeker means having a purpose, setting goals and pursuing one's dreams:

- Life is like a journey of discovery—pursue your dreams.
- Use your imagination to envision what could be.
- Set goals and commit yourself to action.

- Persevere toward your goals despite disappointment and setback.

Confronting challenges courageously means overcoming fears and learning to act decisively:

- Other people also feel afraid sometimes.
- Confront the fears created by your imagination.
- What seems threatening may not really be dangerous.
- You can overcome some fears by helping others.
- Face adversity courageously.
- Sleep peacefully; do not be afraid of the dark.

Growing closer to others refers to developing a sense of kinship with others:

- You belong to a family that loves and protects you.
- You live in a special place.
- Love means showing that you care.
- Reach out and make friends.
- Kindness wins more friends than selfishness.
- Your friends can like others and still like you.
- You may miss your friends when you are not with them.

Coming to terms with loss and grief means coping with inevitable loss:

- Everyone feels sad at times.
- You might feel sad when separated from someone you love.
- Death is an inevitable part of the cycle of life.
- Death is a permanent loss.
- Showing sadness is a way to show you care about a loss.
- Happy memories of someone we loved are a tribute to that relationship and provide us with comfort when we feel sad.
- Funerals provide us with an opportunity to say goodbye to someone we love.

Offering kindness to others refers to such altruistic skills as sharing, generosity, compassion, and helping:

- Offer comfort to someone in distress.
- Take care of someone who is sick or hurt.
- Share with others.
- Be generous.
- Offer others your assistance when help is needed.
- Protect someone who is endangered.
- Rescue others from harm.

Preserving an openness to the world emphasizes awareness and honesty:

- Use all your senses to be aware of the world around you.
- Explore and investigate the world around you.
- People may disagree about what is true.
- Gather evidence to determine the facts.
- Appearances are deceiving.
- Others may try to mislead you.
- Deception destroys trust.
- Fantasies are not necessarily deceptions.
- Not everyone will believe you when you tell the truth.

Becoming a social problem-solver emphasizes understanding consequences and identifying alternative solutions:

- Your actions are linked with the actions of others.
- Identify alternative solutions to a problem.
- Consider the consequences of what you do.

Forming a positive self-image refers to children's attitudes toward themselves:

- You are a special person with a body that is just right for you.
- You are filled with life and energy.
- You have a unique way of relating to the world that makes you special.

- You are an individual with your own likes and dislikes.
- You are growing and changing in many ways.
- We all have natural limitations on what we can do.
- You are a worthwhile person regardless of mistakes.

These eight critical themes will be examined in chapters three through ten.

We never forget stories that resonated with our dreams and feelings. Integrated into our own personal story, they will always be a part of us and our relationship with the world. Beloved stories are a part of the landscape of our childhood, a place where we can return again and again if we preserve the bridges to the childlike parts of our minds. Now, as parents or teachers, we have the opportunity to enrich our children's lives with books and stories of similar quality.

But being concerned that a story communicates something worthwhile is not enough. We should also be concerned whether it is a *good* story. The best of children's literature is good literature, only in miniature. A worthwhile picture book is like a single beautiful rose in a small vase set on a white tablecloth. The beauty of the flower is not diminished by its uncomplicated presentation. The simplicity of the arrangement adds to its drama and elegance.

CHAPTER TWO

Storytime: Making Those Moments Special

For many of us, special childhood moments include stories of delight and wonder—tales of gentle bears and kind rabbits, great heroes facing dangerous foes, mysterious forests, and majestic castles. The special stories that sparked our imaginations and stirred our souls are a part of our history, part of the heritage that shaped the way we view the world.

When we recall the stories of our childhood we may also remember being physically close, snuggling up to loved ones to feel their warmth and affection as we listened to their every word. We may remember the smell of our storytellers' perfume or cologne, the sounds of their voices, the textures of their clothes, and the expressions on their faces. Storytime is powerful because it combines an imaginary experience with loving human contact. It is a gift we can pass on to our children.

Strengthening Relationships

When children listen to a story they want a partner in the experience. Stories presented by talking teddy bears, tape recorders, or televisions are lifeless copies of the real fare. Children want someone who genuinely cares enough about them to take the time to share a story. They don't want someone to lecture them. They want someone to be their partner on their imaginative journey. What children find special about storytime is the devotion, sharing, trust, and comfort they experience in their relationship with the storyteller.

Finding time to be with our children is difficult because of the hectic nature of modern life. We know that childhood is a fleeting moment. The wonderful preschooler with unkempt hair and scraped knees will soon become a young man or woman leaving home to face the world. The early years of childhood provide us with a window of opportunity for making contact with that child, a window that we will never be able to open again once it is closed.

Storytime provides us with an opportunity to share a special moment with our children. When we read or tell a story with enthusiasm we send children a clear message: "I care so much for you that I want to give you the most precious gift I have—my time." During those moments together nothing but the story matters. Everyday distractions facing children and adults are set aside. In storytime, what really counts are being together and sharing a story. Storytime is an act of devotion.

Common enjoyment is the key to a shared experience. Parents can become involved in the drama of the story along with their children. According to C. S. Lewis, most of the great fantasies and fairy tales were not meant for children at all, but for everyone. Enjoyment of storytime depends on liberating the childlike part of ourselves, a part of our personality that has nothing to do with being "childish." Being childlike means delighting in simple things, having fun spontaneously.

Reading to our children can reawaken this childlike part of our minds. Children help us rediscover that something as simple as a good picture book can still be fun. "Tell me a story," is an invitation to journey with a child through the world of make-believe. For a few brief moments we are truly together with our children, sharing humor and sorrow, danger and deliverance along with story characters. Stories can reawaken the innocence of our childhood.

But storytime can be more than a shared experience. We can reveal our own feelings and values in the stories we share. Story characters can become a vehicle for expressing our own real emotions and values. The warmth of an older sister for her infant brother in *The Maggie B.*, by Irene Haas, may be the warmth and affection we feel for those we love. The grouchiness of the young boy in *Alexander and the Terrible, Horrible, No Good, Very Bad Day*, by Judith Viorst, may be the irritability we sometimes feel on difficult days. The sadness of the young boy who loses his precious balloon in *I Don't Care*, by Marjorie Sharmat, may be the grief we experience when we are separated from those we value most. Children can sense something powerful happening when we make our story come alive with our own real emotions.

The power of this moment, however, depends on our own willingness to risk revealing the personal part of ourselves touched by a story. If we fear sharing part of our hearts, our story may become a wall that separates instead of a window that reveals. If the words are uttered coldly, without emotion, our story is stillborn—a lifeless shell, a mask. We can allow our own authentic emotions to surface in response to story events. Our laughter, our tears are the stuff of real emotions that, once shared, draw us closer to children.

Children offer something precious to us when we read or tell them a story—their trust. If they could put their faith in us into words our children might say, "Here storyteller, take my mind on a journey; give it wings and lift it into the winds of imagination. Be my guide to places I've never been, to see wonders my eyes have never seen. I trust you. Here, take my mind."

Children want their lives to be enriched by stories, to feel their heart touched by the magic of a book. They don't want to hear shallow and boring lectures or mindless fluff disguised as stories. They want us to respond to their trust with tales of power and delight, of wonder and insight.

Storytime can provide parents and children a comfortable respite from a busy and often stressful world. The words "once upon a time" are a signal to relax. For a few moments parents and children can share each other's company and enjoy a story together. You can see children calm down as a story begins. Their breathing becomes deeper, the worry in their faces dissolves, and muscular tension dissipates. They are relaxed but attentive. As they become drawn into the story their faces may reflect sadness, anger, or fear. They are fully involved with the story's characters.

Few experiences can match storytime for its capacity to bring us closer to the children we love. Offering a story is not just something we do for our children; it is also something we do for our relationship and for ourselves. The most memorable storytime is a moment of enjoyment and wonder shared by both parents and children.

Choosing a Resonant Story

A good story is the basis for an enjoyable storytime. As you browse through a library or bookstore, look for books that have interesting stories. You might search for a story that conveys a point of view or value you would like to emphasize. For example, you might choose Astrid Lindgren's *The Tomten and the Fox* for its focus on a peaceful resolution of conflict. Or you might look for a story that responds to a problem in your child's life. For example, *Baby Brother Blues*, by Maria Polushkin, may help children overcome some of the jealousy they feel toward a younger sibling. Or you might look for a book that is just pure delight, an endearing tale with no apparent message. But in each case you are conducting a search for a special book for you and your children to enjoy together.

Choose a story with a theme that fits you and your children.

As you examine a story, consider how your children might relate to its theme. Would the story touch an important part of your children's lives? Are your children ready and willing to hear its message? Are they familiar with the subject?

A child who is saddened by the death of a loved one might benefit from the emphasis on love and compassion in *I'll Always Love You*, by Hans Wilhelm, or *Christmas Moon*, by Denys Cazet. A child who is frightened of the dark at bedtime might appreciate the peacefulness emphasized in *When I'm Sleepy*, by Jane Howard, or *Night in the Country*, by Cynthia Rylant.

Instead of responding to a specific problem in our children's lives, we may want to use storytime to emphasize an idea or value we want them to consider. We might read *I'll Always Love You* to stress the importance of telling loved ones how you really feel about them. *When I'm Sleepy* is a wonderfully relaxing story that communicates security and protection. If we feel strongly about the peaceful resolution of conflict and the risks of the abuse of power, we might read *The Man Who Could Call Down Owls*, by Eve Bunting, or *The War Party*, by William O. Steele.

Selecting a book to read to young children is a personal decision. Our enjoyment of a story depends on such factors as our own background, our personal values, and how we interpret our children's needs and preferences. We may like a book because we enjoyed it as a child or because we appreciate its point of view. Or we may choose a book because we know the theme will be of interest to our children. These reactions are like filters that color our perceptions of a book's quality.

The personal nature of our own reactions and the individual differences among children make it difficult to agree on the merits of a specific book. Some four-year-olds are ready for a story like *Sleeping Beauty*. They have had experience with complex and intense stories and can put the danger and violence into perspective. Other four-year-old children are not ready for the more elaborate imagery of fairy tales. And, regardless of their age, some children dislike stories that include danger and violence. Parents are in the best position to make an effective choice of stories for their children. General age guidelines for the books mentioned in *From Wonder to Wisdom* are provided in the Bibliography of Children's Books.

Evaluate the quality of the illustrations.

After scanning the book for its vision, examine the illustrations once again. Do they create a mood and atmosphere that complements the book's theme?

If the story emphasizes bedtime serenity and security, the pictures should be warm and uncluttered like those by Lynne Cherry in *When I'm Sleepy*. If the focus is on a courageous struggle against a powerful adversary, the pictures should be bold and dramatic like those by Michael Hague in *The Unicorn and the Lake*. Or if the emphasis is on humor, the pictures should be light and funny like those by James Marshall in *Wings: A Tale of Two Chickens*. Illustrations from each of these books are dramatically different in their artistic style. But each beautifully complements and extends the vision conveyed in their texts.

The amount of detail in the illustrations is also important. According to the Children's Book Council, toddlers enjoy brightly colored pictures of simple, familiar objects. Clear pictures with little background clutter are important because they typically carry the weight of the story for young children. At this age children "read" the story by looking at the pictures rather than paying much attention to the small amount of text. If you took away the pictures the words may not make much sense. As they grow older, children gradually become interested in increasing detail in their pictures. These more complex illustrations enrich an older preschooler's enjoyment of a story.

As you skim the book, see how one picture follows another. Do the illustrations trigger sensory images—sight, taste, touch, smell, and sound? Good illustrators of books for young children create a rewarding visual and aesthetic experience that enriches the story. They tell the story through pictures.

Evaluate the quality of the writing.

As you read the story, consider first the complexity of the text. Is the vocabulary right for your children? A small percentage of unknown words is ideal. Is the length of the story appropriate? Will your children be able to follow the story? Does it make sense?

Infants and toddlers like simple stories that contain only a few words. Older preschoolers like slightly more complex stories with simple plots. During the early school years children are attracted to plots with more sophisticated story lines and character development.

As they become more capable of following a story, children are drawn to colorful, rhythmic language. Rhythm refers to the pleasing flow of words as they are spoken—how the words sound when they are read. Good rhythm has a pleasant tempo and cadence. Read aloud the following short passage from *The Changing Maze*, by Zilpha Keatley Snyder. Hugh, the shepherd boy, has become trapped in an evil greenthorn maze while searching for his lost lamb:

> Hugh heard a bleat, and quickly turned. His lamb was lying at his feet. At first he thought it was dead, but it opened its eyes when it heard him speak. He knelt and touched its woolly head. "I'll take you home where you belong," he said . . . but then he heard the song begin.
>
> A sweetly mild and wondrous sound. Hugh raised his head and looked around. An empty room with green grass floor and greenthorn walls—no less, no more, except that now, on a high domed mound, a strange flower bloomed. It glittered golden, hummed a golden sound, perfumed the air with promises. Hugh took a long slow breath. The sweet smell breathed and called until. . .
>
> His hands outstretched, Hugh climbed the hill.

Can you feel the tempo of these words, their wonderful rhythm as you speak them? Do phrases like "touched its woolly head," "sweetly mild and wondrous sound," and "glittered golden" sound beautiful?

Words and pictures should work together to create vivid sensory images in the minds of listeners. Children should feel they are present as story events unfold. They should feel the wind in their face, smell the stinking breath of the troll under the bridge, or hear the moaning of the wind as it drifts through the trees. Good writing draws children into the action.

Children are the best critics of the stories they hear. Their judgment is not an intellectual exercise. They let us know how they feel when they ask us to read a favorite book. We can see it in their eyes as the story works its enchantment and hear it in their sighs when the story is over. "Wow, that was good. . . . Read it again, Mommy!"

The best books are those with a vision that touches a child's heart while meeting standards of excellence in writing and illustration. These "resonant" stories are *captivating* because they hold a child's attention. They are *enchanting* because they capture a child's imagination. And they are also *satisfying* because, in the span of a few minutes, a place of wonder is created, a stage is set with delightful characters, and a problem or conflict is ultimately resolved. A good story can be a gift of love.

Establishing a Worthwhile Storytime

To make your storytime enjoyable for both you and your children, choose a good time and place, identify with story characters, read or tell the story expressively, be responsive to your listeners, and make a connection between story characters and your children.

Choose a good time and place.

Proper timing and location are important elements for a satisfying storytime. Storytime will not work if the parent is busy or the children distracted by other activities. To become fully involved in a story both parents and children must be able to find the time and space that allows them to relax and enjoy their fifteen or so minutes together.

Setting aside a regular time to read or tell a story provides the basis for a satisfying ritual. Pairing storytime with such activities as bedtime or an afternoon nap can be effective because children can look forward to the story when they are just beginning to settle down. Ultimately, the best time is any time when parents want to share a story and children are willing to listen.

A dependable storytime requires a commitment by parents to set aside a portion of their time every day. A twenty-minute storytime each night seems like a reasonable amount of time, even for busy parents.

Identify with story characters.

Just before you read or tell your story, take a few moments to become familiar with story characters. View the world through their eyes. Sense the loneliness, for example, of the boy with learning problems in *Crow Boy*, by Taro Yashima, or the sadness of the young child who misses his grandfather in *December 24th*, by Denys Cazet. Experience the wonderful contentment of a child who feels loved and secure as she drifts off to sleep in *When I'm Sleepy*, by Jane Howard. Feel the wind in your hair as you sail through the air in a cardboard box with a young brother and sister in *The Gift*, by John Prater; see and hear the exotic creatures that inhabit *The Zabajaba Jungle*, by William Steig. If we can experience for ourselves what story characters feel, then we can make the story real for our children's imaginations.

Read or tell the story expressively.

As you read, use your voice, facial expressions, and body movements to illustrate the feelings and reactions of story characters. Children are affected more by your feeling for the story than by how well you read or tell it. But reading a story can be even more fun if you try to polish some of your story-reading skills.

Don Reynolds of the Central Kansas Library System

suggests these guidelines for increasing the power of your story to transport children into the world you create.

Consider the rate of your speaking. To give emphasis to some points of your story you might slow down; when the action picks up you could read a little faster. Some story characters may also speak faster or slower than others. Consider the following exchange in James Marshall's hilarious *Wings: A Tale of Two Chickens*. A fox has just arrived in a hot air balloon and is trying to lure Winnie the Chicken away from her friend Harriet:

"Care to go for a spin?" said the stranger.
"Oh, I couldn't," said Winnie.
"Oh, come on," said the stranger. "Live a little."
"Why not?" said Winnie.
And she climbed up the ladder and into the basket.
"Blast off!" cried the stranger.
"Stop! Stop!" cried Harriet.
But it was too late.

With the words "Blast off!" the tempo could speed up and then immediately stop at the words, ". . . cried Harriet." At that moment you could pause and then slowly read, "But it was too late."

Use expressive silent pauses. You can emphasize these changes in the speed of your reading with expressive silent pauses. Pausing adds drama to the story by separating ideas and giving emphasis to what follows. Brief pauses at critical points in the story also give children a momentary respite from the action and provide them with a chance to reflect on what is happening in the story.

Introduce variations in the pitch of your voice. In the preceding example, Harriet may have a high-pitched voice, while the Fox might speak with a lower pitch. The reverse might even be funnier. Changes in pitch can also denote surprise or give emphasis to a question.

Change the intensity of your voice at various points to give emphasis to story events. Intensity is the degree of strength in your voice, ranging from forceful to soft. If you are reading *Where the Wild Things Are*, for example, and you arrive at the line, ". . . till Max said, BE STILL! And he tamed them with a magic trick . . . ," the words, "BE STILL!" could be read forcefully to give emphasis to the command. Reading with force does not mean being loud. Force is the sense of energy and determination conveyed in the voice.

In contrast, a soft voice conveys serenity or wistfulness. When Patrick tells his mother, "My head is full of Grandpa," in Cazet's *December 24*, you might soften your voice a little to show how much the young boy misses his grandfather. Speaking softly does not mean whispering. You create softness by relaxing your vocal cords and smoothing the hard edges of the words.

Create "word pictures" with your voice. Word pictures sound like what they describe. For example, read the word "hot" so that it radiates heat, "cold" as if it's covered with frost. "Floating" could sound as though it is drifting, "sad" as though someone is about to cry. Picture words are fun but can be overdone. Too many can be distracting and tiresome. Employ them occasionally to help create vivid sensory images for your listeners.

Children do not expect you to be a gifted actor or actress when reading or telling a story. Changing the rate, pitch, and intensity of your speech and creating word pictures does enrich enjoyment of the story. The key is to add enough drama to make the story sparkle, but not so much as to distract listeners by calling attention to your fancy manner of speaking. The focus should always remain on the story.

Be responsive to your listeners.

Storytime can be a wonderful moment of closeness between parents and children. For this intimacy to occur, though, parents have to be aware of how their children are reacting to the story.

During storytime, parents can pause a moment to clarify a misunderstanding or confusion. They can snuggle closer to a child who is frightened or saddened by story events.

They can vary the way they are reading the story if the child's attention wanders. Storytime can be a shared moment of tenderness if parents remain aware of how their children are responding and then build on that experience to create a vivid story.

Being responsive may mean involving children in storytime. Research by Linda Leanord Lamme and Athol B. Packer on how parents and children relate to each other during storytime shows some interesting trends as children grow older. At some point between six and nine months children show interest in a book by turning its pages and making noises and gestures to accompany a story. By the end of their first year infants may become even louder and more emphatic in their responses, cooing along with the story reading, making animal sounds to accompany animals in the story, and laughing outright at funny parts of books. Many infants can turn one page at a time of a familiar story, especially if the book has cardboard pages.

During their second year, active toddlers typically dislike sitting still for long periods so, except for naptime and bedtime, short stories remain the best choice. Children at this age love to point to illustrations in a book and have the parent respond. They like to chime in on rhymes, name things and characters, or make sound effects to the story. By the end of the second year children who have listened to brief, simple stories have learned what to expect from storytime. They know that something interesting is between the covers of a book. They may have learned to count on storytime as a predictable part of their day, a time when they can relax and enjoy the story offered by their parents.

As soon as they become familiar with the story line, young children will become more actively involved in the storytime. They may spontaneously offer an example from their own experience ("I have a doggy too!"), make up some of their own words, name story events, laugh, exclaim, question the text, and put themselves into the story. They may even interject elements from another story. At this point children reestablish themselves as a contributing storytime partner.

Partnership is the key to an effective storytime. Children want to be a part of the story experience. They want to share the power of telling a story even though they cannot read. Storytime can be an invitation to children to assume the storyteller's mantle of power, to give life to ideas, to touch another person's mind.

Children will occasionally become very excited about sharing an idea associated with a story. Their imagination has wandered off the story's path and will not return until the idea or experience is shared. Reading a book like *Christmas Moon* may, for example, trigger pleasant memories about their grandparents, memories they want to share right now, not later. At these moments you might set aside the book and let them tell you about their ideas. As they talk you can refer back to the story.

When children are ready to return to the story you can pick up the thread once again. Think of a story as a river. A child's comments do not have to obstruct the flow of the story. They can be like tributaries that merge into the drama as it moves along. Your story is then given strength by these small streams of children's thoughts.

Make a connection between story characters and your children.

The importance of storytime does not have to end when you complete the story. There will be many other opportunities to contrast what happens in a story with your children's lives.

The intent is not to quiz children about what they hear but to make a parallel between child and story. If a child does something courageous, for example, you might say something like, "Doing that took a lot of courage, just like the young girl who risked her life to save a baby panda in that book, *Once There Were No Pandas*." During a conversation about a time when your child was afraid you might refer back to the little monster who was afraid of humans in *The Monster Bed.* If you are talking about love and affection you might refer to the young girl who made a special gift for her blind grandfather in *Happy Birthday, Grampie.*

You might also relate the story to your childhood. When did you act courageously? You might have stood up to a bully or spoken up for a friend who was being unjustly punished. How about the times you were afraid? Maybe you were afraid of monsters, of going home from a friend's house at night, or of being laughed at if you did something wrong in class. And how about love? Can you remember what it felt like to be "in love" when you were a young child? Sure, we call it puppy love now. But you could feel its power then, the desire to be close to someone, to have them pay attention to you and like you. Your children will enjoy hearing about these experiences and how they relate to the stories you read.

Involving children in activities related to story themes is another way to expand on storytime. Games, art activities, and visits to interesting places provide opportunities for deepening an understanding of story themes. After reading *Once There Were No Pandas* you might involve your children in making something good to eat for residents of a local nursing home. This act of kindness is in the spirit of the young girl's sacrifice in Margaret Greaves's book. Your children might make drawings of "scary things" after hearing *The Monster Bed.* After hearing *Happy Birthday, Grampie* they might make a special gift for their grandfather. Activities take the ideas treated abstractly in stories and discussions and put them into action.

Discussions and activities build bridges to stories. They allow us to reaffirm what we think are the most significant aspects of the stories we share. Used in this way, storytime is not an isolated experience cut off from the rest of children's lives. It is an integral part of their existence that illuminates their world, brings them joy, and draws them closer to the ones they love.

Every person has a yearning to be a king or queen and wear a crown of gold, to be a hero with a courageous spirit.

Within every person's heart is a secret kingdom, a store-house of dreams that lingers in the mind. Storytime gives us all permission to journey to that place of wonder.

Storybreaks

In addition to the more than 250 children's books re-viewed in *From Wonder to Wisdom,* each of the remaining eight chapters provides a few "Butterberry Hill" short sto-ries you can *tell* your children. Each simple story relates to the theme and key ideas for that chapter.

Choose a theme or idea that concerns you and find a Butterberry Hill story that relates to that concern. Read the story to yourself several times. Don't try to memorize the story word for word. When you tell the story feel free to use your own words. Embellish it with additional detail, describing, for example, the weather, clothes worn by characters, or the surrounding scenery. Paraphrase character statements. Instead of saying, "Then Grandpa Jake said. . . ." use voice changes to signal who's talking.

Choose a good time and place to tell the story—just before bedtime, while driving in a car, or while going for a walk. Reexamine "Read or Tell the Story Expressively" in chapter two for suggestions on storytelling skills. Have fun with the storytelling.

Brief Sketches of Butterberry Hill Characters

JAKE BUTTERBERRY	An elderly widower who never had any children. Lives alone but is very happy. Kind, loves children.
LUCY MERRIWETHER	An elderly widow. She and Jake are good friends. Loves to cook.
AMY	A friendly young girl. Can be a lit-tle aloof at times.

CASEY	A friendly young boy. Often feels insecure.
RODNEY	Mrs. Winterbones's nephew. Very arrogant. Can be very nasty.
LITTLE DIRTY DOROTHY	A spunky child. Likes to rough-house. Lives with her father.
MRS. WINTERBONES	The wealthiest person in Butterberry Hill. Very snobby.
FARNSWORTH	Her bumbling hired hand.
PENELOPE PIG	Very touchy about being a pig. Aspires to be a "lady."
BRIARBUTTON RABBIT	An energetic character who may not have much patience.
WITCH WART	A well-meaning witch who lives on the edge of Butterberry Hill. Her spells often backfire.
SEYMOUR CREATURE	A scary-looking but harmless character with an unknown background. Wants desperately to be accepted.

CHAPTER THREE

From Sleeping Beauty to Scuffy the Tugboat:

Becoming a Goal-Seeker

My first childhood friend was a dreamer. Bobby shared his hopes with me one afternoon while we sat on a curb and tossed stones into a gravel street. More than anything else in the world my friend wanted to own a ranch and raise horses when he grew up. How about me? Would I like to join him? This was no meaningless boast made to pass away the time on a lazy summer afternoon. No, here was serious stuff, a promise Bobby had made to himself. He described his dream secrets with warmth and enthusiasm, a vision of gentle rolling hills, lush woods, and a ranch better than anything we ever saw on television. Me too, I thought. Maybe I could have a ranch right next to his. The future! What wonderful opportunities it held for us during those warm summer days. We looked forward to a tomorrow that beckoned with the promise of success and happiness. We nursed our hopes and aspirations in the privacy of our own imaginations.

Of course, adult logic would insist that our chances of owning horse ranches were extremely poor. But focusing on the specifics of Bobby's goal overlooks the most important point about its importance. Children who have a positive vision for themselves embrace a future filled with hope. They believe in their hearts that what they aspire to will someday be within their reach, that the pledge they have made to themselves will be fulfilled.

Specific goals change as a child grows older. A pre-schooler, for example, may first insist he will be a cowboy when he grows up. During grade school he may change his mind and decide to own a ranch. As a high-schooler he might set aside this goal in favor of becoming a doctor. He might change his mind again during college and decide to become a university professor. Regardless of the specifics of the goal, what remains consistent across all ages is the child's enduring optimism and self-belief.

Psychotherapists Charlotte Buhler and Victor Frankl believe that having a meaningful purpose in life is the basis for reaching personal fulfillment. At any age, our dreams and aspirations bring meaning to life and imbue action with energy and enthusiasm. From an infant struggling to reach a toy hanging from a mobile over his crib to a nation exploring the cosmos that surrounds our planet, we are by birth goal-seekers and star-reachers.

Children bring something special to life that enables them to act with purpose. Making an effort to reach a goal is a demonstration of an inner strength, a determined spirit that resides deep within a child's personality. We see this vitality in an infant's determined effort to reach a toy hanging from a mobile, a four-year-old rocking and feeding a doll, a kindergartner building a tower of blocks. These children are not holding back and letting the world wash over them. They are moving forward to greet the world, to learn from it and change it by their own willful acts.

Without such confidence and energy, the place within children's hearts where dreams are nourished will wither and die. Children begin their lives fascinated by the banquet of experiences life has served them. But this eagerness to participate and discover can be crushed by an uncaring and unresponsive environment. Nothing is sadder than the hollow-eyed, vacant look of a child without hope, the look of one who has come to believe that the future will be a barren landscape of burned-out dreams.

What we do and say to children can make a difference. We can play an important part in a child's search for a personal dream. Parents and teachers can provide opportunities for children to experience success and gain confidence in their growing capabilities. "Look at the hole I dug, Mommy!" a preschooler shouts. Her mother responds, "Oh, Sarah, what a deep hole! You worked hard to dig that!" Her mother's response gives recognition to the child's efforts and confirms her feelings of personal power.

When we talk to children we can also convey our faith in their future. A kindergartner tells his father, "Daddy, I am going to buy you a house when I grow up!" His father responds, "That would be exciting! There are so many things you will be able to do when you grow up." These comments recognize the child's excitement about his future and the choices he will have some day. What we say is important because young children believe what we tell them.

How Stories Contribute to Goal-Seeking

Stories can affirm a child's future. Stories emphasize the importance of pursuing goals in a variety of ways. The story might focus on a character who sets a relatively simple goal and then strives to achieve it. For example, a young boy works hard to win a bike race in *Wheels*, by Jane Resh Thomas, and a young girl wants desperately to learn how to ride her bicycle but is frightened of taking a risk in *What's the Matter Sylvie, Can't You Ride?* by Karen Born Andersen.

Some stories focus on characters who have more elaborate goals, individuals who are willing to make a great journey to achieve their noble purpose. The voyage may be an exploration, as in *Where the River Begins*, by Thomas Locker; a quest for something precious, as in *The Weaving of a Dream*, by Marilee Heyer; or a dramatic rescue, as in *East of the Sun and West of the Moon*, by Mercer Mayer.

The best stories are inspirational because they tell children that success, despite adversity and self-doubt, is within their reach if they continue to persevere. Stories may introduce children to heroes and heroines who travel to a faraway land to find a precious object or carry out a dramatic rescue. Take, for example, the prince who seeks Sleeping Beauty. For one hundred years Sleeping Beauty, her family, and her subjects have been in a deep, enchanted sleep. The kind Star Faerie cast this spell to prevent the Blue Faerie from carrying out her threat of death. Sleeping Beauty and her subjects would remain in this deep, peaceful slumber until one who "loves her more than life itself" should find her and wake her with an innocent kiss.

Many years later, in a faraway land, a young prince hears of the hidden kingdom and its beautiful princess and makes a pledge to lift the enchantment. After a long and difficult journey he finally arrives outside the forest that surrounds the castle. To reach Sleeping Beauty he has to challenge a clever dwarf, make his way through a foul swamp filled with vipers and other strange and beautiful creatures, and slash his way through a forest of deadly thorns. Once inside the castle he finds Sleeping Beauty and awakens her with his kiss.

As in all fairy tales, *Sleeping Beauty* combines multiple themes: overcoming fear, taking revenge, resisting temptation, and performing a rescue, to name a few. The theme of determined purpose is central to this fairy tale. The prince has a dream—to reach Sleeping Beauty and lift the enchantment. Nothing will distract him from his goal or frighten him away. We admire him for his tenacity, his noble heart, and his willingness to make sacrifices and risk his life to reach his goal. Like the young prince, we, too, can make the choice to pursue worthy goals.

Another story of a dream pursued is the familiar tale of *Scuffy the Tugboat*, by Gertrude Crampton. Scuffy was one of the heroic characters of my childhood. "A toy store is no place for a red-painted tugboat ... I was meant for bigger things," he declares. So the man with the polka-dot tie and his son let Scuffy sail a gentle brook high in the hills. Unfortunately, the stream quickly carries Scuffy downstream away from his two friends.

At first, Scuffy is all too happy to embark on his solitary adventure. But he soon finds that the stream, then the river, and finally the sea have their dangers, too. Along the way, Scuffy encounters a curious cow, a logjam, a storm, and a crowded port. Fortunately, the man with the polka-dot tie finds Scuffy before he drifts out into the ocean and returns him safely home.

Scuffy's voyage spoke directly to my own apprehensions. Even as a preschooler I knew some day I would have to leave home and embark on my own personal journey through an uncertain and challenging world. Scuffy's daring voyage and safe return was a message of hope as I contemplated my future. Scuffy found himself in trouble because he was not truly ready to venture into the wider world. But the next time left beckoned, I knew his journey, like my own, would be successful.

Stories can encourage children to view their lives as moving toward a positive goal, a future within their reach if they work hard and maintain a worthy heart. Stories of a dream pursued convey powerful messages of anticipation children may incorporate into their personal stories:

- Life is like a journey of discovery—pursue your dreams.
- Use your imagination to envision what could be.
- Set goals and commit yourself to action.
- Persevere toward your goals despite disappointment and setback.

Life Is Like a Journey of Discovery— Pursue Your Dreams

The Journey is a powerful metaphor in stories. Life challenges us to assume the mantle of the hero and leave our home to venture into the world. Along the way, we have to pass many tests, overcome many obstacles, and face opponents who might harm us as we pursue worthy goals. At times we may feel as though we are lost in an unmerciful wilderness; at other times we may feel as though we have finally found our way home. Kind forces and benevolent companions may help us through difficult times. And each of us wants our story to have a happy ending, to complete our personal journey.

Sometimes the journey is a simple pursuit, one that satisfies a curiosity. Like Scuffy the Tugboat we want to know what is just downstream, or down the block, or over the hill. Two children are curious about what lies just over the horizon in *What Is Beyond the Hill?*, by Ernst Ekker. Does the world stop there . . . just beyond the hill?

No, the world does not stop there.
Beyond the hill, there is another hill.
And what is beyond the other hill? Does the world stop there?
Beyond the hill is another hill and another hill and still another hill. But the world does not stop there.

Children are provided with a view of an expanding world in which hills give way to mountains, and mountains to stars. The world is an immense and majestic place, beckoning children to seek what lies just over the horizon.

Two children and their grandfather seek to find the origins of a river that flows by their home in *Where the River Begins*, by Thomas Locker. Josh, Aaron, and Grandfather follow the river up to the foothills of the mountains and into a dark forest where they set up camp for the evening. The next day, they find the river's origin in a still pond, high in an upland meadow. Their search is over. On the return trip, they learn the real source of the river's power when a thunderstorm rolls through the valley. Thomas Locker's beautiful oil paintings vividly capture both the majesty of the river and its special place in nature.

Sometimes we might imagine our journey a wondrous adventure. A brother and sister, for example, embark on a fantastic journey of the imagination in *The Gift*, a wordless picture book illustrated by John Prater. The two children climb into a discarded cardboard box, which magically lifts them into the air. John Prater's bright illustrations provide a moving picture for the mind, a sense of floating and flying as the two children soar through the air in their box, chasing trucks and trains, searching the depths of the ocean for sunken treasure, and exploring a dangerous jungle. The enchanted box then returns the two young adventurers safely to their home.

Our journey may also require us to take risks, make sacrifices, and confront danger. *East of the Sun and West of the Moon*, Mercer Mayer's version of the classic Frog Prince tale, tells of a beautiful maiden's quest for self-redemption. The story begins with a journey to save her seriously ill father. So the maiden sets out for the home of South Wind to obtain a silver cup full of clear, healing water from his spring. After a long journey, she arrives at the South Wind's home but finds him gone and the spring clouded over. An enchanted frog greets her, though, and promises to clear the spring if she grants him three wishes. She agrees and returns home with the precious water.

The frog's first wish, to visit her at home, is easy for her to accept. But after seven visits, the frog makes his second wish—that she be his bride. She refuses and, in a fit of rage, kills the frog by hurling it against the wall. The frog suddenly turns into a handsome and noble youth. But because of her broken promise he is carried away by demons to wed a hideous troll princess in a kingdom "east of the sun and west of the moon."

Now the maiden begins a second perilous journey, this time to find this magical kingdom and rescue the prince. Along the way she discovers several wondrous creatures willing to help her reach her goal: The Salamander, who lives in a chamber of fire, gives her a small tinderbox; Father Forest gives her a small bow and arrow; and the Great Fish gives her one of his scales. North Wind carries her to the troll kingdom. The maiden then uses each of her gifts to free her beloved and destroy the troll princess and her family. Through perseverance and courage, she has atoned for her faithlessness and proven her true love. Mercer Mayer's illustrations have a rich depth of color that brings energy and life to this grand adventure.

Use Your Imagination to Envision What Could Be

Acting out of a sense of purpose and fulfilling a personal dream begin with the creative processes of the imagination. Imagination is the talent for seeing beyond reality to allow the mind to connect ideas in novel ways. An active imagination liberates the thought processes of the rational side of our minds. Imagination allows us to consider new possibilities, rehearse new courses of action, and see things as they could be.

In *Partners in Play: A Step-By-Step Guide to Imaginative Play in Children*, psychologists Dorothy and Jerome Singer suggest that "our human capacity to plan ahead, whether for moments, days or years, is built to a certain extent around our playful daydreams of possible events in the future and our role in them" [p. 3]. Psychologists Brian and Shirley Sutton-Smith view play as a rehearsal of possibilities. They believe that a flourishing imagination given expression in dramatic play during the first five years of life establishes the stage for a child's personal dream. The basics of the dream—self-confidence, self-worth, belief in the power to affect one's destiny—are formed during the early childhood years.

Imaginative stories keep children's minds open to possibilities. They thaw rigid ways of thinking and encourage creativity and flexibility. *The Mysteries of Harris Burdick* is a wonderful example of Chris Van Allsburg's feasts for a child's imagination. In this wordless picture book, readers are treated to fourteen mysterious pictures drawn by "Harris Burdick" to accompany a series of his short stories. Alas, these short stories have disappeared along with Mr. Burdick, and now readers are challenged to provide their own explanations for his pictures. Van Allsburg's soft, lumines-

cent illustrations will stir the deep pools of anyone's imagination, regardless of age.

Imagination allows us to leave the constraints of the
immediate moment to create a place with more exciting
challenges. *The Castle Builder*, by Dennis Nolan, illustrates how children practice mastering threats in their
imaginative play. A young boy builds a massive, elaborate
sand castle on the beach. Stepping back to admire his
creation, he imagines entering the castle, where excitement
and danger await. First, he tames a ferocious dragon. Next,
with the dragon's assistance, he drives away a fearsome
band of Black Knights. Within his castle the young boy
can exercise great power, except over the steadily advancing tide. As the sea reclaims his creation, the young boy
completes his simple fantasy of make-believe with the promise, "Tomorrow I will build an even bigger castle."

Children often feel at the mercy of powerful forces. Others are bigger than they are and often exert control over
their actions. The world may seem at times to be a threatening place filled with unexpected dangers. But in stories,
children can cast themselves in central roles of heroes
and heroines. This acting out in the imagination helps
to strengthen children's sense of personal power and
competence.

In *The Amazing Voyage of Jackie Grace*, Matt Faulkner
has crafted a delightful story of a young boy's imaginary
journey. Just as Jackie settles in for his bath, a wizened
old captain runs across the bathroom's tiled floor and jumps
into the tub. Of course, this unexpected visitor startles
Jackie.

"Hey, what's going on?"
"Sorry, laddy. There's a big blow coming in and my
crew and I are stranded. And your mom said we could
use the tub."

Two comical crew members join the others in the now-
crowded tub. Jackie insists that his visitors leave. After all,
it is his bath time. But as we turn the page we discover

that where there was once a bathroom wall, a dark and ominous storm is now rolling toward the group.

So Jackie finds himself hijacked on the high seas, tossed about by a furious storm, and then attacked by a pirate ship. While the rest of his crew cower in confusion, Jackie takes charge. Despite a ferocious attack by the pirate cannon, he dives into the water and swims to the pirate ship. In a hilarious confrontation with the captain, Jackie wins control of the helm and invites his seafaring friends aboard. The old captain then asks Jackie to join his crew. Jackie is so proud that he can even hear the wind call his name. . . . Or is that his mother calling?

In Karen Ackerman's *Song and Dance Man*, an old man uses his imagination to recreate the excitement of earlier years. Grandpa was a song and dance man who performed on the vaudeville stage. He enjoys telling his grandchildren about his past. One day, he takes them up to the attic and shows them his old costumes. He takes his gold-tipped cane, turns on the lamps to serve as spotlights, and sprinkles a little powder on the floor. Then, for a short while, before an adoring audience of three, he puts on a dazzling performance of songs, dances, and jokes. The children sit entranced, transported to the "good old days" when their grandpa was master of the old soft shoe. Stephen Gammell's charming illustrations swirl with energy and color.

The Polar Express is Chris Van Allsburg's haunting and beautifully illustrated story about a boy's continuing belief in the magic of Christmas. One Christmas Eve a mysterious train arrives in front of the young boy's house to take him and other children to the North Pole. There he is singled out by Santa Claus to receive the first gift of Christmas—a silver bell from Santa's sleigh. Unfortunately, the young boy loses his precious gift on the return trip.

On Christmas morning, though, he finds the bell under the tree. There is a note: "Found this on the seat of my sleigh. Fix that hole in your pocket." Signed, "Mr. C."

I shook the bell. It made the most beautiful sound my sister and I ever heard.

But my mother said, "Oh, that's too bad."

"Yes," said my father, "it's broken."

When I'd shaken the bell, my parents had not heard a sound.

At one time most of my friends could hear the bell, but as years passed, it fell silent for all of them. Even Sarah found one Christmas that she could no longer hear its sweet sound. Though I've grown old, the bell still rings for me as it does for all who truly believe.

The Polar Express is Van Allsburg's appeal to all of us to retain our childlike capacity for wonder. Scientific discovery has not eliminated imagination, mystery, and drama in the world. If we think these qualities are frivolous and insignificant we may unwittingly cripple our children's capacity for creating and rehearsing possibilities for the future. The creative mind that can conceive of a marvelous adventure in a cardboard box, find mystery in a single picture, or keep wonder alive as the spirit of Christmas can also see the world as it might be and then act to make that vision a reality.

Imagination complements rational thinking. A rational person without imagination is imprisoned within the confines of the immediate moment. The imaginative person without rationality lacks direction and self-discipline. Insight becomes possible only when imagination and rationality work in concert. Good judgment, originality, flexibility of thought, and problem-solving are all dependent on a healthy imagination.

Set Goals and Commit Yourself to Action

Some stories challenge children to make decisions about what is important, to take a stand and commit themselves to action. These stories show characters who have strong beliefs about right and wrong. They act decisively. They are deeply satisfied with their accomplishments because of their personal involvement in setting their goals.

Commitment is possible only if children believe their

goal belongs to them. They must "own" their goals. Little energy or enthusiasm can be brought to pursuing someone else's vision. Coercion or manipulation undermine any opportunity to draw satisfaction from success. Children have two choices when faced with this pressure—to sacrifice their own identity by pursuing the wishful fantasies of another or to reject and rebel against those expectations.

Brian McConnachie portrays a child's curiosity, resourcefulness, and determination to follow her own path in *Lilly of the Forest*. Everyone in Dun Gannon Gil Gook makes doghouses. But Lilly is tired of painting happy dog faces over their entrances. When she complains of being bored, her father makes her sit alone at the edge of the forest. She wanders off into the woods to find adventure. Lost and frightened, she begins to build a little shelter. The forest animals volunteer to help, and soon she has an enormous and beautiful home. By this time, her parents have become quite concerned about her absence and have entered the forest to search for their daughter. When they visit the "enchanted princess of the forest palace," her parents discover that Lilly is their host. Instead of returning home, they decide to remain with her in her forest home where they would ". . . never run out of interesting things to do."

Lilly is bored with her job because she has never made a personal choice to be involved in that activity. Children will admire Lilly's decision to strike out on her own. They will also appreciate Lilly's reconciliation with her parents and their decision to join her in the forest.

As they begin to think about what they might do, either in the next moment or far in the future, children gradually begin to make choices about what is important to them. In *A Father Like That*, by Charlotte Zolotow, a young boy shares his image of the ideal father. Although he has never met him, he can describe what he thinks his father would have been like if he had been a part of his life. "He'd rather go down to the store and have a Coke with me than sit around having beer with some other fathers. He'd never call me a sissy if I cried. He'd just say, 'Never mind, old fellow, you'll feel better later on.'" As we listen to his wishful longing we sense sadness and disappointment rather than anger and bitterness. His mother responds, "I'll tell you what. . . . I like the kind of father you're talking about. And in case he never comes, just remember when you grow up, you can be a father like that yourself!"

Instead of dwelling on the past, the mother shows her son that his wish reveals powerful values and talents that could become a part of his future. He does not have to depend on someone else to fulfill his dream. He can make his wish come true by becoming the kind of father he values. His mother recasts his loss as a potential strength.

Play provides children with opportunities to set goals. To young children, building a block tower or digging a hole are short-term goals worthy of their effort. *The Real Hole*, by Beverly Cleary, shows how determined a young child can be. One morning four-year-old Jimmy sets out to dig the "biggest hole in the world" in his back yard. While he digs, several family members and friends offer suggestions for what he might do with his hole. Jimmy, though, likes it just the way it is. When his father suggests they plant a tree, Jimmy agrees, for only a real tree would be appropriate for his real, grown-up hole.

Developmental changes in children's commitment to goals are affected by time and complexity. During their fourth and fifth years children gradually become more capable of engaging in independent action. They are able to dress themselves without adult supervision, brush their teeth, wash their faces, and use the toilet by themselves. They can play games with rules and solve some social conflicts on their own. During these later preschool years, children take pride in tangible accomplishments—digging a hole, building a tower, painting a picture. Such activities are important to children because of the simple planning, effort, and skill necessary to complete them and the sense of accomplishment that follows.

As they mature during their grade-school years and become more capable of reflecting on themselves and their futures, children can set goals that require more patience.

Some stories show children patiently working toward a long-term goal.

In *The Patchwork Quilt*, by Valerie Flournoy, a young girl decides to help her grandmother work on a beautiful quilt. At first Tonya can only watch in appreciation as her grandmother begins to construct the quilt from squares of scrap cloth. But when her grandmother falls ill Tonya decides to finish the project herself. With the help of her mother and the rest of the family she diligently cuts and sews until her grandmother can resume the task.

The completed masterpiece is a kaleidoscope of reds, greens, blues, and golds, blended throughout the quilt. To show appreciation for all of Tonya's hard work, her grandmother and mother give her the quilt. Tonya cherishes the quilt, not only because there is something of everyone in her family in it, but because she made the decision on her own to pick up the scissors and needle and thread and complete the project. Yes, other family members helped her along the way, but they never took control of the activity.

Some stories show children pursuing more abstract goals—to become a wonderful dancer, a skilled artist, or a loving father or mother. In *Miss Rumphius*, Barbara Cooney tells a gentle story of a young girl who shapes her destiny around her grandfather's challenge. As a young child, Miss Rumphius envisions a life similar to her grandfather's, one that will allow her to visit faraway places and live by the sea.

"That is all very well, little Alice," said her grandfather, "but there is a third thing you must do."

"What is that?" asked Alice.

"You must do something to make the world more beautiful," said her grandfather.

"All right," said Alice. But she did not know what that could be.

The young girl grows into a woman who sets out to fulfill her first two dreams of travel and life by the sea. Much later, when she is ready to settle down, Miss Rumphius accomplishes her final and most important challenge by sowing beautiful blue and purple and rose-colored flowers along the coast near where she lives. And like her grandfather before her, she passes the challenge of making the world more beautiful on to her niece.

Miss Rumphius was personally devoted to making the world more beautiful. She found her grandfather's expectation an inspiration, not a demand. She committed herself to this goal, not because she had to, but because she wanted to return something beautiful to a world that had given her so many opportunities.

Persevere Toward Your Goals Despite Disappointment and Setback

Important story characters do not just sit and think or discuss abstractions with others—they act. They may begin a long journey, rescue a pet, explore a mysterious forest, battle a giant, or help a parent with farm chores. They persist in their purpose despite obstacles and setbacks.

Hans Christian Andersen's classic tale of *The Steadfast Tin Soldier* emphasizes persistence toward a goal. This tragic tale of the little tin soldier with only one leg touches some of the deepest emotions of both parents and children. We admire his courage and his determination to return to the lovely paper ballerina. After falling out the window, he has to overcome many obstacles: the boys who sent him sailing down the gutter in a newspaper boat, the river rat who threatens him for not paying a toll, and a great fish who swallows him whole. Eventually, he does return to the home where his adventure began.

Our happiness at his reunion with the paper ballerina is soon tempered, however, by the couple's tragic end in the flames of the fireplace. Yet the brave tin soldier's determination lingers on our minds, giving us strength when we meet misfortune. Children admire the tin soldier for his courage in overcoming his limitations and meeting the challenges that test his resolve.

STORYBREAK

Amy's Effort

Once upon a time, in the wonderful town of Butterberry Hill . . .

Amy felt very sad. The boat she was trying to build had just fallen apart. "Every time I try to make something it breaks," she told herself. "I am a failure." She decided to go visit Witch Wart.

Just about at the time when Amy's boat was breaking, Witch Wart was worrying about her sister, Witch Goosebump, who lived in Pumpkin Valley. Witch Goosebump had a terrible case of the sneezes. She became afflicted with the sneezes after accidentally breathing in the fumes of a magic potion that consisted of boiled hogweed and fishfeathers. All she could do was sit in bed with a pile of tissues while she sneezed after almost every breath.

Witch Wart made her sister some special medicine to cure the sneezes but was unable to deliver it because she had too much work to do. She could hardly walk across her room, much less all the way to Pumpkin Valley. Who could deliver the medicine for her? Just at that moment, Amy knocked on her door. "Why, Amy could do it," Witch Wart thought.

Witch Wart invited Amy in and asked her to deliver the medicine to her sister Witch Goosebump in Pumpkin Valley. Amy told her, "I can't do that. I am a failure!" But Witch Wart pleaded for her help, insisting that she could do more than she thought. "Well, I will try, but don't be mad at me when I fail."

Witch Wart reached into the special "goodies" bag under her bed and gave Amy a tiny crystal snowflake, a feather, and a little silver spoon. "Here, these will help on your journey." Amy put them in her pocket and then left with the medicine.

She walked and walked and walked. "I'll never make it," she said to herself. "I am a failure." She passed Moonsweep Mountain and took a narrow path all the way through the Ominous Woods. Then she came to the Great Blue River. But the bridge was out and there was no way to cross.

"That's it. I failed!" she thought. She turned to go back, but then she remembered Witch Wart's gifts. The crystal snowflake was beginning to feel very cold in her pocket. When she took it out to look at it she could see frost beginning to form on it. Then she had an idea. She took the snowflake and threw it on the water.

As soon as the snowflake hit that water the Great Blue River instantly turned to solid ice as far as you could see. Amy carefully went down to the riverbank and looked at the frozen river. She knew that thin ice is very dangerous, and she didn't want to fall in. But the ice was so thick that she could walk across it. As soon as Amy walked across to the other side, the ice vanished and the river began to flow once again. "I've got to get to Pumpkin Valley," she thought.

Soon she came to a huge canyon. She looked for the bridge, but it had fallen in. Amy took the feather Witch Wart had given her and threw it into the air. The feather turned into a great eagle which picked her up and carried her across the canyon. As soon as the eagle set her down, it turned into dust. "I've got to get to Pumpkin Valley," she told herself. So off she went to continue her journey.

Then she came to a range of huge mountains. Pumpkin Valley was just on the other side. Amy took out the little silver spoon and threw it on the ground. . . . Nothing happened. She dug a little hole with it. . . . Nothing happened. She stuck it in the ground and sang a song to it. . . . Nothing happened. "Now I'll never get over the mountains," she said to herself. She thought she would be a failure after all.

But then she looked up at the mountain and thought, "BUT I'VE GOT TO GET TO PUMPKIN VALLEY!" So then she started to climb. She climbed and climbed, over big rocks that scratched. She slipped and caught herself. She pulled herself up and climbed again. She climbed and climbed. She was so tired. Her muscles hurt. But still she climbed. And then finally she was at the top! There below her was the little town of Pumpkin Valley.

Going down was much easier. She found Witch Goosebump's home and gave her the special medicine to cure her sneezes. Witch Goosebump was so happy! She reached under her bed for her bag of goodies. "Here," she said, "are some special gifts to help you get back to Butterberry Hill." "No thanks," said Amy. "I can get back to Butterberry Hill all by myself."

And you know what? She did.

The classic Aesop's fable, *The Hare and the Tortoise*, illustrates the rewards of sticking to a task and the risks of complacency. The hare becomes distracted by his overconfidence. But the tortoise never loses sight of his goal. "Slow and steady wins the race," Aesop tells us.

Even *The Adventures of Simple Simon*, beautifully illustrated by Chris Conover, regales children with the value of bouncing back again and again, always trying something new.

> He washed himself with polish
> And gave his face a shine.
> Then he buffed his shoes with soap
> And hung them on the line.
> He took some water in a sieve,
> But soon it all slipped through.
> And now poor Simple Simon
> Bids you all "Adieu!"

Children love to hear of Simple Simon's absurd antics. But beneath the surface of this silliness is a character who never becomes discouraged by mistakes. What delights children about this rhyme is not just the funny things Simple Simon does, but the upbeat tempo of his happy-go-lucky and persistent effort.

In *The Great Escape*, Philippe Dupasquier has crafted a delightful wordless picture book about a prisoner determined to elude his captors. Once the little man escapes from prison, the madcap chase is on. No matter where he goes or where he hides—department store, museum, or theater—his pursuers remain hot on his trail. Along the way, he takes time to return a cat to an old woman, feed an elephant, and help a frightened fox. The prisoner never gives up, regardless of how hopeless his escape might look, and neither do the police. Dupasquier's illustrations flow from top to bottom and from one page to the next with energy, wit, and intelligence.

Little Fox Goes to the End of the World, by Ann Tompert, is a charming story of a child's self-confident perseverance.

"Someday," Little Fox announces to her mother, "I'm going to travel to the end of the world." Little Fox then describes her daring and imaginative journey. Along the way she tames angry bears and frightens threatening tigers, crosses icy mountains and hot deserts, and captures the wind as she sails the open sea. Once she establishes her independence, Little Fox is quite willing to return home where her mother waits with her favorite dinner.

Two ants have to overcome repeated challenges to find their way home from a mysterious kitchen in Chris Van Allsburg's *Two Bad Ants*. At first they are a part of a group seeking the marvelous crystals in a faraway place. After a long and arduous journey they scale a huge mountain, pass through a dark tunnel, and finally discover the sparkling treasure. But the two "bad" ants become separated from the other ants when they stay to gorge themselves on the sweet crystals.

After falling asleep they are scooped up from their treasure and thrown into a boiling brown lake. One challenge after another faces them in their effort to return home: a burning dark place, a waterfall, a whirling storm, a strange force. Chris Van Allsburg offers children a totally new perspective of a familiar activity. Being caught up in the busy activities of a human fixing breakfast—making hot chocolate and fixing toast—can lead to a mysterious and challenging chain of events for two spunky ants.

On a more serious note, *Follow the Drinking Gourd*, by Jeanette Winter, shows how former slaves were willing to face danger and even death to pursue their goal of freedom by following the Underground Railroad. One of the conductors of the railroad, an old sailor named Peg Leg Joe, traveled from one plantation to another and taught the slaves an innocent folk song, "Follow the Drinking Gourd." Hidden in the lyrics, though, were instructions for reaching the railroad and following it north. We accompany one group of slaves on their dash to freedom, beginning with their flight from the plantation with a pack of dogs in close pursuit, to their trip up the Ohio River, and to their successful arrival at the Canadian border. Their journey is a vivid reminder of how inspiring a worthy goal can be.

Some stories caution children about the blind pursuit of goals. Another tale by Chris Van Allsburg, *The Wreck of the Zephyr*, tells the story of mysterious longing and frustration. At the edge of a cliff, high above the sea, a child discovers the wreck of a small sailboat. How did it get there? An old sailor tells him the story of a young boy's obsessive desire to become the greatest sailor in the world, how he discovered a place where sailboats could be made to fly, and how his impatient attempt to harness that power led to failure and bitter disappointment. Through *The Wreck of the Zephyr* Van Allsburg tell his listeners that a greedy and blind pursuit of goals may very well end in failure. Success is more likely if goals are pursued with patience and hard work.

Summary

G. K. Chesterton said, "You cannot tell a story without the idea of pursuing a purpose and sticking to a point." Stories can be an important part of our effort to convey to young minds that life can have a purpose, that every person can have a special dream to guide their actions. Yes, of course, there will be setbacks and obstacles. But these inevitable failures and distractions can make children stronger, more noble. In our hearts, each of us can be a hero determined to persevere despite the odds. To fulfill their dreams, children have to face their worst fears and approach life courageously. We will turn to this issue in the next chapter.

CHAPTER FOUR

From The Little Engine That Could to Where the Wild Things Are:

Confronting Challenges Courageously

Most of us can remember what it meant to be afraid during our childhood. Terrifying images of a vivid nightmare, the menacing glare of a neighborhood bully, creepy spiders and sticky cobwebs in a basement cellar, and other frightening experiences passed relentlessly through the landscape of our childhood. We may set these memories aside in the far recesses of our minds, but we never truly forget them. Deep down, part of us will always remain the young child, trembling upon hearing distant thunder or frightened of what may be hiding under our bed. Authors like Stephen King understand our fascination for the fears of our childhood and know their power over our imaginations.

Fear can cripple action, but it can also provide opportunities for courage. Even when we felt the most helpless we may have sensed the faint beginnings of courage growing within. We didn't always run away. There were moments when we were determined to stand firm against the threat. We calmed ourselves after a nightmare, refused to run when a bully approached, or descended into the cellar to get a can of peaches. These little acts of bravery occurred suddenly, sometimes taking us by surprise.

These moments provided us with a hint of our true nature, one that is truly noble, strong, heroic. The adults who surrounded us may have been unaware of our little heroisms. And our own fears may have cast doubt on this inner strength. "Deep down, you are really a coward," we may have told ourselves. This fear of weakness is an illusion that masks a true capacity for heroism. Fear is not the enemy, for it makes courage possible. The challenge is to act despite fear.

How Stories Contribute to Overcoming Fear and Acting Courageously

Sometimes the characters in stories we read or hear provided us with models for courage. I loved *The Little Engine That Could* when I was a child. The Little Engine believed in himself and persevered despite the obstacle of the hill and the ridicule of others. Yes, he proclaimed, "I think I can; I think I can; I THINK I CAN!" I found this message inspirational, especially during asthma attacks in the middle of the night, when every breath was an act of quiet determination. The Little Engine had to carry supplies up a steep hill; my challenge was to sustain a fragile hold on life. During the worst attacks I, too, might tell myself, "Keep on going; don't give up . . . take one more breath. I can make it. I THINK I CAN!" And I did.

All children have to face and confront fear. Every child longs to be like Max in Maurice Sendak's *Where the Wild Things Are*. After being sent to bed without his supper Max imagines a journey to the land where the Wild Things are. There the Wild Things challenge him by roaring their terrible roars, gnashing their terrible teeth, and rolling their terrible eyes. Max does not run away. Instead, in a loud, firm voice he commands, "BE STILL!" He then tames them

. . . with a magic trick of staring into all their yellow eyes without blinking once and they were frightened and called him the most wild thing of all. . . .

Max inspires children. Like Max, all children have to confront fear and its whispers of discouragement and doom in the land of their own Wild Things—the arena of their minds. To these fears they must also insist, "BE STILL!"

Parents may worry that books with dragons, witches, giants, and other frightening creatures will scare their children and make them have nightmares. Some children are frightened of such stories. But others hunger for heroes who overcome such foes. The defeat of frightening images in a story context may provide them with encouragement to face their own fears. When they applaud the knight's daring they may be cheering themselves.

Children love stories with nasty, threatening, ugly creatures because they also love heroes and their deeds of courage. Portraying something negative allows us to more clearly emphasize the positive. How can we emphasize courageous action if the forces opposing story characters are not convincingly dangerous? If we dilute our stories with weak characters, we also rob our children of the opportunity to witness great courage and heroic effort.

Heroes can help children work through their real fears. Their efforts to overcome an obstacle or vanquish a threat provides children with a model for confronting their own apprehensions, both in their imagination and in reality. For example, a child who is terrified by the dog chained in a neighbor's back yard may be attracted to *Where the Wild Things Are, Peter and the Wolf,* or any other of many well-known stories that focus on a young person overcoming a threat. Successful outcomes in these stories are reassuring because they send the message that determination and intelligence can successfully oppose danger.

Stories can discipline imaginary surrogates for a child's most terrifying fears. Within the landscape of a story, heroes confront dragons, giants, and witches, expose their cruel nature, and soundly defeat them. Monsters are brought out of the closet or from under the bed and confronted. Light is cast upon darkness, pushing the shadows away. When you finish such a story with the words ". . . the end," the child's response is a noticeable sigh of relief. Now she can rest easy. The defeat of one fear on an imaginary plane can hold out hope for the defeat of another in the waking world.

Andre Favat points out that dangerous story elements like stinking trolls under bridges, deadly witches, and terrible battles between knights and dragons are far removed from our lives in terms of both time and place and are less frightening for those children able to differentiate between fantasy and reality. On the other hand, stories that capitalize on children's real fears by telling *realistic* stories of danger may be much more frightening than any fairy tale. A child may be terrified by a story about the kidnapping of a real little girl because the story comes too close to reality. The evening news or violent television programs may present more horrifying possibilities than traditional fairy tales. Unless they are being warned of a specific realistic danger, children are better off if they hear stories of witches, dragons, and giants than of burglars, child molesters, and kidnappers. With the words, "Once upon a time . . ." children know they can enjoy the story without being reminded of danger waiting outside their front doors.

Age has a significant effect on how children react to scary images. Stories of foul trolls and sinister witches may confuse and frighten three-year-olds, who are likely to confuse fantasy and reality. In contrast, most five-year-olds have a much better grasp of the nature of the world around them and can enjoy the thrill of conflict between witches and princesses, monsters and brave little boys and girls. They are frequent visitors to the land of imagination and know its boundaries. Also, the more intelligent a child, the faster she will be able to recognize real dangers and distinguish them from imaginary threats.

Temperament can also have an effect on how children react to scary stories. Some children recoil from any kind of violence. They withdraw when emotions around them become intense. They worry about story characters who encounter conflict and threat. Children with such sensitive temperaments may recoil from fairy tales with strong images. Yet timid children often have the most to gain from hearing such stories. A gradual introduction to stories of Tough Magic may be the best strategy for impressionable children who are distressed by tales of danger and conflict.

The *setting* for the story is a third critical factor in the potential impact that frightening story images make on children. Stories of Tough Magic, with characters risking their lives as they oppose dangerous foes, may be too intense for children who are drifting off to sleep. The dark shadows of witches, giants, and fiery dragons may linger on the edges of a child's mind and then take shape as disturbing nightmares that push more peaceful dreams aside. At bedtime, gentle stories with peaceful images are best. Stories of great heroes and fearsome creatures are better if left to the brighter light of day.

Stories help children cope with fear in at least three ways. First, stories can show children that they are not alone with their fears. Sometimes the worst fear may seem so terrible that it cannot be put into words. Stories can bring such fears out into the open so they can be acknowledged and discussed. Stories show children that fear is a universal response to danger.

Second, stories provide opportunities for parents and children to talk about fear. As they discuss a story with their children, parents might describe some of the fears they had when they were children and how they learned to overcome or live with them. Stories might also prompt spontaneous comments from children about their fears. While listening to *There's a Nightmare in My Closet*, for example, children may identify a recent nightmare that frightened them.

And third, stories show characters who respond positively to their fears. When they are frightened, children feel confused and powerless to act. Stories show characters who are able to calm themselves and have the presence of mind to take action to resolve a problem. Children might gain some insight into their fear, learn how to avoid danger, or stand up to a threat when necessary. Stories suggest to children that they are capable of acting courageously, too.

Many good stories for children place emphasis on the theme "Face Fear and Act Courageously." These stories convey powerful messages of hope and determination:

- Other people also feel afraid sometimes.
- Confront the fears created by your imagination.
- What seems threatening may not really be dangerous.
- You can overcome some fears by helping others.
- Face adversity courageously.
- Sleep peacefully—do not be afraid of the dark.

In many stories heroic characters have to face a terrible danger and overcome great obstacles to reach their goal and gain their just reward. Children find encouragement in these stories. As they listen, again and again, they will gradually find that these underlying messages of confidence and hope have become a part of their personal stories.

We hope our children will learn to become risk-takers who gradually move from dependence to self-reliance as they grow older. We know that the ability to understand danger and to protect oneself contributes to a child's survival. But fear should be a wise servant, guiding sensible reactions, rather than a master that dominates and bullies. The courage to face inevitable hardship is necessary for a satisfying life.

Other People Also Feel Afraid Sometimes

All children are afraid at one time or another as they grow up. They are insecure because there are so many unknowns in their lives. Real or imagined dangers lurk in every shadow, lie in ambush around every corner. Many of these fears protect our children from danger: Children who hear ice cracking as they walk across a frozen pond, or meet a stranger who tries to lure them into a car *should* feel afraid. The physical arousal of fear can be a positive force since it provides the energy to escape threat and avoid unnecessary risks. Fear is like the ringing of an internal alarm that warns of danger.

Fear is also a core emotion that underlies other strong feelings like anger, jealousy, and sadness. Think of emotions as the layered skins on an onion. Each level can be "peeled" away to show another feeling that lies beneath it. For example, a child might hit her brother because she is afraid that he will ruin the tower she is building. Another preschooler cries when his mother leaves him at the babysitter because he fears being left with a stranger.

Infants are frightened by direct experience with unusual events—loud noises, the sensation of falling, sudden movements, flashes of light, people or objects associated with pain, and strange people, things, or situations. Between two and four years of age, children begin to associate some things with frightening experiences. They may, for example, become afraid of heights after falling down steps, fear separation from parents after becoming lost in a supermarket, or avoid furry animals after being pushed down by a dog. Young children are frightened because of specific experiences they have.

Older children's fears often begin with apprehension about death or separation. Preschoolers and young grade-school children tend to view death as a punishment for wrongdoing. They may even believe they will die or their parents will leave them because of their misbehavior. Instead of recognizing and expressing such apprehension, children show their fear of death and abandonment as imagined threats from bogeymen who hide in the dusty caverns under beds, or in play that emphasizes themes of destruction and death.

Some stories reassure children by pointing out that fear is a normal reaction to a perception of threat. They tell children they are not alone—everyone feels frightened of something. They need not be ashamed of their fear. They can talk about their fears without worrying that such acknowledgment will make them worse or lead to ridicule. *A Book of Scary Things* identifies many common childhood fears: spiders, diving boards, monsters under the bed, and the wind going "Ooooooooooo." All these things can be scary, some of them even to adults.

> My mother is a rather brave woman. She isn't afraid of cows. She doesn't get scared when she finds a mouse in the kitchen.
> But a little snake in the garden can scare her.
> My father is brave too. He isn't afraid of hornets or a fire in the oven. But he's afraid to go high up on a ladder.

Author Paul Showers demystifies many of these fears with reassuring information and suggestions for how to respond safely. Children and their parents can look and laugh about some of their fears, and see that sometimes it's even good to be afraid.

Even the brave old woman in *The Little Old Lady Who Was Not Afraid of Anything*, by Linda Williams, was startled by the sudden appearance of a strange creature. While on a walk in the forest to collect herbs and spices she is followed by a pair of animated shoes. The shoes are joined by a pair of pants, a shirt, two white gloves, and a hat. To each of these things she demands, "Get out of my way. . . . I'm not afraid of you." But when a very large, very orange, very scary pumpkin head appears, the little old lady runs home as fast as she can.

A moment later she answers a knock at her door. But by now the little old lady has regained her courage:

> "I'm not afraid of you," said the little old lady bravely. "What do you want anyway?"
> "We have come to scare you!"
> "You can't scare *me*," said the little old lady.
> "Then what's to become of us?" The pumpkin head suddenly looked unhappy.

The little old lady arrives at a perfect solution by suggesting that the animated clothes become a scarecrow in her

garden. The sounds each of the clothes make as they follow
the old woman tend to heighten the spookiness of the
story. But a satisfying and humorous conclusion is likely
to defuse the tension built up in the previous pages.

A turtle can be quite unhappy if he is afraid of the dark
inside his own shell. *Franklin in the Dark*, by Paulette
Bourgeois, introduces listeners to Franklin's special dilemma. Every night, his mother shines a flashlight into
his shell. But Franklin is still afraid. So he goes looking
for help. A duck frightened of deep water offers him water
wings. A lion frightened of loud sounds offers him his
earmuffs. A bird frightened of high flying offers him a
parachute. But Franklin is not afraid of water, loud sounds,
or heights. When he returns home, he tells his mother
about the other animals and their fears. "Oh," she said.
"They were all afraid of something." Later that night . . .

Franklin's mother gave him a cold supper and a warm
hug. And then she sent him off to bed.

"Good night, dear," she said.

Well, Franklin knew what he had to do. He crawled
right inside his small, dark shell. He was sure he saw
creepy things, slippery things, and a monster. But he
said a brave "Good night."

And then, when nobody was looking, Franklin the
turtle turned on his night light.

Franklin puts his fear into better perspective after listening
to others describe their own apprehensions. He can face
the dark because he feels less alone. His mother never
belittles his fears. Her calm and patient support shows
assurance that her son will master his fear in his own time
and way.

Will It Be Okay?, by Crescent Dragonwagon, provides
children with a glimpse of a young girl expressing her
fears and finding reassurance from her mother. The young
girl identifies a worry and her mother counters with a
soothing answer.

"But what if snakes come in the night?"

"You keep a flute by your bed and play a song, and the snakes hear, and are quiet, and happy, and love you."

Again, and again, the child responds to the mother's encouragement with ". . . but what if . . . ?" Big dogs, thunder, lightning, being hated, and bees provide good reason to worry. As the child shares her worries with her mother she is also taking the children who hear the story into her confidence. Many of their fears will be similar to the concerns she expresses. Her mother's patient and reassuring answers will strengthen their own sense of security in the world.

Children who worry about separation will appreciate *Left Behind*, by Carol and Donald Carrick. Christopher is separated from others in his grade-school class during a subway trip. Despite his initial panic and helplessness, he is able to calm himself and find a policeman. The policeman takes him to his station, where his coworkers try to find his teacher. Now Christopher has a new set of worries. Will Mrs. Snow be angry with him? Would the other kids think he is dumb? But these fears vanish when she arrives.

> He was glad to see her even if she might be angry. "I was scared you'd never find me," he said.
> Mrs. Snow looked relieved. "I was scared, too."

Children will be reassured by the help Christopher receives from the policemen. When they are frightened there will be someone they can reach out to for help—a parent, teacher, relative, or a policeman.

In *Ira Sleeps Over*, by Bernard Waber, a young boy overcomes his fear of ridicule by learning that he shares a common interest with a friend. Ira's first invitation to sleep over at Reggie's house poses a real problem. Should he take Tah Tah the teddy bear? His sister claims that Reggie will laugh at him if he does. So Ira leaves his bear at home.

That night, in the middle of a scary story, Reggie climbs out of bed and retrieves his teddy bear. He still needs something special to reassure him when he is frightened. So Ira runs home to get his teddy bear, too. Children appreciate Ira's conflict between wanting to cling to a comforting part of his past and wanting to appear mature and self-confident.

Confront the Fears Created by Your Imagination

Children learn unrealistic fears in many ways. Sometimes what we say can alarm them. Unthinking adults may terrify children with insensitive comments. Some adults use a child's imagination as a weapon to force compliance. A babysitter, for example, tells a child that an ugly witch will come and eat her up during the night if she continues to misbehave. A parent warns a child that his thumb will fall off if he continues to put it in his mouth. In each case the adult uses a child's imagination as a bludgeon to gain compliance.

Young children learn to protect themselves from some dangers. But because of preschoolers' limited understanding, lack of real power, and vulnerability, they can easily let their imaginations go wild as they react to what they see and hear. They may misinterpret or misunderstand danger. Monsters are created as stand-ins for some of their worst fears. What kind of monsters are hiding in the darkness of a closet? Will a wolf crawl through the bedroom window? Will bad men come to take their mommy or daddy away?

Some stories show children successfully confronting an imaginary fear. For example, in Mercer Mayer's *There's a Nightmare in My Closet*, a young boy is initially frightened of the nightmare who hides in his closet. But one night he confronts the monster when it appears. He discovers that the huge, repulsive-looking nightmare is really a timid, frightened creature in need of a friend. The boy takes pity on the nightmare when it begins to cry, and tries to comfort him by tucking it into his bed. The roles are reversed:

The frightening image is exposed for its weakness, and the timid child gains strength.

Mercer Mayer returns to a similar theme in *There's Something in My Attic*. This time a nightmare in the attic is no match for a brave young girl with a lasso. Her parents try to convince her the sounds she hears above her room are really mice. Unconvinced, the young girl puts on her cowboy hat and boots, grabs her lasso, and investigates the attic on her own. There she finds the nightmare that has been stealing her toys. This time it has her new teddy bear. So she lassos the creature and pulls it to her parents' room. But the nightmare escapes before she can prove her suspicions were correct: ". . . nightmares are very tricky, and sometimes they just slip away. I'll just have to get my bear back tomorrow."

Mercer Mayer's pen-and-ink-with-watercolor-wash nightmares are big, hulking creatures, more to be pitied than feared. In *There's a Nightmare in My Closet*, the nightmare cries when confronted. In *There's Something in My Attic*, it clutches the tiny teddy bear in a touching display of insecurity. They are recognizable as monsters but are incapable of doing harm, just like the nightmares they represent.

John Canty has a young boy confront his fear of shadows in *Shadows*. Benjamin hates the dark. As he lies in bed he thinks he can see fierce creatures living there. When their shadows grow bigger and more menacing, Benjamin is about to flee from his room. But he stops himself.

> "If I run," he says aloud, "it will always chase me. Always and forever. But this is my room, and I won't run from anything!"

So Benjamin turns, and the shadows "whirl and swirl, then melt away." Now Benjamin can return to bed and sleep with newfound security.

What Seems Threatening May Not Really Be Dangerous

Regardless of age, fear paralyzes instead of protects when children misunderstand or exaggerate a danger. Lack of experience can be the basis for this confusion. A four-year-old in my preschool class panicked after cutting her finger because she thought all her blood would leak out. Another child began to worry after I put an ice pack on the bump on his head because he thought I might "freeze his brain."

A farm couple told me that their preschool daughter became extremely anxious and withdrawn when she heard the family would have to sell their farm. The parents knew that the loss of their home would upset her, but they were surprised by the intensity of her panic. A friend of the family later discovered during a casual conversation with the young girl that she believed that someone in her family would have to die in order for a farm sale to take place. At some time in the past she had associated death with farm sales. She might have heard her mother tell her father, "That's too bad about the Olsens. Now that Sam's died I guess Karen will have to sell their farm." Lacking information and maturity, young children can easily form misconceptions about emotional events.

A group of children enjoy scaring themselves on the way to their bus stop one foggy morning in *The Green Lion of Zion Street* by Julia Fields. There is a lion—green, fierce, mighty, proud—crouched on the ridge of the bridge they have to cross. It's made of stone—but who can be sure what's really there in the fog?

> . . . on that ridge,
>   they are going to see something crouched
> up there, lolled up there
> to give anybody a scare.
>   It will raise their hair.
>   Brave or not.

Imaginations can sometimes be too vivid. The children dash across the bridge. The bus is late, so they return to examine the lion more closely.

> The fog is gone.
> The lion is clear
> and all alone.
> Just a lion
> and made of stone.
> Stone.
> Stone!

In the safety of a group, the children use their good sense to reassure themselves.

> We be's looking,
> Checking it out.
> Checking it in.
> We walks backward
> and close to, again.

And as they look, they remind themselves that the statue has eyes that cannot see, feet that cannot move, and a mouth that cannot eat. They realize there is no danger, because something made of stone is not alive. Even though it may look real, especially in the fog, it cannot hurt them.

In *Ghost's Hour, Spook's Hour*, by Eve Bunting, a boy and his dog wake up at midnight and are frightened by unusual sounds and images as they walk through the darkened house. But each of the scary incidents has a good explanation. The *Woooooo* outside Jake's window is the wind. The *Eeeeee* is the moaning of his bedroom door when it opens. The *Craak, slither, whiiish!* against the window is a branch. The whiteness moving out of the dark toward Jake as he carries his dog is only their reflection off a big mirror. Most frightening of all, though, is his parents' empty room. Where did they go?

Father arrives after he hears Jake's and Biff's frightened howls. He tells Jake that he and his mother are

sleeping on the living room couch because of the noise of
the tree branch against their bedroom window. Donald
Carrick's illustrations are dark and ominous as the boy
and his pet explore their home. The final illustrations with
the bright glow of the candle next to the living room couch
provide a reassuring contrast to the eerie darkness in the
rest of the house. Settled securely next to his parents in
their makeshift bed, Jake is now ready to drift off to sleep.

Lucille Clifton writes in *Amifika* about how fear can
follow misunderstanding. Amifika could hear the music in
his mother's voice when she talked about his daddy coming
home. He also heard her talk of getting rid of things his
father has never seen in order to make more room in their
small apartment. "I be the thing they get rid of," he concludes. After all, what father could love a child he can't
remember? So Amifika waits and dreads the moment when
he will be removed from his family.

But when his father arrives, the man's happiness and
tender embrace removes all doubt from Amifika's mind
about the love that exists between them. Children who
hear *Amifika* will learn how a mistake in judgment can
cause unrealistic fears. Parents may also use it as an
opportunity to talk about past and present misunderstandings in their own family.

You Can Overcome Some Fears by Helping Others

Being courageous should not be associated with physical
strength or control over others. Courage does not mean
bullying someone. Berniece Freschet introduces us to a
real scaredy-cat who learns about being brave in *Furlie
Cat*, humorously illustrated by Betsy Lewin. Furlie is afraid
of squirrels and birds and even his own shadow. He is
ashamed of himself, so he begins practicing being brave.
Furlie makes fierce faces in the mirror, confronts his shadow,
and practices his growls on a mouse in the attic. He experiences his first taste of power when he inadvertently frightens Oscar the dog. From that moment on, Furlie enjoys

scaring everyone he can and becomes the biggest bully in the neighborhood.

But when a young bear cub growls back at him, Furlie lets out a screech and scrambles to the topmost branch of the nearest tree. That night, as he clings to his narrow perch, Furlie hears the strange and scary sounds of a screech owl swooping through the trees and night hunters moving through the forest below. For the first time he feels truly frightened and ashamed of how he must have made others feel when he bullied them. The next morning Oscar passes by and wags his tail when he sees Furlie up in the tree. His presence encourages the repentant cat to leave his safe perch. Together they return home.

In *Fang*, by Barbara Shook Hazen, we meet a child who is frightened of the bulldog next door, big kids on the corner, big waves at the beach, thunderstorms, and the monsters in his closet. That's why he picks Fang, his big fierce-looking pet dog, to be his protector. Unfortunately, Fang is frightened of even more things than his young master. So the boy tries to teach his pet that babies, bath water, and his own reflection are not really dangerous.

> Then I hug him, and tell him I love him anyway, even if he is a big coward, instead of big and brave.

As he reassures his pet the young boy also gains insight into his own fears. Now he can face that bulldog, those big kids, waves, thunderstorms, and monsters, because he realizes they are not the threats he imagined them to be.

Michael, by Liesel M. Skorpen, illustrates how a child can set aside fear when someone or something needs help. Michael is afraid of storms. One night when thunder and lightning rage outside his window he sees a baby rabbit in his yard. Despite his fear, Michael safely braves the wrath of the storm to save the terrified animal. Michael does not eliminate his fear—he rises above it, finding courage within himself and taking decisive and reasonable action. Children learn from *Michael* that fear does not necessarily prevent them from acting responsibly and helping others.

A young child helps an unusual friend during his first plane trip to visit his grandmother in David McPhail's *First Flight*. As he boards the plane he is joined by a life-sized teddy bear who needs reassurance and supervision. The big lovable bear's awkwardness helps to emphasize the self-control and assurance of the young boy as he masters a new experience. The boy can buckle his seat belt, but the bear needs help. The boy neatly eats his meal, but the bear makes a terrible mess with his honey. The boy goes to the bathroom by himself, but the bear makes a fuss and bounces around the cabin during a moment of turbulence. The capabilities of the young boy are made more apparent in comparison to the antics of his nervous friend.

Courage means moving forward despite fear. It does not mean an absence of fear. Ann Cameron's book *Harry (the Monster)* shows how courage can enable one person to overcome fear to help another. Harry is a young monster who lives in a cave with his friend Frank the bullfrog. Harry loves his purple hair, orange ears, and green tongue. He looks forward to growing bigger and stronger every day. But despite being a monster, Harry harbors a great fear of the Small People. Frank is sympathetic and helps Harry post a warning outside his cave: "Stay away from this cave! A monster lives here and he is brave."

When the Small People (who are afraid of monsters) arrive to explore the cave, they fail to see Harry, who is hiding under his bed covers. When they grab Frank to take him back home with them, Harry overcomes his fear to save his friend. Children like Harry because they can sympathize with his fear of the unknown. Harry also demonstrates that they can act to help someone even if they are afraid.

In some stories courage means standing up to a threat. In *Harry and the Terrible Whatzit*, by Dick Gackenbach, a young child overcomes his fear of the basement by confronting a monster. Harry is certain something terrible lives in the dark, smelly cellar. When his mother goes to the basement and fails to return, Harry summons his cour-

STORYBREAK

Rodney's Threat

Once upon a time, in the wonderful town of Butterberry Hill ...

Amy, Casey, and the rest of the kids in the school were all excited because their teacher, Mrs. Golightly, was getting married. Amy looked and looked for a wedding present. She finally found a pretty blue scarf, and she had just enough allowance money to pay for it herself. She brought it home, put it in a box, and wrapped it in bright pink paper.

All the kids brought their presents to school the next day and put them on a table in the classroom. But then Rodney did the most terrible thing. He was very angry with Amy because she would not let him ride her new bike. So when everyone went out to play, Rodney snuck back into the classroom, opened Amy's present, took out the scarf, hid it in his pocket, and put a rotten, squishy old banana in its place. He carefully wrapped the box so that it looked as pretty as it was before he opened it. "Won't Mrs. Golightly be surprised when she opens Amy's present and finds a rotten, smelly old banana!" thought Rodney.

Rodney would have gotten away with his nasty trick. But just as he was putting the squishy banana in the box, Casey walked into the room. He had returned to the classroom to get something out of his desk. "What are you doing to Amy's present, Rodney?" he asked. "A joke, that's what!" Rodney said. "And if you tell I'll beat you up; I'll give you a knuckle sandwich!" Rodney laughed and went outside to play.

Poor Casey! If he tells the teacher, then Rodney will beat him up. If he keeps quiet, then she will think Amy gave her a spoiled banana for a present. Just then Mrs. Golightly and all the children entered the room. "Time to open the presents!" the children shouted. Mrs. Golightly thanked them all for their kindness and reached for a present to open. Casey's heart beat fast, and Rodney grinned from the back of the room. Her first choice was Dorothy's present—a little silver bell. The teacher thanked Dorothy and reached to open another present. This time her hands found the box with the pretty pink paper. Casey's heart beat faster, Amy smiled with pride, and Rodney was starting to giggle. Mrs. Golightly's hands began to unwrap the box.

Just as she was about to open the present, Casey jumped up and shouted "STOP!" "Why, what's the matter, Casey?" Mrs. Golightly asked. Casey stood up and took a deep breath. Rodney stopped giggling. Now he was staring right at Casey, his eyes narrowed and seething with anger. Casey took another deep breath. And then he told Mrs. Golightly what he saw Rodney do to Amy's present.

"Rodney, what do have to say for yourself?" said the teacher. Rodney jumped from his desk and pleaded, "No, Mrs. Golightly, I didn't do that! Casey is just blaming me." But at that moment all the children near Rodney began pointing at the little bit of the blue scarf poking out of his pocket. Mrs. Golightly told Rodney, "That was a terrible thing to do, Rodney. Go to the back of the room, put the scarf back in the box and rewrap it just like it was. You also have some explaining to do after school today." Boy, did Rodney ever get into trouble for that dirty trick.

Casey sure was scared. He thought Rodney would beat him up for sure. But then he remembered a saying Grandpa Jake had told him:

> When you are afraid
> And think you might cry—
> Say, "I will do what I can,
> "I will stay and try!"

Rodney was waiting for him the next morning on the way to school. "OK, Casey-flacy, now I'm going to beat you up!"

Casey repeated Grandpa Jake's words to himself. He told Rodney, "I will do what I can—I will stay and try." Rodney was surprised because he thought Casey would run away. So he puffed himself up again and shouted, "OK, Casey the pasty. Here it comes, a knuckle sandwich!" But still Casey held his ground. Again Rodney shouted, even louder this time, "You better run!" But Casey did not run. "Listen, you, Rodney!" he said, feeling braver with each word. "What you

did was wrong. Don't you ever do that again. You hear!"
Rodney took a step back. "Maybe, maybe not," he said. He
turned and walked away.

You see, Rodney was a bully. But he liked to use words and
threats to scare others to do what he wanted. He was too
afraid of getting hurt if he really got into a fight. That's why
he left when Casey refused to run away. Casey went on home,
feeling happy that he had the courage to do what he knew
was right.

---

age to go and find her. When he confronts the Terrible
Whatzit in the basement Harry makes an interesting discovery: The creature shrinks if his intended victim is un-
afraid. Children learn from Harry that what is frightening
may not be so terrible if it is confronted and understood.

Face Adversity Courageously

When does courage emerge in childhood? In *Children's
Fears*, clinical psychologist Benjamin Wolman points out
that courage is based on security during childhood. Children must first count on others before they can begin to
depend on themselves. They need the assistance and protection of parents, teachers, and other adults in their com-
munities. When accompanied by encouragement, this
support will nurture self-confidence. Later, as adults, they
will first look to their own ability to deal with a threat,
and then to their friends, relatives, and neighbors to help
if needed. Adult security depends on self-confidence reinforced by support from others; children's sense of security
depends on support from others reinforced by their own
self-confidence.

The protection of others provides children with an umbrella of security under which they can gradually develop
self-reliance. But parents and other adults cannot always
be there to shield a child from disappointment or danger.
At these moments even young children have to draw on

their inner strength or fortitude to move ahead. Benjamin
Wolman argues that, with our encouragement, children
will gradually make the shift from being dependent on
others for their safety to assuming responsibility for their
own well-being.

Learning to persevere begins during early childhood.
Our children show evidence of courage the first time they
start to walk, fall down and bump their noses, and then
stand up to try again. On the first day of kindergarten
they may set out bravely for new adventures despite mis-
givings and tears. Or as they lie in bed, listening to the
sudden crackling of thunder, their room lit by bursts of
lightning, they may tell themselves, "You are safe—no
harm will come to you or your family. It's just a scary
storm." Fear is typically associated with childhood. Courage, though, is often overlooked because we tend to assume
that children are passive and dependent.

William Steig provides us with two delightful books about
children who have to draw on their courage and determination in order to succeed. In *Brave Irene* a young girl
volunteers to deliver a gown her mother made for the
duchess to wear that evening. First she has to battle freez-
ing wind and snow as she crosses Farmer Bennett's sheep
pasture. The wind rips the package from her grasp and the
beautiful gown is swept away. She steps in a hole and
hurts her ankle. But she plods on, dragging furrows in the
snow with her sore foot.

The sun sets and Irene soon becomes lost. She sees a
lighted area ahead, down a hill that must be the palace.
But just as she pushes forward she falls off a little cliff and
is buried in the snow. The thought occurs to her that
maybe she should just give up.

> Even if she could call for help, no one would hear her.
> Her body shook. Her teeth chattered. Why not freeze to
> death, she thought, and let all these troubles end. Why
> not? She was already buried.
>
> *And never see her mother's face again?* Her good
> mother who smelled like fresh-baked bread? In an explo-

sion of fury, she flung her body about to free herself and was finally able to climb up on her knees and look around.

She then uses the box like a sled to race down the hill. As she walks nervously toward the palace she is surprised to find the gown hanging from a tree. Irene proudly delivers her prize. During her long and difficult journey, she chose never to submit to her adversity. Irene was successful because she had a goal and had the courage to persevere.

In *The Zabajaba Jungle* we meet another hero who can stand beside brave Irene. Leonard has to cut and slash his way through the Zabajaba Jungle. "Why is he there? He himself doesn't know. He just has to push on." Along the way he has to avoid hungry plants, rescue a big butterfly from the jaws of a hungry flower, and travel through the insides of a petrified monster. When he wakes up in his hammock the next morning, the ground below is filled with a legion of writhing snakes. But he is lifted up and away by the butterfly he had rescued.

There are more challenges. After he takes a sip of nectar from a yellow flower, Leonard is captured by a gang of mandrills who accuse him of breaking the law. Fortunately, he escapes at his trial by distracting his captors with fireworks. As he flees, Leonard finds his parents trapped in a large glass bottle and saves them as well. *The Zabajaba Jungle* is a dreamlike adventure featuring an exceptionally brave young boy. Like brave Irene, Leonard is determined to succeed regardless of the obstacles.

In some stories, courage means overcoming one's own self-doubt. In *What's the Matter Sylvie, Can't You Ride?*, by Karen B. Andersen, a young girl overcomes her fear of falling to learn to ride her bicycle. Sylvie wants to ride, but she just can't keep her feet on the pedals. So day after day, Sylvie remains seated on her bike, defeated and forlorn as she watches the rest of the world glide by. Just when she decides to give up in frustration, she suddenly finds herself racing down the dreaded hill. "Hey, this is it!" she yells. "I can do it!" As soon as Sylvie sets aside her worries, she finds the energy to take a chance and learn a new skill.

Fairy tales are, of course, an excellent source for stories of courage. *The Loathsome Dragon*, retold by David Wiesner and Kim Kahng and illustrated with remarkable paintings by David Wiesner, tells the story of the determined Childe Wynd who sails to the shores of Bamborough Keep to free his sister from a wicked spell. A jealous queen has transformed the fair maiden Margaret into a loathsome dragon who wanders the kingdom, devouring all in its path. Only three kisses from Childe Wynd will restore her form. Her brother hears of her plight, and with three and thirty of his bravest men he sails to Bamborough Castle. The queen attempts to stop him by magically forcing the Loathsome Dragon to attack his ship when he reaches the harbor. But Childe Wynd outsmarts the queen by finding a better place to land. He then approaches the dragon who beckons him to kiss her on the forehead. The brave knight overcomes his fear and suspicion to set his sister free.

Irene, Leonard, Childe Wynd, and Sylvie share a determination to overcome fear to reach a goal. Their courage may inspire children to draw on their own reservoir of courage to overcome self-doubt.

Sleep Peacefully—Do Not Be Afraid of the Dark

Bedtime can be frightening for some children because their imaginations can project their fears into the darkness. Bedtime stories can be a reassuring ritual that provides a soothing transition between the hectic activities of the day and preparation for sleeping. Some stories focus specifically on children's concerns about darkness. One of the best is Reeve Lindbergh's *The Midnight Farm*. Mother and child sit together on the edge of the child's bed. It is the middle of the night and the child is not yet asleep.

> Here is the dark when day is done,
> Here is the dark with no moon or sun,
> Here is the dark when all lights are out,
> Here is the heart of the dark.

So begins mother and child's tour of the farm at midnight. There is reassuring familiarity to the big dark stove, the cats playing with a glove, the raccoon family in the dark of the maple tree. They visit their geese, horses, cows, and sheep. All are comfortable and at peace in the dark.

> Here is the dark of the midnight farm,
> Safe and still and full and warm,
> Deep in the dark and free from harm
> In the dark of the midnight farm.

Reeve Lindbergh's tender lullabye uses the word *dark* repetitively—"dark of the chair in the hall," "the dark by the big wood stove," "dark in the barn at night"—to strip the word of its frightening connotations. Beautiful full-color pen-and-ink drawings by Susan Jeffers recapture the richly shaded hues of a peaceful farm at midnight.

Night in the Country, by Cynthia Rylant, begins with,

> "There is no night so dark, so black as night in the country."

But there is life in that night country: owls swooping among the trees, night frogs singing songs, an apple falling from a tree behind your house. Rabbits eat the fallen apples, a raccoon mother licks her babies, and a cow nuzzles her calf. Each of these images is meant to reassure children about the night, to show them that all is peaceful and secure. Young children can be easily frightened by night sounds they cannot see. So Cynthia Rylant makes the sounds less strange and threatening by identifying their origins.

Other stories focus on sleeping itself and calm children through peaceful imagery and repetition. *When I'm Sleepy* is a wonderfully soothing story that will help children drift off to sleep. Jane Howard invites children to imagine how it would feel to sleep like other creatures.

> When I'm sleepy, I wish I could curl up in a basket or fall asleep in a downy nest.

When I'm sleepy, and I stretch and yawn, I wonder how it would be to sleep in a swamp or a hollow log or crawl into a cozy cave and sleep all winter.

Lynne Cherry's illustrations have a delightful texture to them, like reaching out to touch a soft, warm blanket. They show a young child asleep in a position similar to the animal resting with her. In most instances the child actually snuggles up to the animal. But in every situation she is perfectly comfortable. The story concludes with ...

When I'm sleepy, and my eyelids keep falling shut, I'm so glad I can go to sleep in my very own bed under my own warm blanket with my head on my own soft pillow.

Lulled by the repetition and reassured by the child's comfort and safety, most tired children will be ready to drift off to sleep by the end of the book—that is, if they are still awake.

Mirra Ginsburg introduces children to a delightfully soothing Armenian song in *The Sun's Asleep Behind the Hill*. This bedtime lullabye serenades children with images of life settling down for the night.

> The sun shone
> in the sky all day.
> The sun grew tired
> and went away
> to sleep behind the hill.

The sun is followed by the breeze, the leaves, the bird, the squirrel, and, finally the child we have seen playing in the park. With each page, illustrations by Paul O. Zelinsky show night gradually spreading its mantle of darkness. But then the moon appears to cast a cool glow over the land while the mother carries her sleeping child home.

Half Moon and One Whole Star, by Crescent Dragonwagon, with illustrations by Jerry Pinkney; *Once: A*

Lullabye, by bp Nichol, with illustrations by Anita Lobel; and *The Dream Child*, by David McPhail, are excellent examples of other delightful bedtime books. Each of these titles can help children set aside the cares and tensions of the day and relax as they get ready to drift off to sleep.

Summary

The Cowardly Lion in *The Wizard of Oz* is crippled by fear because he underestimates his own strength and exaggerates the threats he faces. Here is the Lion, king of beasts, who trembles in fear of any real or imagined danger. If he could only get a medal from the Wizard then he would be transformed from a coward to a courageous creature worthy of his title. But after meeting the Wizard, he learns that he always had the capacity to stand up to threat. His courage appeared in time of real need, even though he failed to recognize his strength. He never really needed the medal. The Lion demonstrated his bravery long before he meets the Wizard.

As parents we are like the Wizard of Oz. Our children look to us for guidance and strength. We, in turn, deeply love them and wish to protect them from threat and disappointment. If we could, each of us would assume the power of the Wizard and award our children an enchanted medal, a piece of tinsel that would enable them to avoid danger and overcome adversity.

But such a gift would distract our children from the real source of the courage that resides within themselves. If we could keep them from all harm, our protection would become a trap, sapping them of strength in a stifling web of misguided love. Finding strength and courage is ultimately a solitary pursuit, made possible only by tightening one's belt and facing inevitable trouble.

Every child, indeed every person, has a choice: to respond to life either as a victim trembling in a corner or as a gallant fighter facing adversity with hope and determination. Parents can provide support and encouragement. But ultimately children themselves will be the authors of their own personal stories.

What remains in our children's minds long after we are gone are recollections of the stories that we shared and memories of the moments when we allowed them to glimpse what was within our hearts. Our stories can be messages that resonate over time, gentle encouragements that linger in the back of their minds. And then in their darker moments, when the going gets rough, our children may say to themselves, "I think I can, I think I can, I THINK I CAN!"

CHAPTER FIVE

From Hansel and Gretel to George and Martha:

Growing Closer to Others

Hidden away in the dusty attic of every human mind is the fear of being overlooked by others. To go unrecognized is to be a nonperson, insignificant in the world, a phantom drifting invisibly through crowds of people, untouched and alone. We yearn for recognition—the friendly smile of a waitress, the warmth of a handshake, the tenderness of a child's hug. Every social contact is a confirmation of who we are and what we mean to others. Our friends are like mirrors who provide us with reflections of our true nature. Without this confirmation our sense of self lacks substance, like a mirage shimmering on a lonely desert. Isolation shatters our self-worth.

The desire to reach out, to make connection with others, begins with the parent-infant relationship and quickly expands to include brothers and sisters and then friends. The two kinds of relationships—with parents and with peers— are dramatically different. According to Swiss psychologist Jean Piaget, involvement with parents is based on a *unilateral* exchange of ideas and expectations. Power is essentially one-way, from parents to children. Parents tell children what to do. When necessary, they set limits and provide guidance. Preschoolers view their parents as powerful authority figures whose beliefs cannot be disputed. No matter how loving, the parent-child relationship is characterized primarily by restraint and expectations of obedience.

Involvement with peers, however, is based on a *mutual* exchange of ideas. According to Piaget, children believe relationships with peers are based on equality and cooperation. Power can be shared. Children can argue with their peers. They are free to disagree, to try to change each other's minds and even come to blows. Children engage each other as equals in the social arena. Success depends on their own quick wits and resources, not assistance from more powerful adults.

A parent's love and acceptance can be something children count on, a bedrock of security that they can return to again and again. But the affection of friends has to be earned. A child's struggle to make and hold friends is essentially a solitary effort. We cannot protect them from the conflict, the hurt, the dashed hopes and disappointments that are an inevitable part of social engagement. There will always be the party invitation that never arrives, the best friend who finds someone else more interesting, the playmate who would rather fight than share.

No matter how affectionate and supportive we might be, we will never be a substitute for our children's friends. Our children can relate to friends as equals and as partners. Friends will teach them social skills. Friends will listen to their deepest secrets. Friends will provide them with insight into themselves. Friends are their future.

How Stories Contribute to Growing Closer to Others

Stories can help to nurture values and ideas that contribute to a child's relationships. Stories can emphasize the importance of loyalty, sacrifice, trust, and understanding that are an important part of one's kinship with others. Stories can provide children with insight about how friendship may begin and end. They can prepare children for disappointment and provide suggestions for resolving conflicts.

Loyalty and cooperation between brother and sister, for example, are clearly evident in the Brothers Grimm fairy tale *Hansel and Gretel*. Initial abandonment by their father establishes a tragic context in which the bonds of love and dedication between Hansel and Gretel can stand out in dramatic relief. Imprisonment by the witch introduces another element of danger. Hansel and Gretel survive these threats because they help each other. They persevere despite the danger of the dark and ominous woods or the threat of the sinister witch. Only by working together can they finally make their escape. Neither sibling dominates nor takes advantage of the other. Hansel comforts his younger sister when they are left in the forest. He tries to find a way to return home by tracing a path out of the woods, first with small white stones and then with bread crumbs. Gretel also contributes by saving her brother from certain death when she outsmarts the witch and pushes her into the oven.

Devotion between children is the core theme of *Hansel and Gretel*. Children love the story because it portrays their own intense feelings about the importance of support and loyalty between close friends. Hansel would never abandon his sister in the woods or insist to the witch, "Eat HER, not me; SHE will taste better!" Gretel would never escape and leave her brother behind to suffer at the hands of the witch. These actions would shock children because they are inconsistent with their beliefs about friendship and loyalty.

A different portrayal of the joys and challenges of friendship is provided by James Marshall in his "George and Martha" books. George and Martha are two endearing hippos whose friendship is constantly being tested, not by danger, but by everyday misunderstandings and imperfections.

The first in the series, *George and Martha*, includes five short stories. Story number one, "Split Pea Soup," examines honesty. Martha loves to make split pea soup, but George hates it more than anything else in the world. He only pretends to like it because he does not want to hurt Martha's feelings. One day, after eating ten bowls of the soup, George can't make himself continue. So he pours the rest of Martha's soup into his shoes, hoping that she will think he finished his meal. Martha is watching from the kitchen, though, and discovers how George really feels about her soup. When she confronts him with his masquerade, Martha admits that she hates the soup too. She only likes to make it. "Friends should always tell each other the truth," Martha concludes.

George and Martha adapt to each other's needs and personalities. Their affection for each other is obvious despite their little misunderstandings, jealousies, and arguments. Because they really care for each other they try to work out their problems. George and Martha demonstrate that conflict is a part of any enduring relationship and that honesty, responsibility, respect, and caring are key ingredients for successful friendships.

Worthwhile stories provide children with numerous examples of individuals forming relationships, overcoming conflicts, and providing support to each other. These stories provide insight about love and friendship and convey values emphasizing loyalty and affection:

- You belong to a family that loves and protects you.
- You live in a special place.
- Love means showing that you care.
- Reach out and make friends.
- Kindness wins more friends than selfishness.
- Your friends can like others and still like you.
- You may miss your friends when you are not with them.

You Belong to a Family That Loves and Protects You

The feeling of being wanted, of being accepted, provides the basis for self-esteem. All children want to feel that they are an important part of their parents' lives. Aliki's

Welcome, Little Baby tells of the love of a mother for her newborn child. "Welcome to our world, little baby. We've been waiting for you," she begins. She introduces her infant to the world. "You'll see it. You'll smell it, and feel it too. You'll hear sounds you never heard before." Mother is delighted with her new baby and is excited about his future. Soft watercolor and crayon drawings emphasize the tenderness between mother and her child. This short story is a serenade, a love song celebrating the miracle of life.

Charlotte Zolotow's *Some Things Go Together* is a touching poem of a young boy's attachment to his mother.

> Peace with dove
> Home with love
> Gardens with flowers
> Clocks with hours
> Moths with screen
> Grass with green
> Leaves with tree
> And you with me.

Zolotow's playful verse and Karen Gundersheimer's delightful artwork illustrate the joy that exists between a young boy and his mother. The young boy's statement is a litany of love conveying his deep sense of identification with her. She is an important part of his life.

Love is more than a special feeling between two people. Much of a child's security comes from belonging to an extended family. Some stories affirm children's experiences of family togetherness. Memories of a strong sense of kinship and attachment to the land are found in *When I Was Young in the Mountains*, by Cynthia Rylant.

When I was young in the mountains, Grandfather came home in the evening covered with the black dust of a coal mine. Only his lips were clean and he used them to kiss the top of my head.

Each happy memory—of Grandma making hot corn bread and fried okra and of trips to the swimming hole—shows how connected the young girl felt to her family and the land where she grew up.

"High in a corner of the sky the moon still curves in a wide smile and reaches its long pale arms down to touch the house far below." Nancy Jewell and Leonard Kessler give young children a glimpse of the love and closeness between three generations in *Family Under the Moon*. As the moonlight peacefully blankets their home, memories of yesterday's happy times and plans for tomorrow are shared by family members. Children will appreciate this gentle story that associates bedtime with security, love, and togetherness.

Cynthia Rylant writes about a very special visit in *The Relatives Came*. A family of relatives pack an ice chest full of pop, crackers, and bologna sandwiches, and leave their home in Virginia to visit another family of relatives. They arrive and pile out of their car.

> Then it was hugging time. Talk about hugging!
> Those relatives just passed us all around their car, pulling us against their wrinkled Virginia clothes, crying sometimes.
> They hugged us for hours.

Hugging is followed by a big supper and finally bedtime. The sounds of breathing fill the house. The relatives stay for weeks, tending the garden and fixing broken things. When they leave, the house now seems too empty. But then the host family realizes that they will have their turn to visit next summer and renew their closeness once again. Stephen Gammell's humorous illustrations portray the love and affection felt between three generations of relatives.

These and other stories may affirm children's sense of belonging within the larger family. Through exposure to such stories they may realize that they are part of a caring network. Within their families, they can be loved and protected. They can face the challenges of growing up knowing that they can depend on their families for support.

STORYBREAK

The Most Wonderful Place

Once upon a time, in the wonderful town of Butterberry Hill . . .

Briarbutton the Rabbit decided to leave Butterberry Hill so he could find the most wonderful place to live. He was tired of boring old Butterberry Hill. He wanted to live in the most wonderful place. So Briarbutton went to Grandpa Jake and asked him, "Tell me about the most wonderful place for me right now, Grandpa Jake, so I can go and live there."

Grandpa Jake told Briarbutton, "Go up to nearby Moonsweep Mountain and look carefully. There you will see the most wonderful place for you." So Briarbutton climbed up Moonsweep Mountain and gazed beyond Butterberry Hill across the valley and mountains in the distance. "Somewhere out there must be the best place for me," thought Briarbutton. So off he went.

The first place he visited had shiny new buildings. But the people were not friendly. Who wants to live in a place where the people are all crabby? The next place Briarbutton visited had friendly people. But it rained all the time, and Briarbutton hated too much rain. The next place he visited had friendly people and not much rain. But they had lots and lots of dogs. Everyone knows rabbits are afraid of dogs, so Briarbutton left that place fast.

"Now where could that best place for me be?" thought Briarbutton. "Grandpa Jake told me I could see it from Moonsweep Mountain." Pretty soon, Briarbutton became tired of looking. He missed his own little rabbit hole. He missed Penelope Pig, Casey, and Amy. Why, he even missed Mrs. Winterbones's obnoxious little nephew Rodney.

So Briarbutton returned to Butterberry Hill. He told Grandpa Jake, "I never found the best place for me. You were wrong, Grandpa Jake."

Grandpa Jake asked Briarbutton to show him where he had gone. So Briarbutton took Grandpa Jake up to Moonsweep Mountain and pointed out the direction he traveled.

Grandpa Jake asked Briarbutton, "Look closely now and tell me what is nearest to you."

Briarbutton looked down from Moonsweep Mountain and . . . guess what he saw? Why, Butterberry Hill, of course.

"Someday you may have to leave, Briarbutton," said Grandpa Jake. "But for now, I bet Butterberry Hill's the best place for you."

Briarbutton had to agree, especially after his friends celebrated his return with carrot cake and ice cream, and after he had a nice comfortable nap in his own little bunny burrow.

You Live in a Special Place

Children also form emotional connections with home and land. Home provides them with shelter, security, and a place to call their own. A young bear from *In Our House,* by Ann Rockwell, begins with "This is my family—my mother, my father, and me. This is the house where we live." He then takes us on a tour of his home by naming what the family likes to do in the living room, kitchen, basement, garage, bathroom, and his own little room. "We love our house," he concludes. "It is our home."

Ann Rockwell fills her book with fascinating detail, showing the family engaged in a wide variety of familiar activities. Young children will enjoy naming what the family does: watering a plant, feeding goldfish, cooking supper, setting the table, washing clothes, and getting dressed. A house does not really become a home until it has a history of such everyday activities. Young bear begins his description with "house" and ends with "home." *In Our House* should prompt considerable discussion between parents and children about life in their own homes.

The House on Maple Street chronicles the events that occur at 107 Maple Street over a three-hundred-year period. Bonnie Pryor takes us back to when this location was part of a forest and a stream. Indians who are following buffalo herds make the edge of the stream their home.

Later, settlers arrive and plant crops and build their homes.
A prosperous town gradually grows up around this spot.
Generation after generation change the landscape and leave
traces of themselves behind. This passage of time is portrayed with activities and images familiar to children.

The child's desire for connection extends beyond a home,
to include a sense of place, a fondness for the land that
provides the setting for their lives. *Yonder*, by Tony Johnston, illustrated with full-color oil paintings by Lloyd Bloom,
is a haunting, lyrical portrayal of the time and place where
one family's life began.

> There comes the farmer with a brand new bride,
> Riding down the hills that roll forever.
> Digs a hole, plants a tree and says a prayer.
> There. Just over there.

The farmer and his bride work the land and make a home.
Children, then grandchildren are born. Every birth is celebrated with the planting of a tree. Every event anchored in
the land, "There, just over there." The farmer and his wife
grow old gracefully. And when he dies, a tree is planted to
mark his passing.

Lloyd Bloom's illustrations emphasize the rich green
colors of the land in spring and summer, the brilliant hues
of fall, and the cool shimmering of snow in the winter. The
majesty of the land, with its rolling hills, thick forests, rich
farmland, and meandering river comes alive with color
and depth. We can understand the family's love for the
land.

> Yonder is a farmer on a jet black horse.
> Yonder are the hills that roll forever. . . .

Love of the land is especially significant for immigrants.
Eve Bunting shows the kinds of adversities one family has
to overcome to arrive at their adopted land in *How Many
Days to America*. The family of four flee their native home
after soldiers visit their house. They leave everything be-

hind, departing on a fishing boat in the middle of the
night. First their motor breaks down and the women have
to make a sail by knotting clothes together. Then their
food and water runs out and many on their ship become ill.
Thieves steal what few possessions they have remaining.
But their launch eventually completes its journey to America. And they arrive on a very special day—Thanksgiving.

Love Means Showing You Care

Many stories emphasize the importance of demonstrat-
ing love through word and deed. Some may focus on physical tenderness. *Baby Hugs*, by Dave Ross, tells children
and their parents that hugging is one way of saying "I love
you!" to a baby. All sorts of baby hugs are pictured—feeding
hugs, burp-the-baby hugs, comfort hugs, and play hugs, to
name only a few. Ross concludes with five rules for hugging babies:

1. Hug happy babies.
2. Hug cranky babies.
3. Hug sick babies.
4. When in doubt, hug the baby!
5. Always remember, a baby *never* outgrows the need
   for hugs.

Parents do more than hug to express their affection for
their children. They also smile, talk, and play games with
them. When rapport exists between a parent and child,
each responds to the other's behavior in a positive way.
Learning how to engage others in this give and take is
critical for forming relationships. Making eye contact and
being responsive to the expressions and vocalizations of
others are subtle but important skills that affect how children are likely to be accepted by their peers. Children who
lack opportunities to learn and practice social engagement
with parents may later tend to withdraw from social involvement or be rejected by other children. They seem out
of sync with others. Their attempts to play with other

children may appear awkward as they hit, pinch, or push their playmates to get their attention.

Some stories show how emotional bonds with others are nurtured by common interests and shared activities. Children especially enjoy stories of adults who show their love by taking the time to share an activity together. In *A Walk in the Rain*, by Ursel Scheffler, Josh and his grandmother go for a walk in the rain. Together they splash through puddles, explore nearby woods, and look for mushrooms. Grandmother never seems in a hurry—she patiently answers Josh's questions and is quite willing to let him take the lead on their adventure. Instead of doing something *for* her grandchild, grandmother has found an activity they can enjoy *together*. Their enjoyment of the walk in the rain is enhanced because it is shared. Ulises Wensell's watercolor illustrations capture the dreamy and peaceful feeling of a gentle shower.

Children who know love, who have experienced it and made it a part of themselves, can then give of themselves to others. Many stories show children expressing devotion to family members. One way that devotion is expressed is by caring for another. *The Maggie B.*, by Irene Haas, is the story of a young girl's love for her baby brother. Margaret Barnstable wished on a star one night for a ship named after her ". . . to sail for a day alone and free, with someone nice for company." The companion she wants most of all is her baby brother. Maggie's adventure with James by her side—fixing him a delicious supper, teaching him how to count, and singing him a song—are touching expressions of affection. Irene Haas's beautiful color illustrations are filled with fascinating detail to add a touch of wonder to this simple, poetic tale.

Some stories show how love can be expressed through giving. *The Mother's Day Mice*, by Eve Bunting, shows how three mice brothers approach the task of finding their mother a gift for Mother's Day. Biggest Mouse picks out a fluffy white wish flower; Middle Mouse finds Mother a juicy red strawberry. Little Mouse wants to give her a spray of honeysuckle, but Cat is lying on the porch of

Honeysuckle Cottage. So he will have to choose something else. Unfortunately, nothing else seems to be the right gift. As he and his brothers return home Little Mouse feels sad because he has nothing to give his mother. But along the way he thinks of something special, a unique gift that can be given but not seen or held. For his gift is not a material object—it is a song of love and appreciation. Each of the mice brothers returns with their own special way of sharing their love with Mother. Mother responds to each of her sons with warmth and affection, confirming the value of their thoughtful gifts.

Sometimes love is expressed through helping. Mutual devotion between a young girl and her grandfather is beautifully portrayed in *The Two of Them* by Aliki. The story begins with the child's birth. "The day she was born, her grandfather made her a ring of silver and polished stone, because he loved her already. Someday it would fit her finger." As they both grow older each flourishes from the affection of the other. "He sang her songs, and told her stories of long ago that had been told to him. Some he made up and some were about his love for the little girl. She helped him in his store after school, and loved the smell of the sawdust he sprinkled on the floor when it rained." But time brings about the inevitable. The grandfather first grows infirm and then becomes sick. The relationship has now come full circle. "At night she tucks him in bed and sings to him and tells him stories he had told her. Some she makes up, and some were . . . of her love for him." When he dies, the emptiness left in her heart is filled with grief. It is spring now, and as she sits in his orchard she is reminded of how they worked together to tend the trees and pick the fruit. Memories of those times together and of his love and devotion will never be forgotten.

The Two of Them is a celebration of the capacity for love. The grandfather's love is all-accepting and nonrestrictive. He cherishes his grandchild because she is a part of his life. She returns his deep affection because of his confirmation of her self-worth and her own capacity for love. Children who listen to this story may be saddened by the grandfather's death. But recognition of the preciousness of human life brings a sense of urgency to forming attachments and expressing love. All relationships end some day, but loving memories can remain. By sharing feelings and ideas after the story, parents can confirm their children's capacity for love and tenderness, not just for relatives but for close friends as well.

Sometimes love is expressed through devotion. In *Rebecca's Nap*, by Fred Burstein, a young girl spends an afternoon with her father instead of napping. Rebecca wakes up shortly after falling asleep for her nap. Mother is asleep so Father takes her outside. Together they explore the land around their rural home. Rebecca finds a big fat toad and gives their horse an apple. She also "helps" her father harvest pumpkins. But Rebecca soon becomes sleepy and ready to continue her nap ... this time for real. Father shows his love by taking the time to be with his daughter and responding to what she finds interesting.

Saying "I love you" is important, too. The significance of this simple statement is beautifully demonstrated in *I'll Always Love You*, by Hans Wilhelm. As the years go by and the young boy grows older and taller, his beloved Elfie, ". . . the best dog in the whole world," grows rounder and rounder. It soon becomes too difficult for Elfie even to climb the stairs. Then one night Elfie dies peacefully in her sleep. The boy is heartbroken.

> We buried Elfie together. We all cried and hugged each other.
>
> My brother and sister loved Elfie a lot, but they never told her so.
>
> I was very sad too, but it helped to remember that I had told her every night, "I'll always love you."

The gentle philosophy of revealing what is in our hearts while there's time is warmly conveyed in this book. The story is sad but not tragic. The tears are more than an expression of mourning; they are a celebration of the boy's love for his lifelong companion. The memories of that love will help him survive his grief. *I'll Always Love You* reminds us to take every opportunity to convey our deepest feelings to our loved ones.

Reach Out and Make Friends

Some stories emphasize the importance of forming friendships. *Lizzie and Harold*, by Elizabeth Winthrop, shows how two children begin a close friendship. Lizzie wants a best friend more than anything else. When she asks her mother how she could find a best friend, her mother responds, "You don't really *get* a best friend. Usually they just happen to you." Harold would like to be her best friend, but Lizzie rejects him because she believes only a girl could be her "best" friend. So she continues to search, and Harold keeps trying to change her mind. He walks to school with her and even shows her how to do the "cat's cradle" and other games with string. He seems to always be there, especially when Lizzie needs him.

But eventually Harold gives up. He decides to bring his trick-or-treat candy to school and give it to somebody else who will promise to be his best friend. When Harold's attention turns to someone else, Lizzie soon realizes that she really does like him best of all. On the way home from school that day Lizzie approaches Harold and asks him to be her best friend. Harold is surprised to see this change of heart but is happy to make friends with the one he likes the most.

The idea of having a "best friend" is important to children. The first relationship with parents provides the basic source of self-esteem. But the world is a social arena. Children need the confirmation of a peer who is not a family member. They expect their parents to love them for who they *are*. But their friends like them for what they *do*. Children can sympathize with Lizzie's mother's advice. You don't gain "best" friends by going out and finding them or buying them. Friendship happens because you like each other and enjoy each other's company.

During the preschool years, friends are important because they are partners in play. Grade-school children's perceptions of friends change because of a shift in their own self-awareness. Grade-schoolers are more conscious of themselves and how they compare to their peers. They want more than someone to play with. They want their friends to like them and to recognize their abilities. They also begin forming close, affectionate feelings of "puppy love" for others. Children can be very self-conscious about these feelings. They may think about showing affection to someone but are too embarrassed to admit their attraction, except to their closest friends.

These ambivalent feelings about showing affection are highlighted in *A Kiss for Little Bear* by Else Holmelund Minarik. After receiving a picture drawn by Little Bear, Grandmother sends a kiss back to him—by way of Hen, Frog, Cat, and Skunk (who stops to give the kiss to another little skunk) until Hen steps in to take the kiss to Little Bear. This warm, humorous story about love and affection ends with the wedding celebration of the two skunks.

Children's initial understanding of the basis for friendship begins with a preoccupation with themselves. Preschoolers believe friends are there to help them have a good time. They may say, for example, that a friend is someone who will give them toys to play with. A friend is someone who is nice to them. Older children, however, believe that friendship involves reciprocity—friends help each other and look out for each other's welfare. "We are friends," an eight-year-old may say, "so I helped him learn to play baseball and he showed me how to play Monopoly." Friends "help each other;" they "join together," and they "trust" and "protect" each other. A preschool child who is teased by a bully would not expect a friend to intervene. But a grade-schooler would expect a friend to help. They believe friends should support each other.

This belief in mutual benefit is conveyed in *Ton and Pon: Big and Little* by Kazuo Iwamura. Ton is tall and Pon is little. Each begins by trying to prove that his height is better than the other. Ton, for example, can walk easily through tall grass while Pon has to struggle. But then Ton hits his head on a tree branch that Pon easily misses. This competition to prove who's better stops when Pon retrieves Ton's hat from a sewer pipe, and Ton retrieves Pon's hat from the top of a haystack. The two decide they are lucky to be friends, for what one can't do the other can. *Ton and Pon* shows children that two individuals can be very different and still be best friends. This perspective encourages children to expand their thinking about friendship from one-way assistance to a mutual exchange of benefits.

The second change in children's beliefs about friendship involves a shift from observable or physical qualities to an awareness of their friend's character. A young child may describe his friend as someone who has red hair, cowboy hat and boots, and a sandbox in his back yard. Grade-school children are more aware of their friends' personalities. An eight-year-old, for example, might tell you his friend is funny and can keep a secret.

Children gradually become more aware of their friends as special people. In *My Friend John*, by Charlotte Zolotow, two boys describe their friendship in terms that acknowledge their differences while celebrating their affection for each other. "We always stick together because I'm good at fights, but John's the only one besides my family who knows I sleep with my light on at night." John and his friend know everything about each other. They share secrets, and they always stick together. At this point children begin to be more aware of a personal, hidden self. Friends are important because children are willing to share this secret side of themselves.

The third change in children's thinking about friends involves a shift from the view that friendships are brief interactions to a belief that these relationships can endure over time. Since their concept of friendship is equated with being nice and conflicts are likely during play, young children may begin, end, and then begin "friendships" again in a relatively short period of time. They may suddenly tell someone who refuses to share a truck, for example, "You're not my friend any more," then reverse themselves a few minutes later when the playmate brings them a toy.

Beginning at about age seven, children view friendship as a continuing relationship. Like preschool children they may also have shifting loyalties because of conflict. But their idea of "friend" means a commitment . . . as long as the peace lasts. The idea that a true friendship can endure despite disagreement and other forms of conflict is not likely to appear until late in the grade-school years.

Friendship as commitment and awareness is humorously portrayed in Judith Viorst's *Rosie and Michael*. "She likes me when I'm dopey and not just when I'm smart. He likes me when I'm grouchy and not just when I'm nice." Rosie and Michael have a mutual admiration society that survives emergencies as well as sudden bursts of anger and name-calling. In one situation after another the two accept each other's differences and express their mutual devotion. Children will enjoy the contrasts between Rosie and Michael. Such stories of friendship show the give-and-take necessary to sustain such a relationship.

Kindness Wins More Friends Than Selfishness

Some stories show how to respond sensitively to others who are afraid of making contact. Caring for animals provides an opportunity for children to learn how to overcome such apprehension. Patience is the theme of *The Mare on the Hill*, by Thomas Locker. When their grandfather buys a white mare that was mistreated by its owner, two boys have the opportunity to help her learn to trust people again. When they release her from the barnyard she retreats to a nearby pasture where she has access to food, water, and shelter. The boys understand the mare's fear and patiently accept her retreat.

Time passes; one season follows another. The two boys carry hay and oats up to the mare during winter and try unsuccessfully to lure her back to the farm. When a storm rumbles through the valley that spring the boys discover that the mare has taken shelter in the barn. They have earned her trust. Soon afterward she even lets them feed her by hand. And the boys' gentle patience is finally rewarded when the mare allows them near her newborn foal.

> As we drew closer, the mare looked up at us. In the soft dawn light she seemed proud and welcoming, and she was calmer than she'd ever been before.

Locker's brilliant oil paintings create a magnificent rural setting for the story.

In *Play With Me*, by Marie Hall Ets, a young girl tries to approach the animals who live in a meadow. Her first response is to grab and poke at them. But each time she tries to catch or touch the frog, turtle, chipmunk, and other woodland animals, they run away. When she finally stops trying and waits quietly, each creature cautiously approaches her.

In both *The Mare on the Hill* and *Play With Me* patient acceptance overcomes initial shyness and fear. Instead of forcing their way into a relationship, characters in these stories provide others with the freedom to manage their fears at their own pace.

Your Friends Can Like Others and Still Like You

Some stories show that friendship can endure misunderstandings and jealousies. *One Frog Too Many*, a wordless picture book by Mercer and Marianna Mayer, is a story of jealousy and reconciliation. Big frog is upset. Little frog has joined his happy family, which includes boy, turtle, and dog. But big frog believes one frog is enough for the group. Maybe he will have to eliminate the competition. So he kicks little frog into the water. But when his competitor fails to surface, big frog's relief gives way to guilt. Now his old friends are worried and angry. Big frog realizes he has made a big mistake.

Children can sometimes be like "big frog," jealous of the intrusions of competitors for the family's or peer group's

STORYBREAK

━━━━━━━━━━━━━

Liking Dust

Once upon a time, in the wonderful town of Butterberry Hill . . .

Casey was feeling lonely. He felt that he had no one to be his friend. Penelope Pig and Briarbutton Rabbit didn't like to do the things he enjoyed. Dorothy was on vacation. And Amy told him she did not want to be his friend because he laughed at the painting she made. That left Rodney. He sure didn't like Rodney and his selfish ways. If only Amy would be his friend. Casey decided to ask Witch Wart for help.

So off he went to Witch Wart's raggedy house on the edge of Butterberry Hill. Witch Wart said she had some magical "Liking Dust" she could give him. But whenever she helped someone she expected some help in return. So she asked Casey to dig up a bag of woolly worm roots for one of her potions. They could be found in the ground next to the Great Blue River that flowed through the Ominous Woods not far from Butterberry Hill. Casey agreed and off he went.

Casey knew it would be a challenge to do what she asked, especially the part about walking through the Ominous Woods. But he found the woolly worm roots, dug them up (boy, did they smell!), and put them in a sack. When she received the roots, Witch Wart gave Casey the sparkly Liking Dust. All he had to do was sprinkle the dust over someone's head, and they would like him forever.

The next day, Casey saw Amy playing outside and stopped to talk to her. He was hoping he'd have the chance to use the Liking Dust. Just as he was about to sprinkle it over Amy's head, Rodney walked in and grabbed his arm. "What you got, Casey?" he asked. Just at that moment, Casey's hand opened up and the dust fell over Rodney's head. "Oh, oh," thought Casey.

The Liking Dust began to work its magic. "Casey, I sure like you," said Rodney. "Come over to my auntie's house to play." Rodney grabbed Casey by the arm and dragged him over to Mrs. Winterbones's house. Rodney gave him toys to play with and kept giving him sweet things to eat. Casey left when his tummy began to ache. The next day, Rodney followed him to school, moved his desk next to him, and wouldn't let anyone else play with him at recess. The same thing happened the next day and the day after that. Casey had never liked Rodney before, but now he became absolutely sick of him.

So Casey paid another visit to Witch Wart. For two sacks of woolly worm roots she agreed to help him once again. Now it was twice as much work and twice the smell. When he returned with the two bags, she told him how to stop the magic of the sparkly Liking Dust. Casey would have to pat Rodney's head while saying, "Dust begone, dust disappear—boogally, boogally, boogally cheer!"

Casey walked back home where Rodney was waiting for him. "Hi, Casey," Rodney said. "Let's play. Come over to my house for more candy." "Ah, Rodney, wait a moment," Casey asked. "Stand still while I tap your head." "Yes, anything for my best friend," said Rodney. So Casey tapped his head while saying, "Dust begone, dust disappear—boogally, boogally, boogally cheer!"

As soon as Casey said the word "cheer," Rodney took a step backward. "Get your hands off me!" he shouted. "Oh, what's that awful smell? Were you rubbing woolly worm root on me? Yuk!" Rodney turned and walked away.

"Whew!" sighed Casey. "I think I like Rodney better as someone who's not my friend." As he walked to Amy's house he thought to himself, "The best friend is one who wants to like you back because of the kind things you do. Maybe Amy will want to be my friend if I tell her I'm sorry for laughing at her painting."

So that's what he did. And you know, he was right!

―――――

attention and affection. Young children find it difficult to understand that someone can like them and another person simultaneously. They may feel that a parent's or friend's affection for another inevitably diminishes the love available to them. *One Frog Too Many* reassures children because it shows that love is expansive, that one can like others without diminishing their other relationships.

Freckles and Willie, by Margery Cuyler, demonstrates how shifting loyalties can blind someone to the value of a friendship. Freckles is not only Willie's pet; he is also his best friend. When Willie is lonely Freckles plays with him. When he is cold Freckles curls up at his feet. To show Freckles how much he loves him, Willie makes him a valentine for Valentine's Day. The significance of a valentine takes on a special meaning for Willie, though, when a new girl moves next door. Unfortunately, Freckles is set aside and overlooked because Jane does not like dogs. But when Jane rejects Willie's valentine, he realizes his mistaken loyalty and returns to the friend that accepts him without reservation. *Freckles and Willie* provides children with an opportunity to sympathize with the underdog. They know how it feels to be shunted aside by someone they thought was their friend. The story also suggests caution when they feel like abandoning old friendships for new ones. By rejecting the old relationship they might lose a precious friend.

You May Miss Your Friends When You Are Not with Them

Some stories focus on the sadness children feel when separated from someone they love. *Annie and the Wild Animals*, by Jan Brett, conveys the longing a young girl feels for her absent pet cat. When her cat disappears Annie tries to become friends with a variety of unsuitable woodland animals. The moose is too big to tame, the wildcat too mean, the bear too grumpy. Others who are attracted to corn cakes left at the edge of a snowy clearing are not as soft and friendly as her cat, Taffy. But when spring arrives Taffy returns. But now she is accompanied by three soft and friendly kittens. Annie will not be lonely any more.

The positive consequences of separation are demonstrated in *Patrick and Ted*, by Geoffrey Hayes. When Ted goes away for the summer Patrick is distraught. Without his best friend he has no one to build things with or hear his secrets. But he soon finds other activities and friends to occupy his time, even enjoying playing by himself, ". . . being just Patrick." When Ted returns, the two friends argue a little as they adjust to a new relationship. But their friendship endures despite their conflict. They discover they can remain best friends without being together all of the time.

The importance of a friend stands in dramatic relief during separation. Annie discovers just how much her cat means to her when it runs away. Separation from friends can also force children to develop new interests and skills. Patrick had become too dependent on Ted. Separation provided him with the opportunity to form new relationships and gain self-confidence.

We are likely to have mixed feelings about our children's friendships. We suffer with them when they are ignored or rejected by their peers. We may also occasionally view our children's friends as competitors who lure them from our sphere of influence to their own. One of the greatest gifts of our love may be to recognize the importance of peer friendship and release our children into the social world.

Most parents may feel at times like the kindly Dr. Rabbit in Jan Wahl's *Doctor Rabbit's Foundling*. While walking home, Dr. Rabbit discovers a tiny bamboo basket containing a tadpole. A note attached to the basket reads, "Take care of my child. Signed: The Unhappy Mother." Dr. Rabbit adopts the baby, and under his gentle care she grows into a lovely little frog. She becomes as precious to him as if she were his own special child. But the time comes for her to join the night and stars as all frogs must someday do. At first, Dr. Rabbit tries to keep her from leaving. But his efforts to keep her at home are futile. Once he realizes that she belongs with her own kind he overcomes his grief and sadly releases her to the night. Dr. Rabbit's predicament is similar to the sorrow any parent feels when a beloved child leaves home.

Summary

"Some day my prince (or princess) will come" is not a statement of fact but rather an expression of inner longing. Each of us, as we grew up, held out hope that we would one day find a Prince Charming or Snow White, someone beautiful in our eyes who would cherish us and accept our love in return. Fantasy can give our lives direction for we all need to have dreams that are part of our personal stories. But we cannot live a fantasy or occupy the castles in our imagination. So parents can also read or tell stories that portray the give-and-take in relationships and how to resolve the problems that plague any friendship. Our heart's longing need not cloud our thinking. The greatest gift our love can provide is the capacity for offering love to another person, to pass the gift along.

CHAPTER SIX

From The Nightingale to Christmas Moon:

Coming to Terms with Loss and Grief

Life can seem at times to be filled with contradictions. A storm rumbles across a peaceful prairie; crops planted with care are parched by a blistering sun; a seedling grows in the shadow of a decaying oak tree. What is true for nature applies to human life, too. A marriage begun with devotion gradually disintegrates as a couple grows apart. An adolescent's dream of inheriting a farm that has been in his family for generations is shattered by foreclosure. A child filled with life one moment is tragically snatched from the world by a drunk driver. Our love and joy may seem at times like grains of sand trickling through our fingers, blown by the twin furies of separation and loss. You and I, we are no strangers to sorrow.

The word "loss" derives from an Old English word that means to perish or be destroyed. Loving someone or something means to make it a part of ourselves and our lives. We expand our definition of ourselves to include what is important to us. Loss or separation disrupts this secure sense of self. Like Humpty Dumpty we may feel like we have broken apart and "all the king's horses and all the king's men" will never be able to put us back together again. Even after recovering we may feel fragmented, as though a part of ourselves is missing.

Children know this sorrow, too. We cannot protect them from separation and loss or hide them from death. Children know what it means to love someone or become attached to something. They also know what it means to be separated from someone or something they love. A favorite teddy bear is lost on a trip, a pet runs away or dies, or a parent leaves—sometimes briefly, sometimes never to return. During such moments children do not hide behind the masquerade of propriety and false valor. Their tears flow freely, without constraint.

Instead of attempting to shield children from all misfortune, we might try to help them come to terms with the contradictions that will be a part of the tapestries of their personal stories. "Coming to terms" means that children will gradually understand that separation, loss, and death are an inevitable part of human experience. Coming to terms with loss also means that they take the pain and hurt, set it aside in their hearts, and then resume the effort of living. Significant loss is never forgotten, but it does not have to be permanently crippling.

There are many ways we can help children come to terms with loss. We can hold them in our arms while they cry, help them bury their pets, and let them see us express our grief. Talking is important, too. Children have all sorts of questions about loss and separation. "Where has Daddy gone?" "Why did he go?" "Will he come back?" These are difficult but typical questions young children have when a parent dies or moves away.

If we do not respond to their concerns, then children will be forced to construct their own reasons for their losses. These explanations may be filled with distortions and inaccuracies:

- Grandpa has gone to heaven. He must love God more than me.
- My dog, Woofy, will have nothing to eat when he is in the ground.
- If I was a good boy, then Daddy would not have died.

Young children cannot grasp the abstractions, complexities, and mysteries surrounding death. They need patient, simple explanations from adults who understand how to reassure them effectively.

We don't have to wait for our children to ask questions to help them come to terms with loss. We can talk to them about our spiritual beliefs and give them information that will help them understand the circumstances surrounding death and other forms of loss such as divorce. We can also convey our thoughts regarding loss and grief through stories and follow-up discussions. We can read or tell them stories about others who have faced loss, experienced grief and then recovered.

How Stories Contribute to Coming to Terms with Loss and Grief

Stories allow children to witness another's experience of loss and separation. During storytime they may hear about a child who cries after his balloon floats away, about another who struggles to cope with her parents' divorce, and a third who affectionately recalls basking in the warmth of a grandparent's love. As they listen to such stories, children reflect on what they hear, compare it to their own lives, and learn from the experiences of story characters. Stories can provide information and stimulate discussions about separation and loss.

Children do not have to face misfortune to benefit from stories about separation and loss. Stories can show others surviving death, divorce and other forms of loss. Through stories children can also learn how death is part of the cycle of life that exists throughout nature. Fortified with this knowledge and the support of others who care about them, children will be able to come to terms with large and small losses.

In *The Nightingale*, by Hans Christian Andersen, an emperor learns the true worth of what he has lost. When he is enchanted by the remarkable Nightingale's song, the Emperor of China demands that the famous bird be invited to sing at his court. When the Nightingale arrives, it sings so beautifully that tears fill the Emperor's eyes. The delicate creature refuses all riches for its wonderful song, declaring that the Emperor's tears are sufficient reward.

One day, a clockwork bird glittering with jewels is brought to the palace. Winding it up makes it sing, its tail glittering with silver and gold as it moves up and down. This remarkable machine, with its ability to sing the same tune, over and over again without getting tired, enchants the Emperor and his court. The Emperor is so blinded by the glamor of the clockwork bird that he awards it a special place on a silk cushion near his bed and banishes the living Nightingale from the land. But one evening, the wheels inside the mechanical creature spin around for a moment and the music stops. After a careful examination, the royal clock-maker declares that the machine is wearing out and should be played only once a year.

Time passes and sorrow descends upon the land, for the Emperor is deathly ill. He pleads for music to ease a troubled mind plagued by memories of his good and evil deeds. But the clockwork bird remains quiet, its silence a bitter reminder of his foolishness. Then one day, while he lies in his bed waiting to greet death, the Emperor hears the most lovely song from outside his window. The Nightingale has returned to sing of comfort and hope, to offer a healing serenade.

The Emperor learned the true value of the Nightingale by its absence. The glitter and sophistication of the mechanical bird distracted him from the natural beauty of the living Nightingale's song. The mechanical bird was indeed amazing. But its song was only a pale imitation of the Nightingale's lovely music.

Separation and loss help us appreciate what is truly important. "You don't know what you've got, until you lose it," as the song tells us. Learning this lesson after the loss may be too late.

Stories like *Christmas Moon*, by Denys Cazet, focus di-

rectly on the impact of death on a young child and the
importance of loving support from adults who care. Even
though it's Christmas Eve, Patrick is sad. "My head is
full of Grandpa," he tells his mother. She comforts him
with "moon magic," a secret Grandpa taught her when she
was a little bunny. She turns off the light in his bedroom,
waves her hand through the moonlight, and wiggles her
fingers over his head. Then she runs her fingers through
his hair, hugs him tightly, and kisses him on the cheek.
"Moon magic," she says. Patrick and his mom sit and rock
together while they share memories of wonderful times
with Grandpa. Comforted by his mother's words of love,
Patrick can now relax and fall asleep. *Christmas Moon*
shows how tender memories and a parent's love can provide reassurance to a child experiencing sadness following
a loss. Denys Cazet's softly radiant illustrations in ink
with watercolor wash bring warmth to the emptiness children feel after the death of someone they love.

Stories like *The Nightingale* and *Christmas Moon* can
provide children with information about loss and death.
But they may also soothe the hurt and reduce a child's
feeling of isolation during a time of sadness. Stories focusing on separation and loss offer a number of concepts for
children to incorporate into their personal stories:

- Everyone feels sad at times.
- You might feel sad when separated from someone you
  love.
- Death is an inevitable part of the cycle of life.
- Death is a permanent loss.
- Expressing sadness is a way to show you care about a
  loss.
- Happy memories of someone we loved are a tribute to
  that relationship and provide us with comfort when we
  feel sad.
- Funerals provide us with an opportunity to say good-bye
  to someone we love.

Everyone Feels Sad at Times

Stories provide us with an opportunity to tell children that sadness is a valuable emotion. Loss is an inevitable part of human life. Sadness is not failure. Sadness is not treason. It is not a punishment or a weakness. Sadness is real. It is an acknowledgment that we care deeply about something. Sadness is a signpost pointing to what we really value. It can make us grow stronger by deepening our compassion and motivating us to form worthwhile relationships with others. If we deny our losses and hide our sadness from others as well as ourselves, then we become the illusions we project. Denial of sadness narrows our experience of life to a shallow range of superficial human emotion.

In *Porcupine's Christmas Blues*, by Jane Breskin Zalben, Porcupine is feeling sad and he doesn't know why. His friend Bernard tells him, "It's okay to feel sad. Everybody does, sometimes." Porcupine is thankful for all the wonderful things in his life—good friends, great food, sunshine glowing on him in the afternoon, and the moon at night. He also has his guitar and his songs. But he still feels melancholy. As he reflects on his friend's reassurance he picks up his guitar and begins to sing:

> I got those Porcupine highs
> way up to the skies.
> No blues for me.
> Happy as can be.
> It's Christmas time
> and I'll light the tree.
> I have a pal
> who is good for me . . .

Porcupine leaves his home to wish a good morning and Merry Christmas to his other forest friends. When he returns home he is alone but definitely not lonely. The blues are gone.

Porcupine is fortunate to have friends who accept his

sadness and gently remind him of the good things in his life. He is also able to express his sadness through his songs. Children can sometimes feel like Porcupine. They may miss a valued playmate who has moved away or a pet that has died. Maybe they miss the presence of a parent who is too busy to take time to be with them. When someone asks them, "What's wrong?" they may not be able to explain why they feel the way they do. We can't reach inside children's hearts to manipulate their emotions. But we can provide support by accepting their feelings and showing them we care.

The Lonely Prince, by Max Bolliger, examines the reasons for a child's sadness. Young Prince William is a melancholy figure who never laughs or cries. The king and queen love their son and worry about his welfare. So they eagerly provide him with everything he wants—a hot-air balloon, a lion in a cage, and even command of an army. But the young prince's gloomy mood is unaffected by these dramatic gifts.

Then Prince William meets the gardener's son and his pet rabbit. He is fascinated by the tiny pet and insists that his young subject give it to him. But the young boy is devoted to his pet rabbit and refuses to comply with the prince's demand. This unexpected defiance surprises the prince, and he begins to cry. The gardener's boy takes pity on him and invites him to share his pet. "I can't give you my rabbit because I love him and he knows me, but we can play with him together." The two boys spend the next day playing together with the rabbit. That night, to his parents' amazement, William smiles and laughs for the very first time. He has discovered the best antidote for his sadness—a friend.

The key moment in *The Lonely Prince* occurs when Prince William begins to cry. At the very moment that he discovers something truly important, he is prevented from making it his own. For the first time we see the prince really feel. His crying is an emotional breakthrough that thaws his emotional indifference. Once he begins to express his feelings, happiness also becomes possible. The prince discovers that what he really needs is a friend, someone like the gardener's son, who is willing to share his enjoyable moments. Like *The Nightingale, The Lonely Prince* is a story about the discovery of what is truly important.

You Might Feel Sad When Separated from Someone You Love

Children begin learning about separation and loss during infancy. During the second half of their first year infants may show intense "separation anxiety" when their parents leave them. They have formed a strong relationship with their parents and cannot understand the temporary nature of a separation. With repeated separations and returns, playing games like peek-a-boo, finding hidden objects, and playing with their toys, infants gradually begin to understand that separation does not necessarily mean loss. By the end of their first year they have learned what developmental psychologists call object permanence—they know that objects remain in existence even though they cannot be seen. But children will continue to experience a tinge of fear, a shadow of doubt when separated from someone they love. Maybe they won't really return after all.

In *I Want Mama*, by Marjorie Weinman Sharmat, a young girl feels alone and lonely when her mother goes to the hospital for an operation. She worries about her mother's safe return. "I think Mama's never coming back. She's never going to brush my hair again or find where I put my green socks when I've given up looking," she tells herself. Even though she cannot visit the hospital she calls her mother on the phone. She even makes her a gift. After one of her father's visits to the hospital he tells his daughter that her mother will be coming home in three days. Overjoyed, the young girl rushes about the house to prepare it for her mother's return.

I Want Mama shows how children react when separated from someone they love. At various times the young girl becomes angry, disappointed, and frightened. She fantasizes about visiting her mother and tries to bargain to get her back. "Maybe if I promise to tell the whole truth for the rest of my life, Mama will come back. Maybe she won't." And finally, there is real joy when she discovers that her mother is returning home.

Some stories can provide insight about attachment to a special place or treasure. In *Georgia Music* Helen Griffith tells us about a young girl who learns about the anguish of leaving one's home. She stays with her grandfather one summer in an old cabin near some railroad tracks. She helps him tend his hot garden patch. After lunch they relax under a tree and look up at the leaves and the sky.

> It was so quiet that they could hear the leaves touching each other, and the bumblebees bumbling, and the crickets and grasshoppers whirring and scratching. And every now and then the old man would nod his head under his straw hat and say, "Now, that's music."

In the evening the two of them would sit on the porch and the old man would play tunes on his harmonica. At night they'd go to sleep to the katydids and the tree frogs and the chuck-will's-widows singing. But then September arrives and his granddaughter has to reluctantly return home. When the girl and her mother return the following summer, they discover that grandfather is no longer able to care for himself. So they take him back to their home in Baltimore. Deprived of his garden and old cabin, grandfather spends his days languishing in a stuffed chair and looking worried and sad. But then his granddaughter learns to play his harmonica. He reexperiences in her music the memories of those warm Georgia summers when day and night were filled with beautiful music. Like the grandfather in *Georgia Music*, children can form attachments to a place.

Divorce also causes painful separations in children's lives. *That Is That*, by Jeanne Whitehouse Peterson, shows how a young girl comes to terms with the sudden and permanent departure of her father. When her father leaves to find his "happiness," Emma Rose tries to console her younger brother by playing an imaginative game. After her mother sends her to her room, she again resorts to magical thinking as she performs a "Magical Come-Home Dance" in front of her mirror.

"Mysterious world! Bring my father back! ... One! Two! Three! Four!"

She closes her eyes and feels her way to the window. But when she opens her eyes and looks out into the front yard, her father remains painfully absent.

That night Emma Rose makes a "Remembering Place." She gathers her father's picture, a candle stub, a china bear, a plastic water gun her father had given her for her birthday, and one of his old cuff links. She sets her treasures on one corner of her desk along with a note that reads, "Good-bye, Father. So long." At first she thinks about him almost every day and cannot talk about him to anyone. But over time the hurt gradually eases. Then one day, while making a snowman with her brother, Emma composes a song. "If you are sad and lonely, I wonder why you wander in the night? But if you are happy, I understand, and wish you well." Emma Rose has come to accept her father's disappearance.

That Is That shows how children use their imagination and play to come to terms with separation or loss. Emma Rose's pain has not been eliminated. She still feels deeply hurt by her father's sudden absence. But his departure does not shatter her life. She is able to translate some of her grief into tenderness toward her younger brother, who was also hurt and confused by their father's absence. Caring for him provides her with an opportunity to reach out to another instead of withdrawing into the nightmare of her own pain.

Always, Always, by Crescent Dragonwagon, shows how children from divorced families can feel divided loyalty for their parents. A young girl reflects on the dramatic differences in her divorced parents—her father is an outdoorsman and carpenter who lives in the country, her mother an office professional who prefers the city. Since her parents divorced she has lived with her father in the summer and with her mother the rest of the year. Even though their values make life together impossible, both parents help their daughter realize that their love for her will endure despite the breakup of their marriage. Her significance in their lives is in no way diminished by their separation. *Always, Always* portrays two parents who have come to terms with their decision to part and have set aside their differences to support their daughter.

In *One More Time*, by Louis Baum, a father enjoys a fun afternoon in the park with Simon, his preschool son. On the return train trip to the home where Simon lives with his mother, father and son share a picnic and storytime together. After arriving at the front door, father promises, "See you soon." Simon responds, "See you soon." Parting is much easier when there is the promise of being reunited.

The title of the story comes from Simon's insistence that he and his father sail a boat, read a story, or ring a door bell ". . . one more time." Simon wants to prolong the time he has with his father and to get the most out of their enjoyable moments together. He does not seem to be particularly sad about their separation. Apparently he is used to his parents' visitation arrangements. But it's obvious Simon is not eager to part. He would treasure almost anything he and his father might do "one more time."

While all children are vulnerable to the catastrophic effects of divorce, researchers have noted that there are fairly significant differences between children depending on their sex (boys at all ages tend to take the event harder) and age. Young children are affected by instability in their daily routine and family life and are more dependent on the family as a source of nurturance. Adjustment can be difficult for young children because of the way they interpret the loss. Preschool children may invent macabre fantasies about the reasons for a parent's departure, or blame themselves for the breakup. In the back of their minds they may be afraid that the remaining parent may also abandon them. So they may cling to this parent, even getting up in the middle of the night to see if he or she is still there.

Following divorce young children may show a lessened interest in expressive play, at a time when such creativity is needed for expressing the tension they feel about the loss or separation. They may regress to some behaviors common during an earlier, more secure stage in their lives. Thumb-sucking, wetting or soiling their pants, temper tantrums, and eating problems may reappear, adding to the parent's burden. Many children find themselves desperately seeking support from parents who are trying to pick up the fragments of their lives and face the world once again.

Storytime can be a moment for parents to reassure their children of their love while encouraging them to think about and better understand the sadness that accompanies this change in their lives.

Death Is an Inevitable Part of the Cycle of Life

Preschool children do not sit around and worry about death. They cannot conceive of a time when they were not living, nor can they consider a time when they will no longer be alive. They live primarily in the present. What they do fear, though, is separation and abandonment.

Children cannot easily grasp the inevitability of death because of their beliefs about what constitutes life. According to Piaget, young children's thinking is characterized by "animism," the attribution of life and consciousness to inanimate objects. Initially young children may attribute life to anything that moves. A five-year-old may say that trees cry when they shed their leaves, that clouds floating in the sky are going on a trip, or that a bush billowing in the wind is trying to grab her. During the later preschool years children attribute life only to those things that move of their own accord. Thus, a child may consider a clock alive because it moves by itself. At about seven or eight years of age children begin to restrict their definition of life to people, plants, and animals.

Because of this animism, young children are likely to attribute consciousness to someone who has died. They may believe that dead people still have the use of their senses but cannot move. During a discussion about death, a kindergartner may ask her teacher how dead people get food when they are in the ground. Some children may become afraid of bedtime because they associate such stillness with death. This belief may be reinforced by a bedtime prayer that says ". . . and if I should die before I wake. . . ."

Our stories and discussions cannot force children to understand the universality of death. We can, though, begin to introduce the idea of a life *cycle*, the concept that growth and decay are interconnected. Nature provides numerous examples of changes that are part of the life cycle.

Rosalie, by Joan Hewett, with illustrations by Donald Carrick, shows how an aging pet dog gradually loses many of her physical abilities but remains an important part of a family's life. Rosalie is sixteen years old. She is deaf and moves much more slowly now. But she is still cherished and included in her family's activities. Everyone learns to make adjustments to the changes they see in their beloved companion. They stop and let her rest when they play and continue to talk to her even though she cannot hear. They try to watch out for her when she lies down to rest, and they pay very close attention to her health. Rosalie is changing as she ages, but everyone loves her for being special.

The Dead Tree, by Alvin Tresselt, shows the gradual decline of a magnificent oak tree. For one hundred years the oak tree spread its branches to the sky. But now it's battered by storms and ravished by insects and other forest creatures. A hurricane eventually topples the proud but weakened oak. The tree gradually decomposes on the rich forest ground. As its form changes, the tree nourishes both the seedlings that grow in its shadow and the forest creatures who seek shelter and food. Then in its final form . . . "On the ground there remained only a brown ghost of richer loam where the proud tree had come to rest."

Tresselt's prose is rich with sensory imagery: ". . . the mosses stitched a green carpet softer than the softest wool," and ". . . the brown leathery leaves, shaken down by the autumn winds, moldered under the snow." These vivid images help to anchor the transformation in nature. The death of the tree is not portrayed as an unfamiliar, unjust event. Instead, it is shown to be interconnected with the life that exists all around it.

The generational life cycle is also introduced in *Mrs. Huggins and Her Hen Hanna*, by Lydia Dabcovich. Mrs. Huggins has a happy relationship with her hen Hanna. They cook and bake and clean the house together. They cooperate with gardening and other farm chores. But this comfortable arrangement comes to an unfortunate end when Hanna becomes sick and dies. Mrs. Huggins buries Hanna in a nearby green meadow and returns sorrowfully to an empty cottage. Her tears of grief are soon interrupted, though, by a sound coming from Hanna's nest. A fuzzy chick has just hatched from one of Hanna's eggs. Mrs. Huggins is overjoyed, for her friend continues to live as part of the following generation. *Mrs. Huggins and Her Hen Hanna* provides parents with an opportunity to introduce children to the life cycle. Parents might also talk with their children about their ancestors and how one generation followed another in their family. These stories can supplement discussions and observations parents and children may have about changes in nature.

Between seven and nine years of age children gradually begin to realize that death is a drastic change involving disintegration of the body, but they may still not understand that death is a natural part of the life cycle. At this age children believe death is caused by accident or illness. If they can keep themselves safe by avoiding accidents or illness, they reason, then they may not die. At about ten years of age children realize that death is an inevitable part of all human life.

A young girl tries to prevent the death of her grandmother in *Annie and the Old One*, by Miska Miles, by stopping her mother from completing a weaving. Her grandmother has announced that when the new rug is taken from the loom, she will "go to Mother Earth." Annie does not want the Old One to die. But she is unable to convince her mother to stop weaving the rug. Gradually the rug begins to take form and increase in size. In desperation Annie rises in the middle of the night to unravel a portion of the rug from the loom. But on the third night, the Old One is waiting for her and gently asks her to return to bed.

The next day, as they sit together on a small mesa gazing off toward the rim of the desert, the Old One tells Annie:

> "My granddaughter," she said, "you have tried to hold back time. This cannot be done." The desert stretched yellow and brown away to the edge of the morning sky. "The sun comes up from the edge of the earth in the morning. It returns to the edge of the earth in the evening. Earth, from which good things come for the living creatures on it. Earth, to which all creatures finally go."

These words helped Annie understand that her grandmother's life and inevitable death were a part of the rhythm of growth and decline in nature, that all life is and always will be a part of the earth. She has a new perspective on death, one that provides her with solace. Her mind eased, Annie picks up her grandmother's weaving stick, a final gift from the Old One, to help complete the weaving, as her mother had done and her grandmother before her.

Using stories to talk with children about death does not mean a morbid preoccupation with the end of life. Quite the contrary. Awareness of death can deepen our feeling for those who are dear to us. "If we truly saw that death was imminent for all," the theologian Kierkegaard suggested, "could we be anything but kind, loving, full of compassion all the time?"

Death Is a Permanent Loss

The permanency of death is another difficult issue for children to understand. Psychologist Maria Nagy found that children between the ages of three and five may act as though death is a temporary event. At this stage children may view death as reversible. It is a departure, a state of sleep, a separation, a change in environment, a temporary illness, or a form of limited life. Death is like a journey—you leave, then you return. Comments like "Grandpa has died and gone to heaven" reinforce this idea. Children may expect the dead to recover, or may speak of the dead as though they are alive. Some children may dig up the grave of a pet to see if it is still there. Not until they are about seven years old will most children realize that death is irrevocable. However, researcher Myra Bluebond-Langner's work with terminally ill children suggests that even young children can be aware that their death is a permanent separation from those they love. Under conditions of intense stress, children may realize that death is a final and irreversible fact of life. Stories can gently lay the foundation for this gradual awareness of the permanency of death.

The Black Dog Who Went Into the Woods quietly emphasizes death's finality. Black Dog is missing—"gone into the woods and died," Benjamin says. Other family members look for her, but Benjamin, the youngest in the family, insists, "Black Dog is gone forever." She was deaf and very old and her walk was stiff and painful. She went to the woods because she knew it was time to die. Then one night, when the moon was full, each person in the family dreams something special about Black Dog. As the moonlight touches each of their faces they wake from their dream and whisper their good-byes to their beloved pet. At breakfast the following morning, family members talk about how their special dream visits allowed them to say farewell to Black Dog. With *The Black Dog Who Went Into the Woods* Edith Thacher Hurd has crafted a wonderful story of love, departure, and farewell. The family knows that Black Dog will never return. To come to terms with that loss they have to make a special farewell, to give tribute to the pet who has provided them with so many happy memories. Emily Arnold McCully's softly colored illustrations add to the dreamy quality of the story.

Time for Uncle Joe, by Nancy Jewell, shows a young girl struggling with the death of a special uncle.

> It is spring again, and the lilac bush is fat and green
> and ready to bloom once more.
> Even the lilacs know
> It's time for Uncle Joe.

As she wanders through Uncle Joe's house and garden the young girl recalls their happy times together. His vacant room is sad confirmation of the fact that he will never return.

> "I know Uncle Joe is never coming back. But soon his whole room will be filled with the scent of lilacs. And when I press my face against the fat, purple clusters, Uncle Joe will be here with me again."

The young girl's recital of loving memories is a deeply moving tribute and a gentle reminder to herself of the permanence of her loss.

We can also respond to children's questions and insecurities by explaining what happens to an individual after death. "Where did Grandpa go? Where *is* he!" children want to know. Our response might help them better understand the natural consequences of death.

The Tenth Good Thing About Barney, by Judith Viorst, offers a logical explanation of what happens to the body following death. Barney the cat died last Friday, and now a grief-stricken young boy struggles with saying good-bye. When his mother asks him to remember ten good things about Barney, he can only name nine. Later, as they plant seeds in their garden, the young boy and his father talk about Barney being in the ground. Father notes, "He'll help grow the flowers, and he'll help grow that tree and

STORYBREAK

Dorothy and Snuggles

Once upon a time, in the wonderful town of Butterberry Hill . . .

Little Dirty Dorothy felt very sad. Snuggles, her pet dog, had died. Snuggles had been her friend for many, many years. As long as she could remember Snuggles was always around. But now he was dead. He had lived a full life and was very, very old. But Dorothy was still sad, because she already missed her old friend. She felt a great weight in her heart. She and her father buried Snuggles in their back yard under a beautiful oak tree.

The next day, on her way back from school, Dorothy still felt sad and close to crying. Amy saw her walking along with a sad expression on her face. "Cheer up, Dorothy! Too bad about your dog. Smile and you will be happy!" And then she went on her way. Dorothy tried to smile. But when she tried to smile her mouth hurt, as if she were tugging on its corners. And the weight in her heart began to grow heavier.

Casey tried to cheer her up too when he saw her. "Too bad about Snuggles, Dorothy. But you can get another dog. So don't be sad." And then he went on his way. Dorothy thought, "Who wants another dog? I want Snuggles back. No other dog will be as nice as Snuggles." She sat down under a tree. Her mouth started to tremble, and a tear began to form in the corner of her eye. The weight in her heart seemed even greater now.

Just then, Rodney happened by. When he saw Dorothy's downcast look he said, "You are not going to cry, are you? Crying's for babies!" Then he went on his way. "I must not cry," Dorothy told herself. "I must not cry . . . I must not cry." But with every word she felt herself coming closer and closer to actually crying. And the weight in her heart just grew worse.

Grandpa Jake saw her sitting under the tree. He knew Snuggles had died and that Dorothy felt sad. He went over and sat down next to her on the ground. They both just sat there quietly for a few minutes. Then Dorothy said, "Snuggles died, Grandpa Jake." "Yes, I heard that he died, Dorothy," said Grandpa Jake.

After a few more moments of silence Dorothy spoke up again. "He was my friend and I loved him." Grandpa Jake moved a little closer to her. "Yes, to lose a friend, someone you love is very sad. I bet you feel really sad, Dorothy."

More tears appeared in Dorothy's eyes. Then more tears, and more tears, and then she began to cry. As she cried, Dorothy moved closer to Grandpa Jake. Dorothy cried and cried as the tears rolled down her cheeks. Grandpa Jake reached out and gently put his arm on her shoulder. And still she cried.

In a little while she stopped. "I will miss Snuggles, Grandpa Jake." "Yes, you will. A little part of your heart will always remember him," Grandpa Jake told her. Dorothy wiped the tears from her eyes. "I guess you think I am a crybaby, Grandpa Jake." "No, Dorothy. I don't think that. I think you are a brave person to show how you really feel. And I think you are a loving person to show how much you care for Snuggles."

"Thanks, Grandpa Jake." Dorothy stood up. "I guess it's time for me to get home. My dad needs my help to cook supper." Grandpa Jake stood up too. "I'll walk a little ways with you, Dorothy, if that's okay." "Sure," Dorothy said, as a smile began to appear on her face. As she and Grandpa Jake walked down the street together Dorothy was already beginning to feel the weight in her heart lighten.

---

some grass. . . . That's a pretty nice job for a cat." With his father's help, the young boy has discovered the *tenth* good thing about Barney.

Judith Viorst provides an optimistic response to a child struggling to understand what has happened to his pet. She clearly and firmly points out that the cat is no longer alive. Barney's body has been returned to the earth, where it nurtures life that will later take root there. The young boy is satisfied because this logical explanation resolves his uncertainty.

Spiritual explanations of what happens following the death of a person are extremely difficult for children to grasp. Mordicai Gerstein offers a Tibetan perspective of what follows death in his book *The Mountains of Tibet.* A woodcutter longs to travel and see the world. But he grows old and dies before fulfilling his wish. When he is given the choice of becoming part of the endless universe some call heaven or living another life, the woodcutter chooses to return to earth.

What we hope to communicate to our children about what follows death is deeply personal. We should keep in mind, though, that young children take our comments *literally.* If we say, "Grandma has gone to heaven," a young child will believe that Grandma has left home to go to another worldly place, like the time she visited relatives in Denver. The fact that she won't come back can be distressing, because young children often interpret such loss as a rejection, a confirmation that they are being punished for being bad. We should also be aware that young children can parrot back what we tell them without understanding the meaning of the words they use. Our challenge is to state our beliefs as simply as possible and to be alert to misinterpretations so we can patiently and clearly correct them.

Expressing Sadness Is a Way to Show You Care About a Loss

John Bowlby of the Tavistock Clinic in London found that children moved through three stages of mourning following significant loss. First, they are likely to test the reality of their loss by denying that death has occurred. They may act as though nothing has happened. A preschooler may seem unconcerned when informed of a parent's death, while another may continue to set out milk for a pet cat that was recently killed by a car. At this point children are not capable of registering the reality of the loss. Only later, when repeated appeals similar to "When is Daddy coming back?" fail to ensure the loved one's return, will children move into the second stage of shock, disbelief, and distress.

During this second stage, strong emotions emerge as children become more conscious of the loss. At first, they may become angry. They may demand that the loved one return. Out of frustration, they may lash out at others. When this protest fails they may feel personally rejected. They may personally blame themselves for the loss. Now tears may make their appearance as the permanence of the loss becomes more apparent. When the loss is particularly important and their protests continue to be unsuccessful, children may then withdraw into despair and apathy. A melancholy cloud may seem to follow them everywhere they go. They may have hollow, sad eyes that seem to say, "I have no hope." Their secure world has fallen apart like a house of cards in a blustery Kansas wind.

With time and patient support, though, children can mend the torn fabric of their world and move to a third stage of grief, a reorganization of their lives without the attachment. Only at this stage can children form relationships that may serve as a substitute for the one they lost. An uncle, for example, can now become a father figure; a new pet can join the family.

Can you recall how sad your child was when a toy he liked was lost or broken? Maybe at first he pretended he didn't care. But try as he might, his mask of indifference failed to make the hurt disappear. *I Don't Care*, by Marjorie Sharmat, shows how young children move through these stages of responding to loss. When his blue balloon with a smiling face blows away, Jonathan tries to deny that it had any real importance.

"I don't care. It was just a dumb balloon," he tells himself. "I don't care if it blew away." But when the reality of his loss can no longer be ignored, Jonathan gives in to his feelings and cries. His tears flow freely. He runs around the block and cries, he runs into the house and cries, and then he just sits and cries. And because Jonathan cries as much as he needs to, when he is through crying, he is really through. He has expressed his heartache, allowed the reality of his loss to work its way into his heart, and now he is ready to resume living without his treasure.

Children's beliefs about the significance of their losses may be different from what we believe is important. A toy balloon means little to us. But that's not the case for Jonathan. By accepting a child's view of what is important, as Jonathan's parents did, we may be more effective in helping our children adjust to their losses.

As children gradually open their minds to the fact of the loss they may release their pain through tears. Jonathan's crying helps restore his emotional balance. His parents allow him to react honestly to his loss. They don't insist that he stop, or minimize the significance of his loss. They let him make the adjustment in his own way. Jonathan adjusts fairly quickly because the balloon, though important to him at the moment, was not deeply significant in his life. His response would have been different if a treasured pet, grandparent, or parent had died. Regardless of the objective value of the loss, crying is part of the healing process, especially if a compassionate friend or parent is there to provide support.

The power of tears and the importance of having someone nearby to share the sadness is the emphasis in *Goodbye, Max*, by Holly Keller. Ben could not believe that his pet dog Max was dead. When Max became sick, Ben and his mother took him to the vet and did everything he told them to do. But Max dies while Ben is at school. When he learns of the death Ben's first reaction is anger toward the vet and his mother. He refuses to even consider a new pet. A new puppy, no matter how cute, would never replace Max. Then Ben's friend Zach arrives to help him deliver newspapers. As they walk through the neighborhood the two friends recall some funny moments with Max. Their laughter, however, soon turns to tears.

> "Boy, I miss him," Ben said.
> "Yeah," Zach said, "me too. But he was really old."
> Ben didn't answer.

He sat down on the curb and started to cry. Zach sat
down next to him, and he cried too. Ben cried until he
couldn't cry anymore.

Fond memories and honest tears provide Ben with the
opportunity to accept his loss. He could share his feelings
with a sympathetic friend who provided support and
reassurance.

Zach's response was helpful because he allied himself
with Ben's pain. He didn't try to stop him from feeling sad.
He didn't make suggestions or offer false condolences. He
shared Ben's sadness, feeling not only the loss of Max but
his friend's grief, too. But he also gently reminded Ben
that Max was quite old. He had lived a full life.

With *The Accident* and *The Foundling*, Carol Carrick
documents the denial, anger, withdrawal, and recovery of
another young child saddened by the death of his pet dog.
We first learn about the death of Bodger in *The Accident*.
The accident that killed Bodger was not anyone's fault.
Christopher's pain is first translated into anger toward the
remorseful driver who hit his pet, and later into frustration with his father for not telling him about burying
Bodger. Christopher and his father take their canoe up the
brook to search for a special stone for Bodger's grave. After
the stone is placed at the grave his father recalls a humorous moment when Bodger tried unsuccessfully to catch a
fish. Christopher's giggles turn to sobs and then real tears.
As he gives in to his grief, he lets the strong arms of his
father enfold him.

The Foundling chronicles Christopher's further adjustment to the loss. The story begins with Christopher resisting his father's encouragements to adopt a puppy. The pain
of Bodger's death is still much too vivid. Part of his mind
still wants to remain faithful to his loyal pet. He does not
want another dog, because no other animal could ever
replace Bodger. But Christopher invites another pet into
his life when he finds an abandoned puppy who needs his
care.

The death of a loved one can be the most bewildering of

all. *Goodbye Rune*, written by Norwegian author Marit Kaldhol, is a powerful, sensitive portrayal of how children respond to death and the support they need to help them come to terms with loss. Sara's best friend is Rune. While playing together at the edge of a lake Sara runs home to find her boots. But when she returns, she discovers Rune floating face down in the water. His death is a crushing blow to the young girl. Sara is bewildered and broken-hearted. To help her cope with her great loss her parents and grandparents accept her grief and patiently respond to her questions about Rune's death. Their tender affection and honesty gradually help to sooth her distress. *Goodbye Rune* may appear at first glance to be too intense for children. But Marit Kaldhol shows children that even under these terrible circumstances others will reach out to help them, that they can survive such a loss. Wenche Oyen's watercolors provide a dreamlike soft focus to the tragic events. Because *Goodbye Rune* is a deeply touching portrayal of grief, take the time to talk with children before and after you share it with them.

The Accident, The Foundling and *Goodbye Rune* point out that movement through the stages of grief cannot be forced. Healing can take place only over time in an atmosphere of acceptance and support. During this time we help children accept the reality of their loss or separation by encouraging them to talk about how they feel. Speak honestly about your own experiences of loss and separation. And help children find the words to communicate their distress by giving their emotions names like *sadness, grief, distress*, or *sorrow*.

Happy Memories of Someone We Loved Are a Tribute to That Relationship and Provide Us with Comfort When We Feel Sad

Following the intense emotion that appears early in the second stage of grief, children may be ready to talk about the loved one who has died. They may want to look at photos or describe experiences with the pet or relative.

Reminiscing gives them the opportunity to put the loss
into perspective. Their mind slowly comes to terms with
the loss: "This is someone I loved, but I know he's gone.
This is sad, but I have happy memories about our times
together. My life has been enriched by knowing him."

The power of sharing memories of a loved one is illustrated in *Badger's Parting Gifts*, by Susan Varley. Badger
was so old he knew he must soon die. Badger wasn't afraid
of death, but he was worried about how his friends would
feel when he was gone. So he told them that he would be
soon "going down the long tunnel," and he hoped they
wouldn't be too sad when it happened. But still, his friends
are shocked when Badger dies. Mole is especially unhappy,
for Badger was his very special friend.

To console themselves, Badger's friends gather to talk
about the days when Badger was alive. Mole tells about
the time when Badger showed him how to use scissors to
cut out a chain of figures from folded paper. Frog recalls
how Badger helped him learn to skate. Fox remembers
how Badger showed him how to knot his tie properly. And
Mrs. Rabbit is thankful for Badger's special gingerbread
recipe.

Each of the animals had a special memory of Badger—
something he had taught them that they could now do
extremely well. He had given them each something to
treasure: a parting gift that would become all the more
special each time it was passed on to others.

On the hillside where he last saw Badger, Mole looks to
the sky and thanks his friend for his parting gift.

Reminiscing allows Badger's friends to share their pain
with each other. When children and adults deny their
grief, they drive it deep into their hearts and minds, where
they have to work to keep it from rising to their consciousness. At these moments we may stop feeling anything,
because any emotion can crumble our fragile defenses and
call attention to the grief. Happiness and enthusiasm then
become hostages in the effort to protect ourselves from

pain. Sharing the loss with others allows our minds to gradually open up to the truth of the loss.

In *Nadia the Willful*, by Sue Alexander, a young girl helps her father, the leader of her clan, recognize the healing power of sharing memories. When her favorite brother Hamed disappears in the desert forever, Nadia refuses to let him be forgotten, despite her father's bitter decree that his name shall not be uttered. Her father tries to ignore and eradicate his pain by forbidding any mention of his son's name. But for Nadia every day holds something to remind her of her beloved brother—the stories he told, the games he played. Her father's desperate decree only deepens her pain. But Nadia cannot remain silent for long. She defiantly approaches others of their clan to speak openly of Hamed and all that he did. The more she talks about Hamed, the clearer his face becomes in her mind and the less hurt she feels inside. But her father continues to threaten banishment for any who speak his name. When she confronts him with her anger, Nadia discovers that her father's bitterness is fueled by desperation. He is gradually forgetting how his son looked and sounded and the happy moments they shared. Nadia gently describes for her father the sad and happy times they had with Hamed:

> "Now you see," Nadia said, her tone more gentle than the softest of the desert breezes, "there is a way that Hamed can be with us still."

Nadia shows her father the healing power of memories. To try to forget, to ignore the misfortune, is ineffective because it denies the magnitude and significance of the loss. Nadia had to remind her clan of how her brother enriched their lives. Sharing these memories was a deserving tribute. Nadia was the first to realize that she had to understand her brother's significance for her life before she could come to terms with his death.

As the heart opens up to grief and expresses itself through both tears and anger, sharing memories with another helps to restore balance in a mind fragmented by loss. Prior to a loss our minds are like a nearly completed puzzle resting on a table. Death disrupts this order by hurling this puzzle to the ground and scattering its pieces. Reminiscing allows us to begin reassembling the puzzle, piece by piece, until we make our minds whole once again. Reminiscing about a loved one is part of the healing process.

Funerals Provide Us with an Opportunity to Say Good-Bye to Someone We Love

Funerals can be another way of playing tribute to someone who has died. In *The Dead Bird*, by Margaret Wise Brown, a group of children conduct a funeral for a dead bird they find in the woods. Following the burial and decoration of the grave, the children sing a song lamenting its death and affirming the permanence of the loss.

> You will never fly
> Again in the sky
> Way up high
> Little dead bird.

Then every day until they forget, the children sing to the little dead bird and place flowers on its grave.

A ritual like a funeral brings the group together to share their grief and acknowledge the common loss. In *The Happy Funeral*, Eve Bunting shows how cultural traditions offer comfort to a child who is saddened by the death of a grandparent. When Laura's grandfather dies, the young Chinese-American girl is confused by her mother's words, "When someone is very old and has lived a good life, he is happy to go." Laura's sorrow is brightened by happy memories of a man who taught her how to tie her shoelaces, how to tell time, and how to let the wind lift her kite into the sky. At the conclusion of the funeral, which is a blend of Chinese and American traditions, Laura ponders the meaning of her mother's words. Death can be a peaceful conclusion to a long, fruitful life.

In *A Fish in His Pocket*, Denys Cazet shows how a young

child uses a simple ceremony to make a special farewell. On his way to school Russell the bear stops by a pond and breaks the morning ice to look beneath the water's surface. As he exchanges looks with a school of fish, one of his textbooks falls into the water. He quickly retrieves the book before it sinks. But after arriving at school, Russell and his teacher discover a tiny dead fish inside the soggy book.

After spending most of the afternoon thinking about what to do with the fish, Russell finally arrives at a solution. After school he makes a little paper boat with "Take Care" written on its side and returns to the pond. "Take care," he says as he gently places the dead fish in the boat and sets it adrift. Russell's simple send-off is his way of showing regret for the accidental death of the fish. Like the last chapter in a book it provides him with a reassuring conclusion to the unfortunate beginning of his day.

Summary

Life can offer no guarantee of protection from death. If we live our lives pretending there is no end, we build a fragile house of cards ready to collapse as the reality of our finite nature becomes obvious. Pretense and illusion, not death, diminish the quality of our lives.

Stories and storytime provide a powerful opportunity for parents to reach out to their children with ideas that will help them cope with the inevitable losses in their lives. There are four keys to helping children come to terms with loss: information, emotional expression, tenderness, and reminiscing. Stories and storytime can help us reach each of these goals. Stories provide children with information about the circumstances surrounding loss and can show characters expressing deep feelings of sadness while they gradually make their recovery. Storytime can also be a special moment of tenderness between parent and child and an encouragement for reminiscing.

In the final analysis, death is a mystery. The most important message related to this story theme may be that the honest acknowledgment and examination of pain and worry will not destroy us or our children. In the comfort of a parent's embrace, children can learn to give words to their greatest fears. Through stories, they will discover that they are not alone. The greatest mystery and the most painful contradictions in their life's journey can be shared with others in the human community.

CHAPTER SEVEN

From Saint George and the Dragon to The Changing Maze:

Offering Kindness to Others

Martin hears his mother crying. The two-year-old stops playing with his trucks and runs into the living room. There she is on the couch, her face in her hands, tears streaming down her cheeks. Martin stands and watches her for a few moments, his face a mirror of her sadness. Then he walks to her side and gently pats her forehead. For a brief moment she stops crying. But when she tries to talk, to reassure him that she will be okay, the tears begin flowing once again. Martin turns and runs to his bedroom. In a short while he reappears with his most precious possession—an old and lovingly worn teddy bear named Snuffles. He walks over to where his mother is lying and tucks the bear next to her on the couch.

James has worked very hard on a painting for his mother's birthday. But in a moment of carelessness he spills a jar of water on the gift, ruining it. After a moment of disbelief, James begins crying. Sarah, one of his preschool classmates, tries to reassure him with a hug. But James abruptly refuses her offer of comfort. After soothing James's misery, the teacher calls the group together to form a circle. She then tells the rest of the children, "James didn't want

Sarah's hug when he was sad. I think Sarah might have a hug to offer someone in our group. Would anyone like to have Sarah's hug?" A young boy with cerebral palsy named Dusty responds to the invitation by crawling laboriously across the circle and up on Sarah's lap. After Dusty and Sarah hug for a moment, he turns and crawls back to his spot in the circle.

Six-year-old Cindy hears growling from outside her window. When she looks outside she sees a stray dog growling at her younger brother Jacob. The object of the dog's attention is a peanut butter and jelly sandwich Jacob holds high over his head, tightly clutched in his hand. Cindy immediately runs outside and claps her hands while yelling, "Bad dog! Go away!" The dog backs off for a moment and then retreats with his tail between his legs. Cindy takes her brother by the hand and leads him back to the house.

We are often deeply touched by children's kindness. Their hugs, kisses, and simple words of comfort are wonderful gifts that express their concern for others. We are moved by these tender efforts because we know children like Martin, Sarah, Dusty, and Cindy are trying to reach out beyond themselves and make a difference to someone else.

These acts of kindness have several common elements. First, these children were not coerced into taking action—their comfort or assistance was freely offered. Second, their focus was on responding to another's problem. In each case their effort entailed some cost—the use of a valued toy, the possibility of rejection, the threat of danger. And third, they were motivated by their concern for another rather than by expectations of reward for themselves.

Kindness can have favorable consequences for the person who offers it. As the Chinese proverb points out, "A little bit of fragrance always clings to the hand that gives you roses." Martin, Sarah, Dusty, and Cindy probably felt proud of themselves that they could reach out to others in their time of need. But their responses were not the result of bribes or threats. Genuinely kind acts are voluntary responses carried out to benefit another without expectation of material or social reward.

Kindness is a visible demonstration of commitment to the welfare of others and a confirmation of the value of life. Children's first acts of kindness begin with concern for others, gradually become more effective in reducing or preventing distress, and eventually become incorporated into a broader ethical framework that is part of their personal story. Children learn to be kind by watching how parents act, by experiencing their parents' kindness, and by listening to what parents tell them through conversation, story, and song. Kindness begins in the crib.

How Stories Contribute to Offering Kindness to Others

The stories we heard as children provided us with a vision of what it means to act compassionately toward others. While settled comfortably in the sanctuary of a parent's lap we may have heard about devotion to others. Through our parents' words we may have been introduced to characters who chose commitment, compassion, and personal sacrifice. From Aesop's fable about the mouse who removed a thorn from a lion's paw to the biblical story of the Good Samaritan, stories with themes of human kindness and good will enriched our lives and encouraged us to take a positive role in the social drama that unfolds around us.

Saint George and the Dragon, by Margaret Hodges, is a retelling of the dramatic battle between good and evil portrayed in Edmund Spenser's *Faerie Queen*. George, the Red Cross Knight, responds to the plea by Princess Una to return with her to drive away a dreadful dragon that has devastated her land and its people. Soon after arriving at the walls of her castle the fearsome dragon appears and the great battle begins. Again and again, the Red Cross Knight attacks the dragon, is driven back by its ferocity, and returns to fight once more. In the end, the Knight perseveres and slays the cruel creature.

Trina Schart Hyman's vivid portrayal of the battle between dragon and knight won the Caldecott Medal for the best illustrations in children's literature for 1984. Fascinating detail and rich color re-create the conflict and complement Margaret Hodges' dramatic prose. Here is the dragon with its hideous roars, scales of brass, vicious jaws with three rows of iron teeth, and eyes blazing with rage. The knight provides an impressive counterpoint with his armor glistening in the sunlight, a red cross emblazoned on a magnificent shield, and a sharp sword wielded with determination. Author and illustrator provide us with an inspiring retelling of the timeless legend of a hero who risks his life to rescue others.

The Changing Maze, by Zilpha Keatley Snyder, is a story of risk and rescue with more recent origins. The wizard-king of the Ragged Lands fashions a marvelous but deadly greenthorn maze to hide his gold and beguile the greedy. Those who seek the treasure are ultimately foiled by the constantly shifting and turning paths of the evil maze. Misery and death, not gold, await them when they become lost in its gloomy shadows. Even the king disappears within his own evil creation.

Long after the king and the maze are forgotten, a black lamb wanders down to the valley and into the maze. A young shepherd boy named Hugh searches for his beloved pet. But he, too, becomes trapped in the changing maze when he is lured into the labyrinth by the bleating of the lamb. After wandering in its greenthorn passages, the boy ultimately has to choose between the lure of gold and his pet's life. Charles Mikolaycak's bold illustrations work harmoniously with Zilpha Keatley Snyder's poetic prose to create a haunting drama of courageous choice and compassionate action.

Saint George and the Dragon and *The Changing Maze* are powerful examples of Tough Magic, Jane Yolen's term for stories that stir the human soul with dramatic and timeless images of courage, justice, and deep compassion. They present a clear message emphasizing the value of life and the responsibility we have to help others in need.

These stories vibrate with emotion and offer words of power we can use to create a magical moment for children. As these and similar stories unfold, children and parents will experience profound and worthy human emotions: sympathy for the oppressed, courage in the face of threat, and an eagerness to act according to one's convictions.

Stories promote kindness in at least four different ways. First, stories help children recognize that someone has a need for assistance. This need may be related to different types of problems: alleviation of pain, reduction of poverty, prevention of failure, and deliverance from danger. Stories can increase children's awareness of these concerns and show their impact on people. Children cannot respond to kindness unless they first notice a problem exists.

Second, stories with these themes emphasize *responding* to someone in need. Important characters do not sit idly by while someone is harmed. They become involved. The Red Cross Knight responds to the plea from Princess Una to help her people. Hugh does not sit and mourn the loss of his pet lamb. He conducts a determined search to find and return the frightened animal to the rest of his flock.

Third, stories provide children with alternatives that will allow them to respond more effectively to the needs of others. A child might recognize a problem situation and feel obligated to respond but may be paralyzed by inaction because he simply is not aware of any potentially helpful actions. Children cannot react unless they know how to act. Over the course of listening to many stories children will gradually expand their own personal stories to include many different forms of kindness, depending on the nature of the problem:

Pain	*Poverty*	*Failure*	*Danger*
Comfort	Share	Help	Protect
Care for	Give		Rescue

Fourth, stories provide children with opportunities to evaluate their own abilities and consider the consequences of their kindness for themselves and others. In order for kindness to occur children must decide they are personally capable of responding while protecting themselves. Children will be kind only if they believe in themselves and have some hope of being successful in responding to another's misfortune.

Stories like *Saint George and the Dragon* and *The Changing Maze* can highlight themes of kindness in children's personal stories. They emphasize that it's important to:

- Offer comfort to someone in distress.
- Take care of someone who is sick or hurt.
- Share with others.
- Be generous.
- Offer others your assistance when help is needed.
- Protect someone who is endangered.
- Rescue others from harm.

Offer Comfort to Someone in Distress

Compassion for the suffering of others is a personal quality that contributes to all other forms of kindness. Offering comfort consists of gentle reassurance, emotional support, and encouragement, or any other positive effort to help another overcome distress.

Stephen, a four-year-old in my preschool class, was a gentle, quiet young boy who had an aura of melancholy that seemed to cling to him everywhere he went. Despite his gloominess Stephen was always quick to show concern for others. One afternoon I felt ill and decided to rest indoors while my student teacher took the children outside to play. On his way out of the room Stephen walked over and sat down next to me. "Oh, Stephen, I don't feel so well. I feel sick," I told him. He stood up, put his arm on my shoulder and suggested, "Now, Doctor Smith, you go home to bed. Your mommy will take care of you." I was deeply touched by Stephen's concern for my welfare.

One of the most powerful effects stories can have on children is to trigger deep emotions of sympathy and compassion for the suffering of others. We can see compassion on the faces of our children as they hear of characters who have to cope with misfortune or confront danger. They may feel a little afraid when Saint George faces the dragon or when Hugh enters the maze to find his lamb. Tears may fill their eyes when they first realize that Chien-min has been killed trying to save a bear cub in *Once There Were No Pandas*, or that the Steadfast Tin Soldier has been thrown into the fire at the conclusion of Hans Christian Andersen's fairy tale. Stories like these encourage children to feel deeply, to "suffer with" a character, to vibrate with the emotions felt by another.

A young boy responds tenderly to a grieving old woman in *Miss Maggie*, by Cynthia Rylant. Maggie Ziegler lives in a rotting log house on the edge of Crawford's pasture. Every time he visits, Nat Crawford tries to see the snake that some folks said lives inside her house. But Nat fears Miss Maggie and her strange ways, so he avoids being near her for too long.

Then one winter day Nat decides to look in on Miss Maggie when he notices that no smoke is blowing from her chimney. When she fails to answer her door, Mat overcomes his initial fear and enters the dimly lit house to search for the old woman. He finds her huddled in a corner clutching a bundle of cloth in her hands.

"Miss Maggie?"
The head moved slightly. Or did he imagine it? He walked over and squatted down beside her.
"Miss Maggie? You sick?"
The old woman slowly raised her head. Her eyes were lost in bags of wrinkled flesh, and their rims looked red.
"Henry," she whispered.
"No, it's me. Nat."
She held up the bundle of cloth.
"Henry."
Nat took the bundle from her. He was sure the snake must have died on her. But wrapped in the rags wasn't a snake. It was a starling.

Miss Maggie's pet bird had died. Nat takes her hand and gently leads her across the field back to his home to get his grandad's help. Nat's effort to help Miss Maggie is made even more special because he has to overcome his apprehension about the snake in her house. His tender response to the confused and unhappy old woman is an excellent example of offering comfort to someone in distress. We can sense the dramatic shifts in Nat's emotions, from concern to fear to courage and then to compassion.

This emotional sensitivity has an effect on kindness. Children whose faces show sadness while watching someone in distress, for example, are more likely to help someone than those whose faces remain impassive. The ability to offer comfort to another by soothing their distress is based on a compassionate reaction to their suffering.

Marion Radke-Yarrow and Carolyn Zahn-Waxler, researchers at the National Institute of Mental Health, and Martin Hoffman, at the University of Michigan, found that the earliest reaction children would make to another person's distress was to become upset themselves. For example, an eleven-month-old girl sees a playmate fall, bump her knee, and begin to cry. A very sad expression appears on her face as she intently observes the child who is hurt. After a few moments, she suddenly puts her thumb in her mouth and runs to bury her head in her mother's lap. Infants will even cry more intensely when exposed to the cries of another infant than when exposed to other similar sounds.

By the middle of their second year children begin to respond directly to the problem. They may, for example, hug or kiss a person in distress. In some cases they may even hit the victim, more as an expression of anxiety and frustration than as an attempt to deliberately hurt the other. By the end of the second year children can take more effective action to resolve the problem. They may embrace someone who is crying, enlist help from a parent or teacher, carefully examine their distresses (tears, hurts, facial expressions), or give something to the victim. Their choices are thoughtful but not always effective. They offer things that are associated with their own comfort—a blanket, teddy bear, cookie, bottle, their own parent. At this point they assume that what soothes them will soothe the person in distress.

Older preschoolers and kindergarten children can make more effective adjustments in their care because they are more aware that the other person is different from them. So they may try to find the real source of distress and determine the most appropriate response to help another. For example, Phyllis Berman, a researcher at the National Institute of Mental Health, found that most preschool and early-grade-school children who are given the responsibility of caring for a crying baby will take constructive action to try to reduce the infant's distress. Typical responses include giving the baby a toy, inviting him to play, offering verbal reassurance, saying "Shhh," or "It's okay," or sitting close and talking quietly to the baby. Girls are more likely than boys to touch, caress, or cuddle an unhappy infant.

In *Go and Hush the Baby*, by Betsy Byars, a young boy tries to find ways to comfort his baby brother. Because she is busy painting, Will's mother asks him to hush the crying infant. Will tries his best even though he would rather be outside. He sings songs, plays a game, does a magic trick, and tells his baby brother a story about a prince and princess. His imaginative and playful efforts prove to be too successful, because each time Will tries to leave, his baby brother begins to cry for more. Will is finally able to go outside when his mother brings his brother's bottle. Children who offer comfort to younger brothers and sisters will identify with Will and find humor in his creative efforts to calm the infant. The simple dialogue and illustrations reveal the bonds of tender affection between the two brothers.

The word *comfort* is derived from the Latin words *cum* and *forte,* meaning "with strength." Will comforts his baby brother because he can identify and implement alternative solutions to soothing the infant's distress. He feels competent and anticipates success. We can build this feeling of strength by encouraging our children to think about how they might respond to the distress of others. We can also help them better understand the consequences of their actions for the victim. We emphasize kindness by also expressing our feelings, principles, and expectations for how our children should respond to suffering. Sensitivity and knowledge are both important.

When they are in distress children usually experience the loving and predictable comfort of their parents. Offering strength to another requires such a base of security within oneself. The benefits of adult comfort and reassurance are dramatically illustrated in *Darkness and the Butterfly*, by Ann Grifalconi. Osa is afraid of the dark. When evening arrives she remains inside, sitting in the corner of her home and hugging her knees to her chin, her eyes black with fear. Her mother and grandfather cannot reassure her that she is safe from her imagined dangers.

One day Osa becomes lost while looking for some colored stones. She follows a glittering butterfly to the home of a wise old woman. After helping her with chores Osa describes her fears to her new friend. The old woman hugs her tightly and tells her:

"Oh, I know how you feel, Osa! I grew up here in the woods and sometimes, when I was alone, I used to get scared too—specially at night!"

When Osa admits she feels so small and vulnerable at night the old woman reassures her:

"But look at that little butterfly, Osa; she must think SHE is the smallest of the small . . . darkness pursues her, too—yet she flies on!"

Osa falls asleep. In a dream a yellow butterfly guides her out of the darkness and into the twinkling light of a thousand friendly stars and a glimmering moon. When she wakens, Osa discovers that her dream and the gentle

STORYBREAK

Penelope Looks for Love

Once upon a time, in the wonderful town of Butterberry Hill . . .

Penelope Pig decided to look for love. She looked under her bed. Didn't find love there. She looked in her cupboards. Didn't find it there. She even looked in her closet. Nope, no love there either.

So then she went outside. She looked in the woods for love. She found a bird caught in a bramble bush. She reached into the prickly thorns and let it free. As it flew into the air it sang the most beautiful song. But still she could not find love.

She looked out in a field for love. But all she found was a dog that was crying because his paw was caught in a trap. She let it free and it licked her face with happiness. "Still," she thought, "I still cannot find love."

She passed by a flower that was beginning to wilt in the sun. No rain had fallen for a long time. So Penelope went home for some water to sprinkle on the plant. "AHHHH!" it seemed to say. And the flower gave off the most beautiful smell, filling the air with loveliness. But still no love in sight.

Penelope passed by Grandpa Jake's house. When he saw her walking by he asked her why she was looking so sad. She told him that she was looking for love and could not find it anywhere. She told him, though, about the bird, the dog, and the plant.

Grandpa Jake put his arm around Penelope and told her, "Now Penelope, you cannot find love like looking for a lost penny on your bedroom floor. Love is something you get from someone else because you are special. The bird gave you its love with its singing, the dog with its licking, and the flower with its beautiful smell. Each was thanking you for being so kind. Here's my way of showing my love for you." Grandpa Jake gave her a friendly, gentle hug.

Penelope went home, feeling all warm and happy inside. She had finally discovered how to find love.

reassurance of the wise old woman have given her the confidence to overcome her fear of the dark.

The wise old woman does not belittle Osa's fears or overprotect her. Instead, her gentle and soothing words of comfort help Osa discover her own inner strength and overcome her exaggerated fear of the night.

Stories like *Miss Maggie, Go and Hush the Baby,* and *Darkness and the Butterfly* emphasize the importance of caring for others and making a positive response to another's need. When my son was three years old, he loved Charlotte Zolotow's *Do You Know What I'll Do?*, a lovely story about a young girl's devotion to her baby brother. At one point in the story she tells her brother:

> "Do you know what I'll do in the middle of the night if you have a nightmare? I'll come and blow on it and you'll be happy."

The accompanying illustration by Garth Williams shows the young girl poised at her baby brother's crib, blowing away a spectral nightmare hovering over his head.

One early Saturday morning, when my son was three, we played a game in which he was the daddy and I, still securely snuggled in bed, was his baby. Bill fluffed my pillow, tucked me in, and patted my head. After falling "asleep" I began crying for my "daddy" because I was having a scary nightmare. "I'll help you!" he shouted. He jumped up on the bed and began furiously huffing and puffing the "nightmare" away from over my head. *Do You Know What I'll Do?* left an impression on his young mind.

Take Care of Someone Who Is Sick or Hurt

Offering comfort is not enough if something can be done to alleviate the distress. A hungry animal, a child with a cut, and a sick parent might like to be comforted with gentle caresses and comforting words. But they would also like to have someone take steps to reduce their physical distress. A hungry animal needs to be fed; a child with a minor cut needs a bandage, a parent who is sick might appreciate a drink of water. Taking care of someone means assuming responsibility for his welfare. It means service— taking action to benefit another.

Taking care of someone is a common theme found in children's literature. In *Amy's Goose*, by Efner Tudor Holmes, a young girl befriends and nurses a wild goose back to health after an attack by a hungry fox. When the goose recovers Amy has to make a difficult choice between keeping the animal for herself or freeing it to join the rest of the flock that is about to head south. Her decision to release the goose shows more concern for its welfare than for her own wishes.

Other stories show a similar willingness to restore another's health. A group of island residents take care of a young girl with a broken leg in *Island Rescue*, by Charles E. Martin. And in *Ben and the Porcupine*, by Carol Carrick, a young boy and his father perform emergency surgery on their pet dog to remove the porcupine quills that bristle from around his nose.

The tragic consequences of indifference to another's plight are portrayed in *The Old Man and the Bear*, by the German author Janosch. The townspeople believe an old man is a fool because he spends his meager savings to purchase birds at the market only to free them or care for them if they are too ill to fly. One bitterly cold winter the old man seeks the help of a bear to help him care for a sick finch. The bird survives, but the exhausted and impoverished old man dies. The following winter, the starving bear and finch seek shelter and care from the villagers:

> The bear lay down outside the church door and kept the bird warm in his paws. The bird sang to him. When the people came out of the church, the children called out:
> "There's a bear, Mommy! We must feed him! Maybe he's an enchanted prince!"
> But the parents said, "A prince! Ridiculous! Besides, there's plenty of time to feed it tomorrow."

But when they came back the next day, the bear and the bird were no longer there. An angel had carried them off to the stars.

The Old Man and the Bear is a haunting fable about love, kindness, and sacrifice. Janosch challenges his listeners to become more than passive observers, to take decisive action when we recognize another's pain. The children in the story want to feed the bear immediately, but their parents prefer to wait . . . until it's too late. The sick, the hurt, the destitute need care immediately, not when it fits the schedule of the person who could make it available. Tomorrow means never to someone who needs help now.

Share with Others

Sharing means experiencing or possessing something in common with another. Children share when they allow a friend to play with one of their toys. Sharing is also possible with resources. For example, a child may hand a playmate one of her crayons so that he has something to draw with too. Unlike generosity, sharing is not permanent. A child would expect the toy or resource to be returned.

The ability to share is based on a secure sense of ownership. Young children can have problems when they confuse sharing with giving something away. A toddler may be cautiously willing to share a teddy bear with a friend, but he may not allow another to touch it if he thinks handing it over means he is giving it away.

As toddlers become more aware of themselves, their possessiveness is linked to the boundaries of their emerging identities. What they own, what is truly theirs, becomes associated with who they really are. A two-year-old's increased interest in claiming toys may be a sign of his increased self-awareness rather than of selfishness. We may promote sharing more effectively in the long run if we first help children express their possessiveness and then encourage them to make arrangements for common play with others.

New brother or sister, for example, may disrupt a child's sense of personal identity by making him insecure about his space and toys. In *Don't Touch My Room*, by Patricia Lakin, a young boy has to adjust to a new member of the family. Aaron has a special room filled with all sorts of wonderful things—trains and buses, trucks and books—that are all his own. But now a new baby is coming and Aaron will have to share his room. Aaron is afraid, not just of losing ownership of his belongings, but of losing his self-worth and privacy. His possessions are an integral part of his identity. Patricia Brewster's colorful illustrations show the progression of Aaron's adjustment from initial insecurity to acceptance and then affection for his baby brother.

Children as young as three years of age have some idea of what it means to own something. If you give them a toy and tell them it belongs to them they will act as if they own it. But if they are told that the toy belongs to the group they are more likely to share it with others. The idea of ownership is based on clear statements by others, especially those in authority. Young children may believe, though, that they may take something for their own if ownership is not clearly defined by another. So a young child may put a friend's toy in his pocket because he believes that the object will become his by virtue of possession. In a similar way, a parent may find his toddler playing at home with a toy taken from a store shelf. The young child did not *steal* the toy. When he saw it on the shelf he found it interesting and simply picked it up to take it home. At this young age children do not understand the rules of ownership and commerce and do not purposely try to deceive another.

In *Soup for Supper*, by Phyllis Root, the hungry Giant Rumbleton incurs the wrath of the wee small woman when he stumbles into her garden. "Give me back my vegetables—you potato nose!" she demands. An argument follows, and potatoes, cabbages, other garden vegetables, and insults are hurled back and forth. The giant, who is really a gentle creature, eventually realizes that the vegetables really do belong to the tiny, stubborn woman. He offers to help her with her harvest if she lets him share the bounty. So the old woman and the considerate giant form an unlikely alliance to care for the garden and make the best vegetable soup in the land.

Sharing can also mean enjoying another's company. Playing together in a sandbox, creating a city of sand, and populating it with toy trucks and stick people is a form of sharing. So is working together to build a tower of blocks. In John Prater's wordless picture book, *The Gift,* two children share an old cardboard box and a wild adventure. In each of these situations two or more children cooperate in their play with one or more toys.

Some activities involve an agreement about common ownership of some object. The group recognizes that no single person can make an exclusive claim of ownership over what is held in common. In *Mushroom in the Rain,* by Mirra Ginsburg, for example, several small forest creatures take shelter from a hard rain under a tiny mushroom. An ant arrives first and then moves over to make room for a butterfly. A mouse, a sparrow, and a rabbit follow to snuggle together under the protective umbrella of the mushroom. Their sharing is especially important for the rabbit, who manages to hide in the crowd from a pursuing fox. Each creature is willing to make room for another under the mushroom. No one argues or makes a claim of ownership. Each cares about the comfort and safety of the others.

Who really owns the birds? The trees in a park? How about the rain or sunshine or moonlight? *Once There Was a Tree,* by Natalia Romanova, emphasizes how all life shares nature's resources. During a fierce storm a lightning bolt splits an old tree in two. A woodsman sees the broken tree and saws it down so only a stump remains. Then, one after another, first the bark beetles, then the ants, bear, and titmouse use the stump as shelter or a source for food. Seasons change and the stump slowly decomposes as it ages. Each creature can make only a fleeting claim of ownership, for the stump belongs to the earth, and the earth is home to all. Gennady Spirin's luminous illustrations highlight the dramatic changes that occur to the once mighty tree in this subtle tale of sharing.

Be Generous

Generosity is more demanding than sharing because the resource is given to the other permanently instead of temporarily. Children are being generous when they give a friend a few cookies from their lunch box, give a small bag of marbles to a playmate who has none, or use their allowance to purchase a birthday gift for a parent. Generosity means sacrificing a material possession to benefit another.

Gift-giving is a common occurrence in many children's books. One of the most familiar is based on the popular Christmas carol, *The Twelve Days of Christmas*, magnificently illustrated by Jan Brett. This favorite of the holiday season is a love song, a serenade of affection offered by a suitor to his lady. In addition to the familiar partridges in the pear tree, maids-a-milking, and the other extravagant gifts, Jan Brett has provided in the left and right margins a glimpse of a family's busy Christmas preparations and "Merry Christmas" in eleven languages.

A more personal view of generosity is presented in Louise Moeri's *Star Mother's Youngest Child*. Star Mother's youngest child wants to visit Earth to celebrate Christmas the way people do. After much pestering Star Mother agrees to give him his wish, since he will soon have to take his place among the constellations. Shortly afterward, a bitter old woman who lives alone on the edge of a forest is visited on Christmas Eve by a young boy with spiky yellow hair and a large nose. The suspicious woman invites the child into her poor home.

During their evening together the old woman and the young child have a profound effect on each other's lives. The woman rediscovers her capacity to love; the child experiences the delights of modest earthly pleasures—a little sugar on hot mush, a simple turnip-and-ham-bone stew, a

Christmas tree decorated with bright yarn and broken beads.

Christmas would not be Christmas without presents. So the old woman gives her young visitor her most precious possession—an old silver buckle, the only thing of value left to her by her mother. The child is thrilled with her gift. But now dusk has fallen, the first stars are glimmering in the sky, and it is time for him to join his brothers and sisters. So, despite the old woman's protests, the child with the spiky yellow hair wishes her good will and returns to the night. After his departure the old woman discovers her gift under the tree.

> Carefully she opened the string, and lifted back the paper. And as she did so, out came the sound of bells, and the sound of laughter, and the smell of hambone stew and baking bread, the light of a candle, the light of stars . . .
>
> "I'll keep it forever," the Old Woman said.

Star Mother's Youngest Child is a special, timeless story that captures the innocence, wonder, and sacrifice that are the real spirit of the holiday season. The dramatic transformation of the Old Woman's bitterness and loneliness to love and kinship, and the Youngest Child's impatience and ignorance to appreciation and fulfillment is vividly documented in Louise Moeri's text and Trina Schart Hyman's detailed black-and-white illustrations.

The Star Child does not passively wait for the Old Woman to be kind. His innocent curiosity and persistent expectations gradually warm the Old Woman's spirit and allow her to rediscover and express the kindness that lies buried in her heart. Like the old woman in *Star Mother's Youngest Child*, children are more likely to give when others, especially their friends, encourage them to be generous.

The Star Child's and Old Woman's gifts are special because they meet each other's needs. In *Wilfrid Gordon McDonald Partridge*, written by Mem Fox and illustrated by Julie Vivas, a young boy offers a unique present to an elderly friend. When his father tells him that Miss Nancy has "lost her memory," Wilfrid Gordon sets out to find and return it to her. Residents of a nearby retirement home tell him what a memory is: something warm, something from long ago, something that makes you cry, something that makes you laugh, something as precious as gold. Wilfrid then gathers several cherished objects to give to his elderly friend: a warm egg, a shell, a medal, a puppet, and a football. As she holds each item, Miss Nancy recalls a wonderful time from her past. "And the two of them smiled and smiled because Miss Nancy's memory had been found again. . . ."

Some stories of generosity emphasize the ultimate positive consequences that may occur from making a sacrifice. In *The Paper Crane*, by Molly Bang, a poor store owner serves a wonderful meal to an old and penniless stranger. Before he leaves, the old man responds to the owner's generosity by folding a paper napkin into the shape of a crane. When he claps his hands the crane becomes a living bird that dances. His restaurant begins to thrive once again, filled with guests eager to see the strange and wondrous bird.

A young girl wins the hand of a king through her generosity in John Steptoe's African tale, *Mufaro's Beautiful Daughters*. Two sisters, Manyara and Nyasha, each seek the favor of the king who has invited "The Most Worthy and Beautiful Daughters in the Land" to appear before him. Manyara leaves home first during the middle of the night. Along the way she refuses to feed a hungry boy and ignores the counsel of an old woman. On her arrival at the magnificent city Manyara is summarily rejected by the king for her selfishness.

Nyasha departs the following morning. When she sees the young boy, she gives him a yam she had brought for her lunch. When she meets the old woman, she thanks her for her advice and gives her a small pouch filled with sunflower seeds. On her arrival at the king's palace, Nyasha is given a warm welcome. The king had magically assumed the images of the hungry child and old woman to test the character of those who sought his hand. Manyara failed the test. Nyasha's spontaneous kindness met with his approval.

Justice is a common theme in children's literature. Generosity and selfishness have dramatic consequences. The material rewards associated with marrying the king would be unimportant to Nyasha. The love and respect demonstrated by the king were much more significant to her. But most importantly, Nyasha's generosity had positive consequences for her own self-esteem and well-being.

Like other forms of kindness, generosity is based on a secure sense of self. Some of this security is the result of feeling a part of a community of others who are willing to be generous in return. A young girl has her generosity tested in *Country Bear's Good Neighbor*, by Larry Dane Brimner.

> "Good morning Country Bear.
> What's in the bowl?
> You want to borrow some apples?
> Certainly!
> That's what good neighbors are for."

But the Country Bear returns, first for some sugar, then an egg, and finally some cinnamon and butter. His neighbor does not react so generously the next time he visits.

> "Absolutely not!
> Don't even ask, Country Bear!
> You have my apples.
> My sugar.
> My flour.
> My walnuts.
> My cinnamon.
> The butter.
> The milk.
> AND
> The only egg."

But the Country Bear returns not to ask for more but this time to give. Surprise! Country Bear has a delicious cake to share.

There are limits to any person's generosity. The young girl gives and gives without complaint. Fortunately, Country Bear wants her to have some of the cake her kindness made possible. Children have a strong sense of reciprocity. "Friends should be nice to each other," they reason. Even though the friendly neighbor provides the food without expectation of reward, the picnic provides a satisfying conclusion to her hospitality.

Spontaneous generosity can also be an important part of being neighborly. *Once Around the Block*, by Kevin Henkes, shows the ready concern of a young child's neighbors. Annie is bored, so she decides to take a walk around the block. Mr. Stewart invites her to walk barefoot through the grass he is watering. Miss Potter gives Annie two warm chocolate-chip cookies when she passes by her house. Mrs. Douglas hands her a rose, and Barney the mailman lets her jingle his keys. When she returns home Annie shares her bounty with her family. She gives the extra cookie to her papa, the rose to her mother, and jingles papa's keys for baby Phil. "And after dinner she ran her toes through the grass while the sun set."

Annie lives in a world filled with friendly people. Each neighbor she meets is interested in how she feels. They care about her and want to help. Annie responded to their attention by passing their kindness on to others. She could be generous because of the loving bounty she received from neighbors. In a similar way, children who feel loved and secure in their relationships are more likely to generously return that affection to others.

Offer Others Your Assistance When Help Is Needed

Helping means assisting another to reach a goal. Children help when they lift a younger child to get a drink from a water fountain, assist in the preparation of dinner, open a door for someone who is carrying something heavy, and hold tools for a parent who is fixing the dishwasher. In each case children offer their time and labor to contribute to another's effort.

Helping is a common theme in children's literature. The helper is often a person with special power whose assistance is needed by the main character in the story. The fairy godmother in *Cinderella*, as retold by Amy Ehrlich and magnificently illustrated by Susan Jeffers, is one of the classic helpers in children's literature. With the touch of her wand Cinderella is transformed from serving girl to beautiful princess. With a wave a pumpkin and six mice become a magnificent coach drawn by fine white horses.

Special helpers in other stories also come to mind: the Seven Dwarfs in *Snow White*, the Tinman, Lion, and Scarecrow in *The Wizard of Oz*, and the Star Faerie in *The Sleeping Beauty*. Stories like these hold out a promise to children: When times get difficult there are kind people in the world who will gladly reach out to help them along the way.

The Mud Pony, a traditional Skidi Pawnee tale retold by Caron Lee Cohen, tells how a young boy is aided by a mysterious mud pony. More than anything else, a poor young Indian boy wants a pony for his very own. So he fashions one out of mud and loves it as though it were real. When he finds himself stranded after his tribe breaks camp for a buffalo hunt, the boy is overcome with despair about being alone. That night he dreams that the mud pony is alive.

> "You are not alone. Mother Earth has given me to you. I am a part of her."

When he awakes, the white-faced mud pony is alive, tossing her mane and pawing the ground. Again the pony repeats, "My son, you are not alone." She promises the boy that if he does what she requests he will become a chief among his people.

After three days of travel, the young boy and his pony

arrive at their tribe's new camp. All marvel at how he found them despite the great distance he had to travel. He and his mysterious pony lead the tribe as they drive away an enemy and capture many buffalo. Because of these exploits the boy is seen as a leader with a great gift, a great power. Later, when he becomes a chief of his people, the mud pony returns to Mother Earth.

Then as the morning light broke over the wet earth, the chief saw a patch of white clay. And through the wind, he heard a voice:
"I am here, your Mother Earth. You are not alone!"

The Mud Pony is a wonderful affirmation of faith and courage and support. "You are not alone!" is a significant message for all children. In their time of need, someone will be there to help them. The earth is a bountiful place that loves its children. The spirit of the Good Samaritan is alive despite the selfish cynicism of our times. The Mud Pony is the neighbor next door who is willing to help when the roof blows off your house, the friend who watches your children when you are sick, the stranger who stops to offer comfort when you have a car accident. "You are not alone!"

Other stories affirm children's capacity for offering help to others. *The Weaving of a Dream*, by Marilee Heyer, is based on an ancient Chinese legend. An old widow labors for three years to weave a magnificent brocade. But a gust of wind lifts the beautiful work into the sky and carries it off to Sun Mountain. Each of the widow's three sons sets out to retrieve the brocade from the fairies who have taken it. But only the youngest has the love and loyalty that enables him to succeed.

Monster Mary, Mischief Maker, by Kazuko Taniguchi, is a lighthearted look at a character's transformation from selfishness to kindness. Three monsters have special responsibilities: Monster Whirlwind sets the clouds in motion; Monster Starshine scatters bright stars throughout the sky; and Monster Sweetflower colors the flowers. But a fourth, Monster Mary, does nothing but make mischief.

She takes potshots at Monster Whirlwind's clouds, snips the tips of Monster Starshine's stars, and smears black paint all over Monster Sweetflower's flowers. She is a real nuisance. One day, Monster Mary feels rather unappreciated, so she decides to leave the company of her three monster friends. At the outset of her journey she inadvertently helps Monster Rainshower when she tosses a handful of pebbles into his pond. She decides to help two monsters make snowflakes and then actually gives some of her food to a group of hungry Thunder and Lightning Monsters. Each of the monsters she helps gives her a heart to show their appreciation, one in the palm of her hand and one on her cheek and tail. When she returns to her three friends she is a new monster, one who knows that helping someone is much more fun than being destructive.

A more realistic portrayal of helping is provided by David McPhail in *Farm Morning*. "Wake up, Dad, it's almost morning!" A five-year-old girl urges her sleepy father to crawl out of bed so they can begin their morning chores. Father and daughter set out to feed the barnyard animals: first the rabbit, then the horses, the cow, the sheep, the geese, and finally the chickens. Even though the young girl often gets in the way, her father is happy to have her help and company. The soft shades of blue, gold, and rose in David McPhail's watercolor-and-ink illustrations capture the early morning light of dawn and the special feeling of kinship between father and daughter.

Children as young as eighteen months of age have the capacity to help with simple household tasks. Researcher Daniel B. Johnson conducted a study in which mothers pretended to cry when one of his colleagues took a doll from her. Half of the eighteen- to twenty-four month-old children retrieved the doll from another part of the room and returned it to their mothers without prompting. About ten percent physically comforted their mothers.

The children were much less responsive to strangers. But even so, ten percent returned the doll to someone they did not know. Of course, it takes time to learn the necessary skills to help with more complex tasks like caring for farm animals. But like the father in *Farm Morning* we best serve our children with patience while they gain experience with helping.

Protect Someone Who Is Endangered

Protection consists of shielding another from harm, attack, or injury. Offering protection is a complex skill for children because they have to imagine a danger that *might* occur and then take action to prevent it from happening. The kindergartner who takes away matches from a younger sister or removes tiny plastic building blocks from a toddler's playpen shields a younger person from potential harm. He or she knows that playing with matches or putting tiny objects in one's mouth can be dangerous. Offering protection is a challenge because those who need to be defended may show no visible signs of distress that would alert a child to the need for protection. Even though they might be aware of a potential danger, they may not understand how to prevent harm from occurring.

Stories that emphasize protection will strengthen children's values for becoming involved. The classic example of a child who recognizes a danger and takes action to protect others can be found in *The Boy Who Held Back the Sea*, retold by Lenny Hort and magnificently illustrated by Thomas Locker. Jan had never done anything really brave before. In fact, he is often full of mischief. But then he discovers water trickling through an isolated part of the dike that protects his Dutch town from flooding. Jan knows that a small leak could soon turn into a torrent. He returns to town and tries to warn the schoolmaster and constable. But they dismiss his pleas as a harmless fantasy. When he insists that he is telling the truth, the constable tells him to return to the dike and that he will bring help.

When he arrives at the dike Jan tries unsuccessfully to plug the leak. He finally manages to stop the flow by wrapping a handkerchief around his finger and plugging it into the tiny gap in the earthen wall. Storm clouds gather and the evening turns cold. No help arrives. But Jan continues his courageous vigil.

> The hand that held back the sea was numb, but the boy hugged the dog with his free arm. "Someone will come soon," he said, "and think what heroes we'll be." But he wasn't sure he believed it himself.

Old Captain Blauvelt notices the young boy's desperate effort and returns to the village for help. But no one takes him seriously either.

The next morning the schoolmaster passes by and begins to scold Jan for not being at school. But Jan is exhausted and unable to respond. Only then does the schoolmaster realize why Jan is curled up by the dike. The alarm is given and other men arrive with tools to repair the leak. After recovering from his ordeal, Jan's devotion is honored with a great festival.

Jan anticipated what would happen if the trickle of water was ignored. He made a personal decision to seek help, and when that was overlooked, to take protective action despite the discomfort and peril. His sacrifice was even more notable because of his initial disregard for authority.

A group of children protect a timber wolf that has regained its freedom after being captured in *A Wolf Story*, by David McPhail. The children first cheer on the timber wolf as it passes their school bus. Later, when the creature is surrounded by men with guns, the children join hands around the wolf.

> "Get out of the way!" yelled the men. "That wolf is dangerous!"
>
> "You get out of the way!" the children yelled back. "Let the wolf go home!"

The hunters move back and wait, but the children refuse to leave. Government officials arrive shortly and decide that the wolf should be returned to its native habitat. The children celebrate their success by dancing and singing in a circle around the wolf.

Protection requires a resolute will, much like that shown by the children in David McPhail's story. The defense of the wolf brings the group of children closer together as they share a common purpose—preventing an injustice. In contrast to the warlike men, they believe the timber wolf is not dangerous, just frightened and misunderstood.

A young boy is determined to protect a magnificent animal in Donald Carrick's *Harald and the Great Stag*. When Harald sees the great stag in the Baron's forest he runs to tell of his discovery to his friends the hunters. His pride turns to fear when he realizes that his boast has only served to encourage the hunters to track down and kill the magnificent creature. Instead of returning home as he is told, Harald reenters the forest in order to protect the stag by throwing the hunters off its trail. But Harald, covered with the scent of animal, then experiences for himself what it means to be the pursued. When a snarling dog finds him hiding in a tree, Harald learns first hand the terror of the hunt. But then an old hunter pulls the dog away, and the pack of dogs and their masters leave to search elsewhere. Later, Harald meets the old man once again and makes an interesting discovery.

> "You saw me in the tree, didn't you?" Harald said.
> The Hunter nodded.
> "That's why you pulled the dog off."
> The old man nodded again. "I thought you would want to know that your Stag still runs free," he said.
> Harald's heart leapt. Then a huge smile spread across his face. "You've been his friend all along."
> "Now he has two," the old hunter said as he slipped back into the forest.

Harald makes the decision to take responsibility for the safety of the stag. His knowledge of the forest and of hunting enable him to take action to save the life of the magnificent animal. Carrick's beautiful illustrations convey the pomp and drama of a forest hunt and the terror of a life-and-death chase.

Rescue Others from Harm

Rescuing is slightly different from protection because harm has already occurred and intervention must be made to stop further injury or abuse. Protection involves responding to a potential threat. Rescuing goes beyond prevention to actually saving someone from further harm. For example, a child grabs a neighborhood bully who is hitting her younger brother; another throws a blanket over a friend whose clothes are on fire. A third carefully enters a street to lead a toddler back to the safety of the sidewalk. Rescuing means that children make direct contact with victims and take action to free them from danger. Performing a rescue may also involve personal risk. In each of these examples, rescuers place themselves in potential peril. A bully, fire, or busy street all present some danger to would-be rescuers. This makes rescuing the most difficult and challenging form of kindness.

Parents want their children to feel confident enough to intervene when someone is being harmed. But at the same time, they are also concerned for their children's safety. Most parents would want their children to consider their own capabilities and the potential costs of taking action when they go to the aid of another. Some may urge their children to not intervene if the victims are strangers or if there is any risk to offering assistance.

Children's literature provides numerous examples of characters who free others from confinement, danger, violence, or evil. The unicorn is a symbol of innocent strength and assistance in Marianna Mayer's *The Unicorn and the Lake*. A venomous serpent preys on the animals who live on the banks of a beautiful lake. The plight of the animals is made even more desperate by a drought that threatens to destroy their home. Then from his mountain home the unicorn hears of their distress. He lifts his head skyward and pierces the clouds with his sharp horn to make rain fall upon the land. But the serpent and its cruelty remain. The unicorn leaves his mountain home to confront the brutal creature.

> The serpent, coldly luminous, lay watching nearby. He alone held the ancient memory of evil, and it had given him mastery over the others. But now he felt his power ebbing away.

In a climactic battle of sharp, cloven hooves against steel bands of muscle the unicorn drives the serpent from the land.

Once There Were No Pandas, by Margaret Greaves, is a retelling of the Chinese legend of how the panda got its spots. Young Chien-min becomes a friend to the pandas after wandering into the forest and removing a thorn from a bear cub's paw. Chien-min is always welcome in the forest following this act of tenderness. Then danger strikes.

While caring for three of the she-bear's cubs Chien-min spots a hungry leopard with fierce topaz eyes and a wide whiskered face hiding in the bamboo. Her shout of warning comes too late as the leopard pounces on one of the cubs. Determined to rescue her beloved Niao Niao, Chien-min hurls a stone at the attacker. Distracted for a moment, the leopard drops its prey and turns on Chien-min. At that moment the furious she-bear arrives, and the leopard makes a hasty retreat. Unfortunately, Chien-min lies still on the ground, struck and killed by the leopard's huge claws.

On hearing of the tragedy the white bears of the forest gather to mourn the loss of their dear friend. As they beat their paws on the rich earth and then against their chests and wipe the tears from their eyes, they leave great black smears across their faces and bodies. As tribute to the young girl's sacrifice the pandas have kept this distinctive black and white coloration.

The Unicorn and the Lake and *Once There Were No Pandas* both emphasize the value of using one's strength and ability to aid others. "Do not sit idly by when others are faced with danger," they encourage. "Take action to stop the unfairness or cruelty."

Other forms of rescue may require less risk. A child extricates a pet who has become tangled up in its leash; another stops a peer from teasing a shy classmate. A third goes to find a teacher to stop a playground fight. In a series of fascinating studies, researcher Ervin Staub examined children's willingness to help when they think they hear a classmate fall from a chair in an adjoining room. He found that children who felt a responsibility for responding to the victim's distress and had some idea of how to help were more willing to investigate the distress.

A Fairy Went A-Marketing, by Rose Fyleman, is a celebration of personal devotion and responsibility.

> A fairy went a-marketing—
> She bought a little fish;
> She put it in a crystal bowl
> Upon a golden dish.
>
> An hour she sat in wonderment
> And watched its silver gleam,
> And then she gently took it up
> And slipped it in a stream.

She buys and then releases a colored bird and gentle mouse, and gives her winter gown to a frog to keep him warm at night. Jamichael Henterly's illustrations provide wonderful detail and texture to the forest and its creatures in this tribute to a fairy's generous spirit.

A Fairy Went A-Marketing is refreshing for its perspective on money and ownership. The fairy purchases the animals and winter gown. But freedom and warmth are more important to her than the accumulation of riches. She knows the real value of what she buys, not for herself but for having the opportunity to act compassionately.

Sometimes a rescue may mean refraining from unintended cruelty. In *The Lady and the Spider*, by Faith McNulty, a young woman stops herself from carelessly destroying a living thing. A spider has taken residence in a head of lettuce in the woman's garden. As she plants, cultivates, and waters her vegetables she is unaware of the tiny creature who remains unaffected by her work.

But then one day the gardener removes the head of lettuce and takes it to her kitchen. While cleaning its leaves she finally notices the little spider clinging to a raft of lettuce. As she moves to casually discard the spider in the trash she stops to study the creature—its tiny dots for eyes, the delicate movement of its slender legs.

> "Isn't it wonderful," she thinks, "that a creature so small can live and love life, find food, and make a home just like me!"

Holding the leaf carefully the young woman returns the spider to its home in the garden.

The Lady and the Spider asks children to reconsider the casual destruction of any living thing. All life is wonderful and special. Faith McNulty portrays the spider and its environment realistically. But we are still drawn into the drama of its struggle to live in its garden home and survive the greater danger posed by the woman herself.

A sudden act of kindness to save another from embarrassment can be another form of rescue. In *Angelina on Stage*, by Katherine Holabird, a young girl becomes jealous of her brother when they both get parts in a ballet. She has the part of a dancing fairy who flies across the stage suspended by wires; her brother gets to be an elf with a small speaking role. Angelina does not have any lines to give, and during rehearsals her brother becomes a favorite of the famous star Madame Zizi. But on opening night when she sees him panic on stage Angelina forgets all sibling rivalry to come to his aid. *Angelina on Stage* shows that kindness is much more rewarding than competition.

Some stories convey to children that others stronger than they will watch over and rescue them if they are threatened. Children know they are vulnerable. They need adults who are willing to keep them from danger. Children who develop a sense of competence under the umbrella of adult watchfulness are more likely to protect and rescue others. *Good Night, Pippin,* by Joan Goodman, is a delightful story of bedtime reassurance. Little Pippin is not sleepy, so Mama tells him a story of the time she rescued him from a band of marauding pirates. Mother follows this adventure with another about the time Pippin's father rescued him from an evil Wizard. Pippin is still not sleepy, so Mother tells him one more story about the time he saved them from a spaceship full of Galacticans with freeze beams. Mother's stories convey a great sense of love and devotion. "If you are ever in trouble we will do everything we can to help you," they seem to say. She affirms his own inner strength for helping those he loves.

Rescuing another in an emergency is the highest form of principled action. There can be no clearer sense of devotion to life than to intervene when someone is threatened by danger. Some of the greatest children's stories are tributes to those who take risks and make sacrifices to help another.

Summary

Kindness means becoming involved and assuming responsibility for action to benefit another. Because of the extent of this intervention there can be a conflict in the messages we send to children:

- Be generous but don't give away too much.
- Protect someone but don't do something dangerous.
- Help but don't boss someone.
- Be friendly but don't talk to strangers.

Children can find themselves torn between these apparently conflicting messages. Balanced at a point of indecision between becoming involved or avoiding action, they might find guidance in the values and beliefs conveyed by the stories they hear from parents, grandparents, and teachers.

Children's decisions to become involved are influenced by many factors—how they have been treated, what they have observed, and what they have heard. The images and words of stories can contribute to a culture of caring and personal stories that emphasize reverence for life.

Instead of runners in a race, aren't we really fellow travelers trudging, dancing, and skipping along the bitter-sweet road of life? And when the burden becomes too heavy or the path too difficult, there is no shame in seeking the hand or companionship of others for help along the way. The strength we gain is a gift we can pass on to others when they need our hand.

CHAPTER EIGHT

From The Emperor's New Clothes to Crow Boy:

Preserving an Openness to the World

Each of us began life with total openness to the world. We were amazed by everything—the music of our wind-up teddy bear, the colors that danced before our eyes, the texture of our blanket, the smell of our mother's perfume. The first bug we saw was a mystery; the first toy we threw from our crib an act of magic. We eagerly sampled as much of the world as we could, often under the wary eye of an attentive parent. There were no barriers in our minds to prevent us from exploring and learning. Life was full of wonder.

Very young children do not have rules, expectations, and obligations that interfere with being open to life. Hand an orange to a fifteen-month-old and see what happens. She may take the fruit and throw it into the air or roll it on the floor. She may tap on it with a spoon. If you hand her a slice she might squeeze it and then watch in fascination while the juice trickles through her fingers. She may chew on what remains of the slice, oblivious to any mess she may be making. She does not name the object, explain it away, or discuss its merits. She simply takes the orange and feels, tastes, smells, and sees it.

But this period of expansion also contains the faint beginnings of the gradual closing of a child's mind to experience. Some of this closing is the result of an inevitable loss of innocence. What was new and fresh becomes predictable and familiar. At some point the wonder loses some of its luster. Children may also withdraw from exploration because they are frightened of what might happen. They may not want to touch a puppy, for example, because of an unpleasant experience they once had with another furry animal.

The loss of innocence is also accelerated by language development. The attempt to label, analyze, and describe something can create distance between the person and the sensory experience. If you give an orange to a twelve-year-old she may say, "Thanks for the orange. Can I eat it?" If given permission, she may cut it into precise sections and carefully eat each piece. She does not want to appear incompetent or messy. As she eats the orange her mind may be preoccupied with problems at school or with thoughts of a boy she would like to know better. The older child may appreciate the orange less because she has lost her fascination with its sensory qualities. The ideas that sweep through her mind crowd out her awareness of the appearance, smell, taste, and feel of the orange. She replaces her *experience* of the orange with *thoughts* about it.

Conceptual development and language are important developmental milestones that allow children to engage in abstract thought and communicate with others. But a preoccupation with thinking can displace full sensory awareness. If words become a shorthand substitute for experience, then analyzing, reminiscing, and daydreaming can displace feeling, tasting, smelling, seeing, and hearing.

In addition to experiencing a gradual loss of sensory contact due to a growth in abstract thinking, children also begin to lose this openness by distorting experiences to meet adult expectations. Children may be told what and what not to feel, see, and hear. Authority figures may insist that something unpleasant does not really exist or that something is true when it is not. They may punish

children for expressing unpleasant emotions or expect them
to pretend to feel something that they do not feel. In *Vital
Lies, Simple Truths,* psychologist Daniel Goleman provides
an example of how cultural attitudes can distort experience. He quotes Barney Simon, a South African playwright:

> All white South Africans are brought up in early child-
> hood by black women. I remember the one in our house,
> Rose. . . . You spend your first years on the black wom-
> an's back. You spend your first years with your cheek
> pressed against her neck. You hear her songs, her ver-
> nacular. You go to the park with her and sit among
> other black women like her. You go into her room and
> maybe her lover is there. You develop this knowledge of
> each other. But at a certain point, South Africa tells you
> that knowledge is obscene, and a crime—worse than a
> crime, a sin. You are told to forget what you already
> know.

Distortion occurs in subtle ways, not just in these more
dramatic situations. Take, for example, the common ritual
of greeting that every preschooler learns in our society:

> How are you?
> Fine. How are you?
> I'm fine.

It makes little difference at this moment how either person
really feels. Being frightened, sad, bored, or hostile makes
little difference. I once asked a child in my preschool class
who was crying, "Stephen, how do you feel?" In a quivering
voice between sobs the four-year-old responded, "Fine!"
Everyone, of course, feels "fine." The masks have to be
donned, the script must be recited. Slowly, so very slowly,
children erect barriers between themselves and others. As
the barrier grows larger they may even grow more distant
from themselves.

Diminished openness can make children feel like strangers wandering senselessly in an alien land. When words

replace sensory experience, truth is held hostage by illusion. When reality is replaced by fabrication children become puppets in another's performance. As a result, children who have lost touch with themselves will begin to distrust their perceptions of what really exists. At this point, children do what so many adults have done before them—they sacrifice their individuality for a comfortable herd mentality; they lose their minds.

The erosion of openness underlies pretense, deceit, and dishonesty. In contrast, honesty means seeing, hearing, and feeling through the veils of illusion that surround us. Being honest means being open to experience. Honesty also means acting with integrity—acknowledging the truth to others whenever possible. We want our children to remain fully alive and open to the world. We want them to act with integrity so they will have self-respect and be trusted and admired.

We can nurture these attitudes by allowing them to come into sensory contact with their environment without having to analyze everything they hear, see, and feel. We can promote integrity by providing a good example and by creating conditions at home that fosters their honesty. We can also nurture values and principles that provide the foundation for integrity. Children's books provide opportunities for conveying these concepts. We can read or tell stories that emphasize the wonder and freshness of the world around us and show the consequences of truthfulness and deception.

How Stories Contribute to Being Open and Genuine

Through the imagery created by word and illustration, stories serve to remind children of the great beauty in the world. They may encourage children to look past the superficial and conspicuous to be more aware of what they see, feel, hear, or touch. Stories can also show that truth can be distorted and misunderstood, and that deception is destined to fail.

Stories like Hans Christian Andersen's *The Emperor's New Clothes* emphasize trusting one's own senses and refusing to be drawn into a deception. The vain emperor and his subjects are tricked by two thieves posing as weavers. In return for money, gold thread, and the finest silk, they pretend to weave magnificent clothes for the king. The emperor's mindless councilors are so unsure of their own eyes and so frightened of looking foolish that they praise the cloth they cannot see rather than break the illusion by pointing out the truth. The emperor also accepts the hoax after hearing his councilors praise the "cloth."

> "Dear me!" thought the emperor. "I can't see a thing! How terrible! Am I stupid? Am I unfit to be emperor? Nothing worse could happen to me!"
>
> "Yes, very pretty!" he said out loud. "It has my entire approval!" He nodded in a satisfied way and gazed at the empty loom, not wishing to admit that he couldn't see anything.

Once the emperor accepts the lie, the rest of his court allow themselves to be drawn into the pretense. They are too afraid to disagree. The emperor proudly dons his new "clothes" and parades through town, amid the accolades of residents unwilling to admit what their eyes tell them. But then a little boy shouts, "But he has nothing on!" His simple honesty shatters the pretense. The words suddenly restore the good sense of the townspeople, who then repeat the child's cry. Innocence has overcome illusion.

In *Crow Boy* Taro Yashima shows the painful consequences of misunderstanding and arrogance. No one pays much attention to Chibi (which means "Little Boy" in Japanese). He is afraid to make friends with the other children at school; he sits by himself in class and is left alone much of the time. The other children often ridicule him for his strange ways.

Only after Mr. Isobe becomes his sixth-grade teacher do

the others discover Chibi's unique talents. Mr. Isobe is impressed with Chibi's sensitivity to nature and his artistic ability. He also spends time talking with Chibi when no one is around. When there is a talent show at school everyone is surprised to see Chibi on stage. They laugh in disbelief. What could Chibi offer? But then he begins his performance. Chibi stands on the stage in front of his classmates and in a haunting voice imitates the voices of crows—of newly hatched crows, of mother and father crows, of crows crying when the village people have some unhappy accident, of crows when they are happy. At that moment, the children realize how unfair they have been. They are also deeply touched by the images he creates with his voice. Mr. Isobe tells the class that during Chibi's long walks to and from school he has been a close observer of insects, birds, and many other creatures people take for granted. Chibi's talent is his special kinship with nature.

Both *The Emperor's New Clothes* and *Crow Boy* focus on the power of awareness and truth. In *The Emperor's New Clothes* a young boy speaks his mind because he has not learned to distort what he sees to gain approval. In *Crow Boy* a group of children discover how much they have misunderstood a classmate. These and other books that focus on sensory experience and truth encourage children to incorporate concepts into their personal stories similar to the following:

- Use all your senses to be aware of the world around you.
- Explore and investigate the world around you.
- People may disagree about what is true.
- Gather evidence to determine the facts.
- Appearances are deceiving.
- Others may try to mislead you.
- Deception destroys trust.
- Fantasies are not necessarily deceptions.
- Not everyone will believe you when you tell the truth.

Use All Your Senses to Be Aware of the World Around You

Some books encourage children to use their senses to explore the world around them. In *I Touch* and its companion books, *I See* and *I Hear*, Rachel Isadora uses bright illustrations and simple statements to highlight a young child's sensory experiences.

"I touch my cereal. It's gooey. I touch my lollipop. It's sticky. I touch daddy's beard. It's scratchy."

The steady rhythm of "I touch . . ." in each of the fifteen events emphasizes the child acting as her own agent in exploring her surroundings. The book also includes an element of caution. "I do not touch the cup. It's hot," says the young girl.

Cock-A-Doodle-Doo, by Franz Brandenberg, is a celebration of sound. Beginning with the rooster's morning call, each of the farm animals offers its own unique greeting to begin the day. As they read the book together, parents and children will join together in an exuberant litany of farmyard life. "Croak, croak . . . quack, quack . . . caw, caw . . . ee-ah, ee-ah." Each sound couplet flows to the next in a chant filled with life and energy.

I Spy On Vacation and *I Spy At the Zoo* are visual feasts for young children. Maureen Roffey has filled these books with fascinating detail. There is so much to see when on vacation or visiting the zoo. Each page invites children to find the answer to a question. "I spy a pair of sunglasses on the . . ." or "I spy a keeper with a bucket of . . ." Children will enjoy looking for the answers found in the illustrations.

Some books combine sensory images. Few of us ever forget the sights and sounds and thrill of riding an old-fashioned merry-go-round. This feeling of floating suspended in air, the cascade of colors, the blur of faces passing by are recaptured in *Up and Down on the Merry-Go-Round*, by Bill Martin, Jr., and John Archambault, with cheerful illustrations by Ted Rand.

Galloping through
the mirrored sky,
strings of stars
are whirling by.

A young boy delights in the motion and blur of color, the thrill of feeling his body carried along. The children on the merry-go-round are drawn together by the common parade and by the spectators who wave to them as they pass by. A ticket buys the opportunity to become immersed in a multisensory adventure for a few minutes.

A quieter approach to experience is provided in *Waiting*, by Nicki Weiss. A young girl waits in her front yard for her mother to return. Even a few minutes can seem like forever to a young child. The sounds of the birds, the smell of a rose, the rustle of the wind blowing across the grass, a ladybug tickling her leg, even the images formed by passing clouds remind Annalee of her mother. Her patience is soon rewarded with a happy reunion.

Walking on walls is just one of many experiences Jimmie Jarnigan has to have during his walk home in *Walls Are To Be Walked*. Flying a kite, gazing at clouds, following the cracks on a sidewalk, and looking in birds' nests are only a part of the journey. Nathan Zimelman wrote *Walls Are To Be Walked* after seeing children coming home from school and recalling how it felt to be fascinated with simple things in the world.

For older children, Peter Parnall's detailed pencil-and-watercolor illustrations in *Apple Tree* endow a solitary apple tree with features that echo the life and energy that exist throughout the world. Spring and summer bring blossoms, ants, chickadees, beetles, and robins. When winter arrives the tree provides ripe apples for deer and other wildlife as well as shelter for an old coon. The *Apple Tree* provides children with a glimpse, rich in sensory detail, of the interdependent nature of woodland life.

You can feel the cold and frosty stillness in Robert Frost's classic poem, *Stopping By Woods on a Snowy Evening*. Black and white pencil, pen, and ink illustrations by Su-

san Jeffers provide contrast between the snowy evening
and the "lovely, dark and deep" woods. Jeffers uses color
sparingly to draw our attention to the rotund old man
whose "promises to keep" involve leaving food for the forest animals.

Explore and Investigate the World Around You

Some stories invite children to attend closely to illustrations and focus their attention on some detail or anticipate
what lies hidden beneath an object or what might happen
on the next page. They encourage children to be percep-
tive. With *Sam at the Seaside*, illustrator Jonathan Lambert has fashioned intriguing folds at the end of each page
to create all sorts of surprises for children as they follow
Sam's seaside adventures. On the first page we see him
pulling on a worm . . . but when the page is turned we find
the worm is really a tentacle connected to a huge octopus.
In the next page we see him riding a wave that turns out
to be the nose of a shark. In each situation Sam is bliss-
fully oblivious to all that is really going on around him.
Sam at the Seaside shows that what seems to be familiar
may also be full of surprises.

In *Trilby's Trumpet*, by Sarah Stapler, children are invited to help poor Trilby find his trumpet by peeking behind special flaps in the illustrations. Where has his brother
hidden it? Is it in the breadbasket, the refrigerator, or
under the quilt? Trilby goes from one room to the next
trying to find the trumpet. At the conclusion of the story,
Trilby realizes that his trumpet has been close at hand all
the time.

Ron Maris has provided an equally tantalizing opportunity for young explorers in *Is Anyone Home?* Readers follow a young farm child completing his chores. Each page
offers a door that can be opened to reveal what lies behind
it. Along the way we discover chickens, cats, horses, Ben
the dog, Grandpa, and finally Grandma. *Is Anyone Home?*
encourages children to think about what occurs behind the
scenes.

In *That Olive*, illustrated by Cindy Wheeler, children play a hide-and-seek game with a mischievous cat with bright green eyes and a crooked tail. Andy cannot find Olive, but readers can if they look closely. She is hidden somewhere on almost every page. We follow Andy from one room to the next as he tries to lure his pet out of her hiding place. He solves his problem by setting a perfect trap, one that Olive will certainly not ignore. Olive is hidden so that she is neither too obvious to a reader nor too inconspicuous. Even young children will have the satisfaction of finding her.

Each of these stories encourages children to sharpen their investigative talents. They ask children to become directly involved by looking under something or turning a page. "Don't take anything for granted. Look beneath the surface to discover more," they imply. Because of the emphasis on visual perception, illustrations in these books play a much more important role than the story. Parents and their young children will go back to these books again and again to share enjoyable visual surprises and solve intriguing problems. These "first mysteries" nurture curiosity, wonder, and imagination.

Some books encourage children to express their curiosity by asking questions about what they see, hear, taste, smell, or touch. "Why?" is a common question asked by young children. When they ask "why" they are not simply making an appeal for a precise explanation. They are saying, "Tell me more about it."

One of the most beautiful examples of a loving introduction to the mysteries of nature is provided by Henry Wadsworth Longfellow in his classic narrative poem, "The Song of Hiawatha," in a version illustrated by Susan Jeffers titled *Hiawatha*.

> By the shores of Gitche Gumee,
> By the shining Big-Sea-Water,
> Stood the wigwam of Nokomis,
> Daughter of the Moon, Nokomis.

Nokomis is Hiawatha's nurse and teacher. She introduces him to the comet Ishkoodah, the legends of the fiery water spirits and the shining stars. Under the patient guidance of Nokomis, Hiawatha discovers the secrets and wonders of nature.

> At the door on summer evenings
> Sat the little Hiawatha;
> Heard the whispering of pine-trees,
> Heard the lapping of the water,
> Sounds of music, words of wonder;
> "Minne-wawa!" said the pine-trees,
> "Mudway-aushka!" said the water.

Hiawatha learns the language and ways of birds and of the beasts who live in the forest. Now that he shares their secrets he calls all creatures his brothers.

In *Sarah's Questions*, by Harriet Ziefert, a young girl and her mother begin their stroll on a sunny summer day by playing a game of I spy. On their way home, Sarah is full of questions: "Why do squirrels have bushy tails? Do dogs dream? Why do birds sing? Why do bees buzz?" Her mother responds patiently to Sarah's curiosity. Even Sarah's grandfather is asked to help answer her questions. Susan Bonners's illustrations are filled with rich earth tones and sun-splashed shadows. Everything is green and growing, with breathtaking beauty to stimulate the wonder and imagination of any curious child.

A child's need for patient, affectionate support from an adult willing to respond to his or her curiosity is depicted in *Chester and Uncle Willoughby*, by Patricia Kier Edwards. In each of four vignettes Chester and his uncle sit on their front porch and exchange thoughts and stories. Even though Uncle Willoughby is quite old, he has retained his sense of humor and keen mind. Chester loves to be with him because Uncle Willoughby makes him feel special. While sitting on the porch of an old farmhouse the two take turns playing a game called "What would you do if . . . ?" One would ask a question and the other would answer.

"What would you do, Uncle Willoughby, if a lion came walking up the back steps?"

Uncle Willoughby thought for a while. "Well, first I'd do my best to look invisible. If that didn't work, I'd aim for not looking tasty. I'd try for scrawny and dried-up looking."

Then for his turn, Uncle Willoughby asked, "What would you do if there was an alligator in your bed?"

That one didn't take Chester long at all. "I'd sleep on the floor. What would you do if oranges started tasting like pickles?"

"I'd make us a pickleade."

Chester and Uncle Willoughby go back and forth, each challenging the other to imagine some creative solution to a humorous dilemma.

Uncle Willoughby was also good at telling about things. He tells a story about nothing—what the world would be like if nothing existed. They also talk together about the colors they see around them—the blue of the sky, the green of growing things, sprouting and ready to go. Chester and his uncle have a special friendship. Their playful language games are an expression of how they view the world around them. Through these exchanges they challenge each other, each testing the sharpness of the other's mind and providing an opportunity to get to know what the other really thinks and feels.

Being aware is not enough. Children want to satisfy their curiosity by becoming actively involved in uncovering the mysteries and wonders that surround them. They want to open the door, look under the rock, or climb the tree. Stories can encourage children to continue their exploration of the world around them. Books like *Hiawatha* also reassure children that there will be adults in their lives to respond to their questions and meet their need for information. Every explorer needs a guide.

People May Disagree About What Is True

As a result of their exploration children acquire facts about the world. Snow melts in a warm room, bugs die if they are squashed, glass breaks if dropped on a hard floor. But other ideas are based more on opinion than on fact. Not everyone agrees about what is right or wrong or what is most important. Two people can view an experience from different perspectives and disagree about what happened and what it means. Some stories point out these differences of opinion and the conflict that can follow.

Lee Bennett Hopkins points out in *I Loved Rose Ann* that even two friends can disagree. Rose Ann and Harry like each other despite a stormy relationship. The first half of the story is told from Harry's point of view, the second from Rose Ann's. Each interprets the events from his or her own perspective. The sharp contrast in their view of the same experiences shows how easily behavior can be misunderstood and how confusing relationships can be.

Two giants are the best of friends until they both find and claim a pretty pink shell. What begins as an argument in *The Two Giants*, by Michael Foreman, quickly erupts into a violent contest. Their rage is mirrored in nature as a storm appears and then ravishes their once peaceful home. Now separated by an expanse of water, the two former friends hurl huge boulders at each other. When they leave the protection of their islands to attack each other, the two giants pause for a moment when they discover their socks are mismatched. At this point the two realize they have forgotten the reason for their conflict. Recalling the happy days of their friendship, the giants drop their clubs into the sea and celebrate the end of their conflict. As they renew their friendship, birds and colorful flowers return to restore peace and beauty to their country.

Two Monsters, by David McKee, provides children with a slightly different view of a similar conflict. Two monsters living on different sides of a mountain disagree over whether day is departing or night is arriving. Like the two giants in Michael Foreman's story, they insult and hurl rocks at each other. When their fight levels the mountain between them, each giant discovers what the other has seen.

> "Incredible," said the first monster. "Night is arriving. You were right."
> "Amazing," said the second monster. "You were right. Day is leaving."
> They decided to watch the sunset together.

Initially the monsters fail to realize they are both right . . . each from their own perspective. Once they glimpse what the other sees, their conflict is over.

Wilson Gage provides an outrageously funny view of misunderstanding and differences of opinion in *Cully Cully and the Bear*. Cully Cully the hunter only nicks the nose of a bear with his arrow.

> "By jingo!" thought the bear. "That hunter has nicked my nose. It hurts. It hurts lots. I will teach that hunter a lesson."

So poor Cully Cully now becomes the hunted, with the angry bear in close pursuit. He finds a giant tree to climb, but its branches are too high for him to reach. The bear arrives, and around and around the tree they go.

Their chase becomes a dizzying display of misunderstanding. Who is chasing whom? Who else is running around the tree? Cully Cully is not sure, and neither is the bear. James Stevenson's illustrations perfectly fit the mood of the story. Parents and children alike will laugh out loud as they follow Cully Cully's misadventure.

Preschool children are primarily egocentric in their thinking. This means they cannot see something from another person's perspective. Egocentrism explains why a young child brings her teddy bear to her distressed mother instead of doing something the mother would find reassuring. Stories like *Cully Cully and the Bear* provide a humorous counterpoint to egocentrism by emphasizing how individuals can differ in their reactions to the same situation.

Young children will never fully understand that contrasting opinions about the same thing can all be true. Nor will they ever be capable of setting aside their own views to take the perspective of another. But stories introducing conflict and dissimilar points of view provide children with their first glimpse of how people can disagree over what they believe to be the "facts." As they gain maturity and experience children will have many opportunities to use this insight in the social arena. If they care about others and are willing to make the effort, they may learn what it means to walk in another person's shoes.

Gather Evidence to Determine the Facts

When there is a conflict of opinion or uncertainty about the truth, more information is needed to make a decision or to pass judgment. Some stories introduce children to the idea of gathering evidence to determine truth.

Paul Galdone's version of *Rumpelstiltskin* is an excellent example of this effort to discover the facts. This Brothers Grimm tale about deception, greed, and justice begins with a lie. A poor miller, wanting to impress the king, tells him that his daughter can spin straw into gold. The king then locks the beautiful young woman in a castle room and threatens her with death unless she spins straw into gold.

Since she has no idea how to meet his demands, the poor miller's daughter can do little else than sit and weep. A tiny man arrives, though, and offers to help the young woman . . . for a price. The first night it is a necklace, the second a ring, the third—the greatest demand of all—her first child if she becomes queen. The young woman reluctantly agrees since she can see no other solution to save her life. The king is so impressed with her production of glittering gold that he makes her his queen.

A year passes and the queen is blessed with a handsome baby boy. But one day the little man suddenly appears and insists that the queen fulfill her promise. She begs him to accept anything she owns—the entire royal treasury if necessary—instead of her newborn baby. The little man stubbornly refuses. But then he is moved by her tears and will allow her to keep her baby if, in three days, she can determine his name.

The first night the queen tells him every name she knows. None is correct. The next day she asks her trusted servant to make inquiries throughout the town. That evening she repeats to the little man the most unusual names she heard. But to each he replies, "That is not my name." In desperation the queen sends her servant to search the woods to find and observe the little man. The servant finds him near the top of a hill, dancing on one leg around a great fire, and crying out:

> "Today I brew, tomorrow I bake.
> The next day the young queen's child I'll take.
> Soon far and wide will spread the fame
> That Rumpelstiltskin is my name."

The servant returns to tell his queen the little man's secret. Soon afterward Rumpelstiltskin arrives to claim his prize. When the queen announces his name he becomes so angry that he stamps the ground and buries himself so deep that he is never seen again. Among its many layers of meaning, *Rumpelstiltskin* emphasizes that there is power both in seeking the truth and in knowledge.

Other stories introduce children to simple mysteries that require careful observation and thought to solve. In *The Sign in Mendel's Window*, by Mildred Phillips, a butcher is unfairly accused of stealing a stranger's money. But keen observation and careful thinking enable his wife and neighbors to prove his innocence and unmask the real thief.

The *Owl in the Garden*, by Berniece Freschet, focuses on a disappearance and theft. The sleepy quiet of a garden is shattered by cries of "THIEF! THIEF! THIEF!" Who took one of Bluejay's nuts? "Not I," said the Robin, Owl, and Rabbit. Bluejay's friends are drawn into a search for the thief. "Maybe you mislaid your peanut," asks Robin. No, they were hidden. "Where did you hide your peanuts?" asks Owl. Under a maple leaf. But when Bluejay picks up the leaf hiding her second peanut, she discovers that it too is missing. While they are talking the real culprit is busy at work, getting ready for winter. Nuts on the ground can belong to anyone, especially a hungry squirrel. Owl observes Squirrel innocently taking Bluejay's third peanut, but everyone is too busy with the arrival of cold weather to find Bluejay to tell her the mystery has been solved.

Each of these stories encourages children to gather evidence to solve a problem or resolve a conflict. They are appropriate for kindergarten and early-grade-school children who are capable of gathering proof and drawing conclusions. (Social problem-solving will be discussed further in Chapter Nine.)

Appearances Are Deceiving

Truth is not always apparent. Sometimes it is hidden, sometimes it is misunderstood. Many of the stories we tell children caution them to look behind the superficial veneer of the world and not be distracted by appearances. The frog prince who desperately seeks a fair young maiden whose kiss will free him from the witch's spell and restore his human form is a classic example of misunderstanding.

Beauty and the Beast, retold by Marianna Mayer, is a familiar example of love, longing, and misunderstanding. A kind and beautiful maiden lives with a loathsome beast in order to save her father's life. During her first night in his magnificent castle she dreams of a fine lady in a gossamer dress who approaches her, saying,

"Beauty, I am content with your good will. Do not abandon your kind ways in fear. In your heart you know what is right. *Trust your heart, and search out the truth. But beware of being deceived by appearances.* Bear the trials to come, and your goodness will be rewarded" [italics mine].

Beauty explores the castle and discovers many of its wonders: a magic looking glass, a marvelous room of her own, an immense hall filled with exotic birds, a room of mirrors that provides entertainment.

At first she is frightened by the monster's grim and ugly appearance. Each day he asks her to be his wife, and each day she refuses. His sadness and quiet resignation to the pain of her rejection arouses her compassion. Over time his appearance becomes less and less fearsome.

The Beast allows Beauty to return home to visit her ailing father on the condition she return within one week. But she misses the deadline and fails to fulfill her promise. When Beauty returns to the castle she discovers the Beast lying still on the ground, apparently dead. As she lifts his head to her lap she tearfully professes her love and agrees to marry him. Beauty's offer to wed the Beast suddenly breaks the dark fairy's spell, and he is restored to a handsome prince.

Selina Hastings's retelling of *Sir Gawain and the Loathly Lady* of King Arthur fame is a similar story of misunderstanding. Sir Gawain offers to marry a misshapen, disgusting old hag who has helped save the life of King Arthur. On his wedding night Sir Gawain discovers that the Loathly Lady has been transformed into a beautiful woman. His act of chivalry and personal sacrifice in agreeing to marry her removed half of the spell that doomed her to the disgusting shape. But how to remove the other half? Her fate rests on his answer to a question. Which would he rather have—his wife beautiful by day and hideous by night, or beautiful by night and loathsome by day? The correct response, we discover, is to invite her to make the choice herself.

With *Everyone Knows What a Dragon Looks Like* Jay Williams and Mercer Mayer provide a slight variation on the theme of mistaken identity. The residents of the city of Wu pray to the Great Cloud Dragon to come and save them from the horde of Wild Horsemen who are riding to destroy them. The next morning an old man who claims to be the Great Cloud Dragon arrives at the city gate.

"I have come to help you," said the little fat man. "But if you want a dragon to help you, you must treat him with courtesy. I have come a long, weary way. Give me something to eat and something to drink and speak to me politely, and I will save the city."

Instead of kindness, the Great Mandarin of the city and his advisors respond to the old man's claim with disbelief and rudeness. How could someone old, fat, and poor really be the Cloud Dragon? A young gatekeeper named Han invites the old man back to his humble little home. As the Wild Horsemen approach the city from across a wide plain, Han offers him a simple bowl of rice and a cup of wine.

In return for Han's kindness, the old man decides to save the city. He leaves Han's hut to stand defiantly outside the city gates. As the Wild Horsemen rush toward the city walls the old man creates a furious windstorm that destroys and scatters their army. The old man turns back to the city and announces, "Now I will show you what a dragon looks like." He then rises into the air and changes form, from a fat old man to a magnificent dragon with golden scales, sharp claws, and teeth that glitter like diamonds. Fully transformed, the Great Cloud Dragon vanishes into the deep blue sky. From that day on the people of Wu called Han the Honorable Defender of the City.

"But best of all," said the Mandarin, "we know what a dragon looks like. He looks like a small, fat, bald old man."

Unlike the Beast or the Loathly Lady, the Great Cloud Dragon willingly took the form of an old man in order to test the character of those who lived in the city of Wu. He would save them only if they were worthy of his protection. If Han had not taken the time to show him respect and compassion, the Great Cloud Dragon would have left the city to face inevitable destruction.

Beauty and the Beast, Sir Gawain and the Loathly Lady, and *Everyone Knows What a Dragon Looks Like* remind listeners that appearance is a poor reflection of a person's real identity. True character is not superficial. Hidden behind the veneer of a person's appearance we might find a prince or princess, a scholarly wizard, or even a powerful dragon. Beauty, strength, and wealth are secondary to what resides in a person's heart. If we take the time to get to know someone we might be surprised by both their inner beauty and strength. Body awareness and self-esteem will be discussed further in Chapter Ten.

Misunderstanding of a different kind can be found in *Chicken Little*, retold and illustrated by Steven Kellogg. Chicken Little thinks the sky is falling when an acorn falls on her head. Henny Penny, Ducky Lucky, Goosey Lucy, and Gosling Gilbert soon join in the frantic chorus: "THE SKY IS FALLING!" Foxy Loxy watches the commotion from his hiding place, hoping to catch a tasty meal.

When Turkey Lurkey arrives Foxy Loxy realizes he is outnumbered. So he assumes the disguise of a policeman and locks the group in his van. The six friends realize they have been fooled. "And as for that nonsense about the sky falling," sneers Foxy Loxy, "this is what beaned the dim-witted chick!" With a triumphant laugh he throws the acorn skyward. Unfortunately for Foxy Loxy, the acorn hits the gears of a police helicopter hovering overhead, forcing it to plunge to the earth and crash into the van. Foxy Loxy is then captured by the parachuting Sergeant Hefty. Chicken Little is wiser now for having discovered her foolish mistake. She discovers that what *seems* real may not *be* real. Her foolish mistake illustrates that it might be wise to double-check initial impressions before taking action.

In addition to appearance we can also misinterpret another's actions. *Donna O'Neeshuck Was Chased by Some Cows*, written by Bill Grossman and illustrated by Sue Truesdell, gives new meaning to the phrase "wild goose chase." Donna's problem begins when she pats a cow on its head. But then she has to flee when all the cows start to chase her. The townspeople and other farm and forest animals join in the chase too. Poor Donna, she has no idea why everyone is pursuing her. Exhausted, she finally stops and asks, "Why are you all chasing me?" "Head pats," they respond, "we want pats on the head. You give such incredible head pats." Donna misunderstood their actions. They have no intention of harming her. What they really want are more of her great little pats on the head.

Sometimes the facts can be distorted, especially when a story is passed on from one person to another. In *It's Perfectly True*, Janet Stevens's adaptation of the Hans Christian Andersen tale, a chicken's innocent remark about losing a feather is modified and exaggerated as it passes from one hen to another, from hen to owl, from owl to pigeon, and then from pigeon to rooster. Until, finally, the hen that started it all reads the headline in her local newspaper: "Five Chickens Die of a Broken Heart." *It's Perfectly True* shows how differences in perspective can be unintentionally misleading.

Others May Try to Mislead You

Sometimes truth is hidden behind a mask of deception. Not everyone in the world can be trusted. There are those like Foxy Loxy who seek personal gain by trapping others in a web of lies and illusions. Many children's stories are cautionary tales, introducing young listeners to the consequences of misplaced trust.

Take, for example, the familiar fairy tale *Little Red Riding Hood*, retold and illustrated by Trina Schart Hyman. On her way through the forest to grandma's house Little Red Riding Hood is greeted by a sly and hungry wolf.

She had no idea what a wicked animal he was, however, so she was not at all frightened of him.

The story begins with misunderstanding. Little Red Riding Hood is unaware of the danger that faces her. The wolf learns of her destination and manages to be the first to arrive at her grandmother's house. Poor grandmother—the wolf gobbles her up and then jumps into her bed and wraps himself in her shawl.

When Little Red Riding Hood arrives, she sees the door open. Something seems wrong, and she becomes suspicious.

She felt quite frightened, but she didn't know why. "What's wrong," she thought. "I always like coming to Grandmother's so much. Why should I feel so afraid? Can it be because she is sick?"

She is aware at one level that something is wrong, but at another level her mind refuses to acknowledge the danger. When she sees her "grandmother" she realizes something is not quite right. She is beginning to lose her innocent naïvete and face the truth. But she is still too slow to notice the wolf's treachery. She is still not confident of her own senses.

"Grandmother! What big, hairy ears you have grown!" she said.

"The better to hear you with, my dear."

"Oh, Grandmother! Your eyes are so shiny!"

"The better to see you with, my dear."

"Your hands look so strange, Grandmother!"

"The better to catch you and hug you with, my dear."

"Please, Grandmother, why do you have such big, sharp teeth?"

"Those are to eat you up with, my dear!"

Poor Little Red Riding Hood—with a bound the wolf leaps out of bed and gobbles her up. Instead of believing what her eyes told her, she set aside her own good sense and accepted the wolf's smooth reassurances. Fortunately a hunter arrives, kills the wolf, and frees both Red Riding Hood and her grandmother.

Snow White and the Seven Dwarfs, in a version magnificently illustrated by Nancy Ekholm Burkert, is a similar cautionary tale. Three times the wicked witch tries to kill the beautiful Snow White. First she orders the huntsman to lure her into the forest. When this deception is unsuccessful she then paints her face and dresses as an old peddler woman selling lace garments. When Snow White tries one on, the witch ties it so tightly that the young maiden falls down as if she were dead. But this attempt fails too. Again she returns to the home of the Seven Dwarfs, this time with a poison comb. But for the third time, her attempt to kill Snow White fails.

Outraged but undaunted, the witch disguises herself once more and returns to kill Snow White with a beautiful poisoned apple. When Snow White takes a bite she falls immediately into a deep, deathlike sleep. Thinking her dead, the dwarves place the young maiden in a glass coffin. A prince finds her resting place and falls immediately in love with her. As he carries the coffin back to his castle, the bite of apple falls from Snow White's mouth, and she regains consciousness.

Like Little Red Riding Hood, Snow White is completely fooled by an evildoer's deception. They both fail to recognize danger. Listeners know that the two are being misled. But no shout from the safety of a cozy armchair will alert them to the deceit. They learn only by experiencing the terrible consequences of their ignorance.

Robert Kraus has provided a different context for seduction in *Come Out and Play, Little Mousie*. Cat is hungry and persistent. Every day he tries to entice Mousie out of her hole with a promise of play and games. Mousie finally discards caution on Saturday and comes out to play. Surprise! Cat wants to play, "Cat and Mouse—you run and I catch you!" Mousie is saved at the final moment by a dog who wants to play, "Cat and Dog." But is it really a dog? In this delightful story of deception and consequence, nothing can be taken for granted.

Lying is a form of aggression. By creating an illusion the liar is exercising a measure of power over another person. Deception is a form of mind control. The aggressor crafts an illusion to change another's feelings or behavior to suit his or her own purposes. Lies, of course, can be devastating. "Mommy or Daddy won't tell you, but you are really adopted," a big sister tells her younger sibling. Such deception shatters the stability of a child's world and destroys the security that underlies self-confidence.

George Told Kate, by Kay Chorao, shows how lies can be a form of cruelty. George is merciless in the exaggerations he tells his younger sister. When her parents tell her to clean up her room, George insists, "You'll get spanked if you don't put away every single thing. . . . Cleaning is hard. . . . It will take you a long, long time." With each statement Kate worries more and more, until she is done and realizes her brother was wrong. He also frightens her with scary images of the teacher she will have at school and tells her they are moving when, in fact, they are not. But each time he lies, Kate discovers his deception.

Young children are easily misled because of their egocentrism. Because they tend to view adults as infallible authority figures, they believe what adults tell them. The depth of their understanding of what is real is also very limited. They may believe someone, for example, who tells them they are filled with tar instead of blood or that a snake will grow from their thumb if they keep putting it in their mouth. They lack sufficient knowledge to evaluate what others tell them.

In addition, young children tend to be swayed by appearance. When three-year-olds see two identical groups of pennies, one in a pile and the other arranged in a line, they will probably say the one in the line has "more" pennies than the other. They make this choice because when the pennies are spread out they *seem* like more. In the same way, preschool children may think that someone who looks or acts "nice" can be trusted.

Trying to teach young children who to trust and what to believe is extremely difficult. If we overemphasize deception we can frighten them so they become anxious and insecure about life in general. Stories similar to those found in this chapter may help introduce a certain intelligent wariness in our children. If Snow White, Little Red Riding Hood, Mousie, and Kate could talk they might tell our children, "Use your minds. Trust your senses; don't believe everything someone tells you. If you are not sure about something ask a parent or teacher for help."

Deception Destroys Trust

In addition to using good sense in evaluating the truthfulness of others we might also want our children to be truthful themselves. Honesty is the foundation for satisfying relationships with others. Deception undermines rapport by eroding trust and respect. When deceit rules, trust deteriorates into suspicion, goodwill into hostility.

Tony Ross's retelling of Aesop's classic *The Boy Who Cried Wolf* is a hilarious portrayal of the young boy who suffers the consequences of his deception. At first, the game of betrayal is fun because of the power the young boy feels in frightening adults. But then he really needs their help, and his cries of "Wolf!" are ignored. They do not believe him any more—his words are meaningless, without reality. In Tony Ross's version of the fable, both the naughty boy and the arrogant townspeople face the consequences of their insensitive actions. Instead of simply telling children that lying is wrong, *The Boy Who Cried Wolf* emphasizes the erosion of trust that is a consequence of deceit.

Why do children lie? In some cases they may be trying to protect themselves against punishment or embarrassment. They have learned that being honest can have painful consequences. "DID YOU BREAK THAT LAMP?" shouts a mother to her preschool son. Let us assume he did. But memories of more painful moments begin flooding his mind. In desperation he blurts out, "Not ME! I didn't do it." Once uttered, the lie hangs suspended in midair, advertising guilt like a flashy neon sign. If his mother knows he is the culprit, he has been caught in a deadly trap. In addition to being punished for breaking the lamp he may also be punished for lying.

Lying and guilt are examined in *The Lie*, by Ann Helena. A young girl accidentally breaks a friend's necklace while everyone else is outside. When the teacher confronts the group about the necklace she denies any responsibility. Her friend asks her to walk home with her after school. During their walk home she confesses her guilt. *The Lie* illustrates a child's struggle of conscience in overcoming fear and risking the truth.

Because of low self-esteem children may lie to gain prestige or attention. They want others to think they are important. Lying as a search for approval is emphasized in *Liar, Liar, Pants on Fire!* by Miriam Cohen. Alex is the new boy in class. No matter what anyone else has, Alex says he has something better. For example, when Sara talks about her hamster, Alex tells everyone he has a horse. When the children discover his exaggerations they taunt him with "Liar, liar, pants on fire!" His attempt to gain recognition has backfired. But Jim doesn't join in. He feels no need to ridicule his classmate. Later, at the Christmas party, he feels sorry for Alex and gives him his decoration to hang on the tree. With his little act of kindness Jim helps Alex feel a little more accepted.

There are many children like Alex—they want so much to be liked that they try to create an illusion more attractive to others than themselves. Their lies are more like desperate wishes than acts of aggression.

Fantasies Are Not Necessarily Deceptions

A fantasy is an untruth that can seem real. In our emphasis on honesty we may actually confuse truth with truthfulness. Children sometimes create fantasies that stretch the truth to make it fit with their real experience. For example, the sound of trees creaking in the wind, the howl of a distant dog, and trash cans tumbling in a nearby alley frighten a child on his way home from a neighbor's house. "Something is coming to get me!" the child thinks. "A bear is coming to get me!" races through his mind as he runs home. Once inside he tells his mother, "A bear almost grabbed me!" This statement is not true, but it is truthful. The child believes what he imagined. In the child's mind, what seemed real really happened.

Sometimes children create fantasies out of wishful thinking. When her mother catches her eating a bag of cookies in the bedroom closet, a two-year-old closes her eyes and says, "Mommy, I no here, go away!" In a similar way children have imaginary playmates to fulfill some of their wishful thinking about companionship.

Fiction is a third form of innocent childlike fantasy. According to Samuel Coleridge, fiction is a "willing suspension of disbelief." When we read a book to a child or listen to them tell us a story, we momentarily suspend reality by mutual consent. The words "Once upon a time . . ." signal that what follows is make-believe. In a similar way, children suspend reality in their play. But even though it is not factual, the story or play activity may convey a deeper truth about the child's experience.

Many children's stories focus on the enjoyment of pretending. Grandpa bunny entertains his grandchildren with one surprise after another in *December 24*, by Denys Cazet. It's his birthday but Grandpa's not letting on that he knows. He tries to "guess" the day by dressing up—first like Abe Lincoln, then Cupid, followed by the Easter Bunny, Count Rabbicula (for Halloween), and finally Santa Claus. The game ends after Grandpa comes tumbling down the chimney.

> "Mercy sakes!" cried Grandma. "Are you all right?"
> Grandpa smiled. "Happy Christmas," he said.
> "Grandpa," said Louie, "*tomorrow* is Christmas."
> Emily handed Grandpa his present.
> "Happy Birthday, Grandpa."

James Stevenson introduces young listeners to a grandfather who likes to make a point by telling his grandchildren outrageous stories about his childhood. In *No Friends* he tells Marie Ann and Louie about how lonely he and his brother Wainey were after they moved. *That Dreadful Day* describes a terrible first day at school with his new teacher, Mr. Smeal. And *There's Nothing to Do!* shows what happened when he and Wainey visited their grandparents' dull farm and had nothing to do. These and other stories in the series are the grandfather's hilarious response to Marie Ann's and Louie's complaints: that they have no friends, that their first day in school was awful, and that they are

STORYBREAK

Penelope's Lie

Once upon a time, in the wonderful town of Butterberry Hill . . .

Miss Lucy made a special blueberry pie for Grandpa Jake's birthday party. Right after she took it out of the oven she put it up on the ledge of an open kitchen window to cool. Then off she went to get ready for the party.

Just then Penelope Pig passed by that window on the way to Grandpa Jake's house. Oh, that pie looked so good, so tasty. Penelope could feel the hungry grumbles in her tummy. "Oh, I'm sure Lucy won't mind if I take just a bite."

So she went over to the pie and took a big bite out of it. It was so good! She decided to take a little more to eat on the way to Grandpa Jake's. So she reached down and took a piece to carry with her.

Now Penelope did not know that the pie was for Grandpa Jake's party. She would not have eaten any of that pie if she had known it was for Grandpa Jake. But she didn't know any of this as she walked to his house.

Along the way she met Little Dirty Dorothy. She asked Dorothy if she would like some of the pie she was carrying. Dorothy did not know it belonged to Miss Lucy. She took some, and the wonderful blueberry juice trickled down her chin as she ate it up. Dorothy thanked Penelope for the pie and continued on home to get Grandpa Jake's present.

Meanwhile, Miss Lucy discovered that part of her pie was missing. "It's ruined," she said. "Who would do such a naughty thing?" She saw Rodney, Mrs. Winterbones's nephew, outside and asked him if he saw anyone take some of her pie. Rodney told her no, but promised to try to find out.

Rodney ran ahead and caught up to Penelope. "Penelope, did you see who ruined Miss Lucy's pie for Grandpa Jake's birthday?" "Oh, my goodness," Penelope thought, "that pie was for Grandpa Jake! Lucy sure will be mad at me!"

Then she did another naughty thing. She lied. "No, I don't

know who took the pie," she told Rodney. So Rodney ran on, enjoying his chance to find the wrongdoer.

By this time, Dorothy had Grandpa Jake's present and was on her way to his house. Rodney ran up to her and started to say, "Dorothy, did you see who ruined . . ." But as soon as he saw the blueberry juice on her chin he shouted, "You did! You took it and now you've ruined Grandpa Jake's party. Wait till I tell Miss Lucy!" And off he ran.

Dorothy was confused. She had no idea what Rodney was talking about, and he never gave her a chance to ask why he was saying those things.

When Rodney arrived at Grandpa Jake's house everyone except Dorothy was there. Miss Lucy looked sad because of her mushed-in pie. Penelope felt awful too, that she had taken something that did not belong to her. Rodney stood in front of everyone and announced loudly, "I KNOW WHO RUINED MISS LUCY'S PIE! IT WAS . . ." Penelope felt her heart beat. ". . . LITTLE DIRTY DOROTHY!" "No," said Miss Lucy, "I don't think Dorothy would do such a thing." Grandpa Jake said, "That does not sound like Dorothy. Are you sure?" "Oh yes," said Rodney.

Now Penelope felt even more miserable. Her friend Dorothy was getting the blame for something she had not done. Dorothy did not know the pie belonged to Miss Lucy. Penelope wanted to say it was her fault, but she was too scared.

At that moment Dorothy arrived. Everyone turned to look at her. Do you know what they saw? Blueberry juice on her chin. When Miss Lucy saw that blueberry juice she said, "Oh Dorothy, you should not have taken a bite out of my pie!" "Your pie? Oh, Miss Lucy, I . . ." Dorothy was going to explain what had happened, but she never had the chance. Rodney interrupted. "Now you ruined Grandpa Jake's pie! You can't come to his party."

How do you think Penelope felt now? She knew she should speak up and tell her friends *she* had taken the piece of pie. But what would happen then? What do you think she did?

Even though her heart was beating very fast, she stood up and said, "I took a bite of Miss Lucy's pie. I took the piece and gave part of it to Dorothy. But she did not know it was Miss Lucy's. It's my fault. I am sorry." She sat down and started to cry. Grandpa Jake and Miss Lucy went over to Penelope and hugged her. They were happy to forgive her, especially after she bravely admitted that she was the one who had taken a piece of the pie. That was a naughty thing for her to do, but not a terrible thing. Even so, Penelope felt sad the rest of the day.

The next morning, when Grandpa Jake went to get his paper from the front porch he found a blueberry pie sitting right in front of the door. There was a note next to it.

> *Dear Grandpa Jake:*
> *I am sorry I ruined your pie. My mom helped me make this pie for you last night. I hope you like it.*
> *Love, Penelope*

Grandpa Jake smiled. He went inside his house and poured himself a cold glass of milk to go with a piece of Penelope's delicious pie.

---

bored. Every story is a grand slapstick adventure. By the time he is finished his grandchildren's frowns have been replaced by smiles.

James Stevenson's grandpa tells stories to entertain and enlighten, not to deceive or mislead. He uses fiction to convey important truths to his grandchildren. In a similar fashion, Santa Claus, the Easter Bunny, and the Tooth Fairy are not lies. They can be enjoyable fictions we share with children to convey our love for them and our delight in their childlike appreciation for fantasy. A world without imagination, without fiction, is a world without wonder, without creativity, without discovery. And such a world is a lifeless graveyard of exhausted dreams, the birthplace of despair.

Not Everyone Will Believe You When You Tell the Truth

When children do tell the truth they may not be believed. Some adults may not take what children say seriously. Hattie the Hen knows how it feels to be ignored. In

Hattie and the Fox she spots a fox's nose in the bushes and tries to warn her barnyard friends. But they don't seem to care.

> "Good grief!" said the goose.
> "Well, well!" said the pig.
> "Who cares?" said the sheep.
> "So what?" said the horse.
> "What next?" said the cow.

Hattie gradually sees more and more of the fox. But each time she tries to warn her friends they fail to take her seriously—until the fox dashes into the yard. Author Mem Fox takes a humorous look at trust and truth in this reversal of "The Boy Who Cried Wolf" theme.

In *Albert's Toothache* Barbara Williams reveals the frustration children can feel when they are misunderstood. Albert complains of a toothache. Of course, no one believes him, because, being a turtle, Albert has no teeth. His mother worries about him and his father is angry. "You *should* be worried about a boy who does not tell the truth," his father tells his mother as he leaves for work. No matter how hard she tries, Albert's mother cannot convince him he has no toothache. And Albert is miserable because his mother will not believe him.

But then his grandmother arrives. After patient questioning she discovers where Albert has a toothache: on his foot. A gopher *bit* him when he stepped in his hole. His complaint referred to the gopher's tooth, not his own. Finally someone understands. With a little loving attention and care Albert is quickly on his feet again.

We are so accustomed to children's tall tales and exaggerations that we may not take the time to understand the real meaning behind their words. Albert was telling the truth. But everyone took what he said literally instead of finding out what he meant. As soon as his grandmother asked him, "Where do you have a toothache?" the mystery was solved.

Summary

We all want our children to grow up to be trustworthy and truthful individuals. But teaching them not to lie is insufficient. Being honest means more than telling the truth. Honesty means being *open* to the world as it is, to go beyond superficialities to grasp what lies behind appearances. Honesty means trusting one's instincts and intuition. It means using words to communicate ideas and feelings clearly, with sensitivity and compassion. Honesty may mean finding wonder in a fallen leaf or wisdom in a well-told story.

CHAPTER NINE

From <u>Goldilocks and the Three Bears</u> to <u>Harald and the Giant Knight</u>:

Becoming a Social Problem-Solver

Every generation, it seems, must learn some of the most important lessons in life by experiencing the consequences of their choices. We may want to save our children from this pain by sharing the wisdom we gained from growing up. We remember the confusion, the hurt, the painful results of foolish decisions. If we could only distill the wisdom life provided us and pass it on to our children then they might be spared the suffering many of us experienced. But our attempts to help children learn from our mistakes often seem fruitless. A child burns his fingers when playing with matches. Another becomes sick after eating too much candy. A third breaks a special toy after playing with it carelessly. These misfortunes happened to us when we were young. But despite our warnings our children seem determined to repeat our blunders. Cautionary lectures from parents, teachers, and other adults never make the same impression as unpleasant experiences.

But if we could protect our children from life's bitter consequences we would prevent them from learning the most important lesson of all—that they can survive their mistakes, learn from them, and use their intelligence to stop problems from occurring or to solve them when they do. Maybe this is why they want to discover these cause and effects for themselves.

Children learn about themselves and others through social engagement. The social arena provides them with a laboratory in which they can study and observe how others react to their actions. A young child, for example, may hit another and then stand back to watch how that child reacts. Conflict is an inevitable byproduct of this social learning. In a fifteen-minute span, two preschool friends can play quietly next to each other, start building a block tower together, disagree over how they should proceed, have a fight, get hurt, cry, make up, and then begin playing happily with a box of sandbox toys. Young children move freely between cooperation and confrontation, delight and anger, smiles and tears.

Children are faced with all sorts of challenges in their play. A four-year-old may have to solve many problems in the course of an afternoon at preschool. He meets another child for the first time and makes the first tentative efforts to play together. He wants a truck in the possession of another child and has to find a way to get it. He becomes frustrated with a woodworking project and asks his teacher for help. Later he has to protect himself from a playmate who tries to push him off a bike. This four-year-old's sense of well-being, like that of any other child, depends on how effectively he can respond to these and other problems of everyday life.

Encouraging children to be open and aware of the world around them is not enough. Children have to be prepared to participate in the flow of events that surrounds them—to be a player and not just an observer. Being a player means being a problem-solver, taking an active role in managing conflict and other types of social challenges. Becoming a problem-solver means gradually gaining an appreciation of how other people's goals can be different from one's own. It means having an awareness of how one's actions affect others and of the range of available alternatives for responding to a problem.

Of course, young children lack the maturity and language skills for engaging in sophisticated social problem-solving. They cannot differentiate their needs from those of others or delay gratification while negotiating a conflict. But the rudiments of mature problem-solving are learned during the preschool years. A carpenter, for example, might begin to learn his trade as a toddler who loves to bang a plastic hammer against a wooden peg and assemble large plastic nuts and bolts. He later builds on these initial skills as he grows older and learns to use a real hammer, then a small saw, and eventually a power drill. Skills like social problem-solving are learned in a similar way, little by little, each building on what was previously learned.

Children learn to become problem-solvers by watching their parents and how they manage their problems. They also learn from the way they are treated. The child who is spanked for every misdeed may use violence to try to solve problems with his playmates. Children also gain ideas from what people tell them. They learn from parents who take the time to explain reasons for their limits and encourage them to think of alternative ways to solve problems. Children can also learn to broaden their knowledge of social problem-solving from the stories their parents tell them.

How Stories Contribute to Problem-Solving

The stories we heard while we were growing up may have encouraged us to think about the consequences of our behavior and to use our intelligence and creativity to solve problems. We might have heard about King Midas, who suffered the consequences of his greed. We may have been fascinated by the pig who escaped a hungry wolf by building a home of bricks while his two foolish brothers constructed worthless homes of straw and sticks. Some of us heard about the chicks who never received any bread from the Little Red Hen because they refused to contribute their help. From *King Midas* to *The Three Little Pigs* to *The Little Red Hen,* stories have emphasized the dangers of senseless and selfish action and the benefits of careful, prudent thinking.

Young children are introduced to the consequences of misbehavior in *Goldilocks and the Three Bears.* Poor Goldilocks. Like any egocentric young child she simply took what she wanted. The house looks interesting, so walk in. Hungry? There's food on the table. Who cares if it was meant for someone else? Of course, you have to sit to eat. No problem if you break one of the chairs—just find another. Sleepy? Lie down and take a nap in someone else's bed.

The mischievous Goldilocks seems indifferent to the consequences of her misconduct. But then the three bears arrive and discover that someone has invaded their home to eat baby bear's food, break his chair, and lie in his bed. At that point, as we all know, Goldilocks has a rude awakening. Lorinda Bryan Cauley, Lynn Bywaters Ferris, and Janet Stevens each have their own wonderfully illustrated versions of this humorous fairy tale about property rights and the consequences of misbehavior.

Some stories encourage children to respond to problems with creative solutions. *Harald and the Giant Knight* is a recent story by Donald Carrick that shows how a father and son use their imaginations to overcome danger. Young Harald dreams of the day when he can become a baron's knight. The knights' shining armor and daring exploits provide an attractive contrast to his boring farm existence. But Harald discovers a callous, destructive side to the knights when they assume control of his family's farm to use it as a practice field. They trample his family's crops and eat their livestock. How can he and his father save their farm? There seems no way to rid themselves of their unwanted guests. In desperation they devise an imaginative plan to frighten away the knights by building the biggest and most terrifying "scarecrow" warrior ever seen in the land. Imagination and creativity triumph over physical might.

Goldilocks and the Three Bears and *Harald and the Giant Knight* are examples of stories that focus on consequences and social problem-solving. Each encourages children to think and reflect on the results of their actions. Goldilocks's attempt to satisfy her curiosity, hunger, and fatigue showed an insensitivity toward the Three Bears and got her into trouble. Harald and his father found a non-violent solution to protect their lands from the threat of intruders.

Stories promote problem-solving in three ways. First, they provide a glimpse of what goes on in a character's mind and heart. We get to know characters and come to understand how they feel, what they think, and why they act the way they do. Second, the dramatic elements of stories are often based on a character striving to reach a goal and overcome barriers to success. Problem-solving is the creative engine that drives the plot. Third, the consequences of a character's choices are given dramatic impact within a story. Deceit may lead to ruin, as in *The Boy Who Cried Wolf.* Or the violent appropriation of power can be self-destructive, as in *The Man Who Could Call Down Owls.* On a more positive note, patient kindness can reduce suspicion and fear, as in *The Mare on the Hill.*

Many stories encourage children to think, to use their intelligence to be aware of problems, and to take action after considering alternatives and their consequences. Stories that focus on solving problems may emphasize the following concepts:

- Your actions are linked with the actions of others.
- Identify alternative solutions to a problem.
- Consider the consequences of what you do.

STORYBREAK

Whose Fault Is It?

Once upon a time, in the wonderful town of Butterberry Hill . . .

Rodney pulled the hair of the girl who sat in the desk in front of him at school. He reached right up and YANK! pulled her hair. Wow, was she ever upset! She reached right around and smacked him on the arm. SMACK! Rodney wanted to hit her back, but the teacher was standing right there. So he didn't.

But on the walk back home after school, he saw Penelope Pig. So he called her a name. He shouted at her, "PIGS STINK!" Now, that is one of the worst things you could ever say to Penelope. She felt angry. Before she could say anything back to him, Rodney had walked away.

Penelope sure was upset. How could anyone think such a mean thing about her. She was the cleanest, prettiest pig in the land. But she was still upset. Then she saw Briarbutton the Rabbit working in his garden. "HEY, BIG EARS! DUMBO!" she shouted. Briarbutton didn't mind her saying "Big ears." But he hated being called "Dumbo." Before he could say anything, Penelope was gone.

Now Briarbutton felt like yelling at someone. Just then Little Dirty Dorothy stopped for a visit. "Briarbutton," she said, "could you give me some of your carrots for my vegetable stew?" But Briarbutton was in no mood for being kind. "DON'T BE A MOOCHER! BUY THEM FROM THE STORE!" And he jumped into his burrow.

Oh, no! Now Dorothy felt sad. Briarbutton had rarely been mean to her before. (Oh, there was that time she put bubble gum on his fur . . . but that's another story.) The more she thought about his thoughtlessness the more angry she became. As she walked along, she saw a soda can lying on the ground. Because she was so upset she gave it a mighty kick.

Well, you know what happened? That can sailed high in the air, right toward the house where Rodney lived with his auntie, Mrs. Winterbones, right to the window of his bedroom, where it hit with a mighty crash. The window broke, and the can hit the plastic airplane model Rodney had just put together. The model fell off the table on to the floor and broke into a hundred pieces.

Rodney saw what had happened to his model and ran from the house to find who was responsible for breaking it. He saw Dorothy looking at the broken window. "You have to pay for the window and model, Dorothy." Dorothy insisted, "Rodney, it's not my fault. Briarbutton was mean to me. That's why I kicked the can."

So Rodney went to Briarbutton's home. Rodney told him, "You were mean to Dorothy, and she kicked the can that broke my window and my model. You have to pay for what happened." But Briarbutton insisted, "Rodney, it's not my fault. Penelope called me 'Dumbo' and that's why I was mean to Dorothy."

So Rodney went to see Penelope. She would have to pay. Rodney told her, "You said a mean thing to Briarbutton and he was selfish to Dorothy who kicked a can that broke my window and model. You have to pay for what happened." "But Rodney," Penelope said, "you called me a 'stinky.' That's why I said that to Briarbutton."

"Oh, oh," thought Rodney. "I said 'Pigs stink' to Penelope because that other little girl smacked my arm. I'll go find her to make her pay." But then he stopped and thought some more. What do you think she will say? She hit him because he pulled her hair. He pulled her hair because he thought it would be fun. Who started the whole thing after all? "Oh well," he thought sadly as he walked back home. "Now let's see," he said to himself, "I wonder how much money I have in my piggy bank?"

Your Actions Are Linked with the Actions of Others

Many stories show how one person's actions are linked with the actions of another. Linkage means that there are subtle connections between us in how we influence each other's behavior. Children make this discovery, for example, when they realize they can get a brother or sister into trouble. "Look at this pan, Jimmy!" seven-year-old Patrick says to his three-year-old brother. "If you turn it over you can take this wooden spoon and hit it like a drum." Patrick demonstrates by quietly tapping the pan with the spoon a few times. Jimmy picks up the spoon and copies his brother by wildly banging on the pan. His mother enters the room and angrily scolds Jimmy for making so much noise while his baby brother is sleeping.

If his mother blames him for his younger brother's misbehavior, Patrick might protest his innocence by insisting that he was an innocent bystander. But maybe, just maybe, he was aware of the relationship between his comments about the pan and his brother being scolded. Maybe he knew his brother would get into trouble when he first showed him how to use the pan as a drum.

Almost every day after class Tammy complains to her parents about being pushed down by Michael, another four-year-old in her preschool class. The parents complain to the teacher and insist that Michael be removed from the group. But the underlying reasons for the problem are not as obvious as the parents think. The conflict typically begins when Tammy urges Michael to chase her. "Bet you can't get me!" she taunts. Michael chases, Tammy slows down, Michael grabs at her, she falls down and begins crying, then Michael runs away. Both children share responsibility for the problem. Their actions are linked. To stop the sequence the teachers have to encourage Michael to refuse to respond to Tammy's taunts, while emphasizing to Tammy that she contributes to the problem by encouraging Michael to chase her.

Linkage and responsibility are portrayed in *Why Mosquitos Buzz in People's Ears,* by Verna Aardema. Mosquito tells Iguana a tall tale that sets into motion a series of events leading to the death of one of Owl's owlets. Iguana does not want to hear any more of Mosquito's big lie, so he plugs his ears. Python hides in a rabbit hole after Iguana does not respond to his good-morning greeting. He thinks

Iguana may be plotting mischief against him. Crow sees Rabbit fleeing his hole and warns other jungle creatures of the danger that must be near. As Monkey leaps through the trees to give warning, he breaks a dead limb that falls into Owl's nest, killing one of her young. The grieving Mother Owl is too sad to wake the sun, so the jungle remains in darkness.

King Lion calls a council to find the reason for the tragic death of the owlet. Beginning with Mother Owl he follows the action-and-reaction sequence back to the Mosquito's original tall tale. All the creatures agree that Mosquito is the culprit and should be punished. From a hiding place in a nearby bush, she overhears their conversation and manages to flee before they can capture her. But her guilty conscience remains to this day.

To this day she goes about whining in people's ears: "Zeee! Is everyone still angry at me?" When she does that, she gets an honest answer. KPAO!

Leo and Diane Dillon's bright and colorful illustrations won the 1976 Caldecott Award for best illustrations in children's literature.

Toby's Toe, by Jane Goodsell, is a variation on the same theme. Toby stubs his toe against the bureau when he gets out of bed one morning. Then he steps on his sister's balloon. Meg complains to Mother, who drops an egg on Father's shoe. Father yells at the dog, who then chases the schoolteacher's cat. Miss Perry is so worried when her cat refuses to come down from the roof that she has no patience with her class when she arrives at school. The children in her class become sullen and ill-tempered. When they return home they pass their hostility on to their parents and brothers and sisters.

But what Toby begins he can undo.

Toby Turner had no idea of the trouble he started when he stubbed his toe and stepped—*pop!*—that morning on Meg's balloon. Luckily for Toby he wasn't in Miss Perry's class and he walked home cheerily whistling "Yankee Doodle."

When he sees his sister's popped balloon he feels guilty. He decides to give her his red baseball cap that she wants so much. His generosity sets into motion another long chain of events in the neighborhood that builds to a much happier conclusion. What makes *Toby's Toe* especially delightful are the sounds that Jane Goodsell sprinkles throughout the story. Ouch! Grrr! Pop! Sob, sob! and other sounds of anger and contentment help listeners track the events as they unfold, one after another.

In *One Summer Night* Eleanor Schick shows how a child's happiness can spread unknowingly to others. Instead of sleeping one summer night, Laura puts on a record and begins to dance. Her dancing reminds two sisters in the apartment across the street of a song they know, so they begin singing instead of fighting. Their song reminds Mr. Stein of one of his favorite tunes, so he begins playing his piano. His tune reminds Mrs. Cameron of the time she danced on the stage, so she begins to dance. Gradually, the dancing, singing, and playing spread throughout the neighborhood. By the time Laura's record stops there is a party in the street below her window. She and her mother and brother sit and watch the joyous celebration late into the night without ever knowing their part in inspiring the scene.

Linkage is an important part of many fairy tales. One character's actions may trigger a response by another that creates a whole new sequence of events. In *The Porcelain Cat,* by Michael Patrick Hearn, a wizard sends his apprentice, Nikon, to find the basilisk blood he needs to turn a porcelain cat into a real animal. The Witch Beneath the Hill tells him she has what he needs. But Nikon will have to do her a favor before she will give it to him. He will have to ask the Undine of the Brook for a special shellfish that the witch needs to cure any burn.

The undine is willing to give Nikon the shellfish. But she expects him to provide her with a basketful of red-spotted mushrooms that grow in the wood. In a small clearing lit by a ring of moonlight Nikon finds the mushrooms the undine needs. The Centaur of the Wood jealously guards his domain, though, and catches Nikon taking the mushrooms. Nikon pleads for mercy by explaining his obligations to the wizard, witch, and undine. The centaur too has a need he cannot meet on his own. Because he is cloven-hoofed he cannot climb the trees to obtain their fruit. He will allow Nikon to take the mushrooms if he first retrieves these tasty morsels.

This final act of assistance then reverses the sequence. The centaur carries Nikon back to the undine, who makes the exchange of shellfish for mushrooms. He then returns to the witch's house and exchanges the shellfish for the basilisk blood needed by the wizard. Nikon has finally met his obligations. *The Porcelain Cat* emphasizes the reciprocity that is an important part of our link with others. You help me; I help you. We both reach our goals by assisting each other.

Children cannot be expected to fully understand the complex notion of linkage or grasp the abstract reasons for another's actions. Preschool children are too dependent on their own egocentric view of the world. They cannot examine their own behavior. If you ask a young child, "Why did you hit your brother?" he may be able to tell you, " 'Cause he took my truck!" He cannot describe other reasons, like jealousy and fear, that may have motivated the hitting.

Nevertheless, young children do show an emerging awareness of how one's actions affect others. They can begin to give reasons for their actions, though at a very concrete, superficial level. They know that their actions can trigger predictable reactions from others. They also begin to ask their parents to explain the reasons for what they do. "Why do I have to go to my room, Mommy?" a child may ask. They can understand clear explanations for the rules we establish.

Knowing that our actions are interrelated provides a foundation for problem-solving. Social problems are essentially cause-effect-cause sequences that have to be interrupted. I want the toy so I grab it from you; you want the toy back so you hit me; I cry and yell for Mother; Mother takes toy and spanks you; you cry; and so on. The conflict escalates unless someone dares to break the chain, reflect on what is happening or about to happen, and then take action to prevent or resolve the problem. An important part of this reflection is considering alternatives.

Identify Alternative Solutions to a Problem

Identifying a variety of alternative solutions to a problem is critical for stopping an escalating chain of conflict or overcoming a barrier. Knowledge of alternatives fosters flexibility. If one solution does not work, another might. To the old saying, "If at first you don't succeed then try, try again," we might add, ". . . and try something different."

The socially skillful child can think of alternatives to reach a goal or solve a problem. A five-year-old who wants to play with a truck in the possession of a classmate may begin by simply asking, "Can I play with the truck?" If that opening is unsuccessful he might try distraction: "Look at that airplane. Why don't you be the flier?" If the child refuses, he might try a little incentive: "If you let me play with that truck, I'll invite you to my birthday party." Or he might ask the teacher for help. He may try to use force. He may not say anything at all, blending into the other child's play with additional toys, waiting for the opportunity to play with the truck as soon as the other child sets it aside.

Children who become easily discouraged and withdraw or use violence may not be able to think of other ways to reach their goals. They live up to the saying, "If the only tool you have is a hammer, you may tend to treat everything as though it were a nail." Most of us know both children and adults who carry only "hammers" in their problem-solving toolbox. Their only alternative may be hitting, or nagging, or running to someone else for help. But a single solution may not work. Some people hit back. Some ignore nagging. And someone may not be available for rescue duty. Children may fail to resolve a problem because they cannot envision alternatives that are more effective than their one solution. According to psychologists Jerome Spivak and Myrna Shure, socially competent children prefer finesse to force. When they have a problem they have more than one tool they can depend on. They have learned to think in terms of identifying a range of alternatives instead of a single solution.

Stories help children build a "toolbox" of alternatives. By listening to a wide variety of stories, children are exposed to many different ways that characters respond to problems. Take, for example, the book by Maurice Jones based on the familiar chant utilizing body movement and sound, *I'm Going on a Dragon Hunt*. Dressed in a wide-brimmed hat and knee-high boots and armed with a butterfly net, a young boy begins his search for a dragon.

"Hello, what's this? It's tall grass. Can't walk around it. Can't leap over it. Have to charge through it."

His next obstacle is a river, followed by a tall tree, a deep ravine, and thick mud. In each instance, his first two efforts to cross the obstacle fail while the third brings success. When he arrives at the dragon's cave he decides to return the way he came, but faster.

In simple, repetitive verse, *I'm Going on a Dragon Hunt* introduces young listeners to the importance of alternatives. If you cannot walk around something or jump over it, charging through it might work. If you cannot fly or jump over something, swinging across might work. In other words, try something different when your first effort fails.

This attitude of persistence can also be seen in Lulu Delacre's *Nathan's Fishing Trip*. Nathan is an elephant, and his friend Nicholas Alexander is a mouse. Their problems start when they go fishing together in a small boat.

First, a stubborn fish pulls Nathan's fishing pole into the water. Then the bait escapes. Nathan tries to catch it. Oh, oh! Only one thing can happen when an elephant jumps on a worm in a small boat. SPLASH! Now the odd couple has lost their other fishing rod. Then Nathan arrives at an ingenious solution to catching a fish. But despite all their efforts he lets it go free because he just doesn't have the heart to cook it.

The tomten in Astrid Lindgren's *The Tomten and the Fox* uses kindness instead of force to solve a hungry fox's problem. When a fox is hungry and has young ones to feed, what can it do? It tries to find some hens to eat, of course. And what can the tomten who guards the farm at night do about the fox? He helps the fox find something else to eat.

Each character in the story has opposing needs and responsibilities, the fox to feed its young, the tomten to protect the hens. The tomten's nonviolent choice, to share his dinner with the hungry fox, is a successful solution. He chooses to respond to the needs of the fox rather than focusing only on his own obligations. The lyrical text and soft pastel illustrations beautifully recreate the tranquility of an isolated Scandinavian farm on a winter night.

Gloria Kamen emphasizes cooperative solutions in *The Ringdoves*. This Indian fable begins with a group of ringdoves who escape capture by rising as one to fly away carrying the hunter's net with them. They fly to the burrow of Zirak the mouse, who gnaws at the net and frees the doves. A crow is impressed with Zirak's kindness and tells him he, too, would like to be his friend. Zirak's initial suspicion for his natural enemy is overcome by the friendly creature's sincerity. He and crow befriend a gazelle fleeing from the hunter's trap. The threesome later devise a clever ruse to fool the hunter and rescue poor tortoise, another of their friends.

Thinking of alternatives requires flexibility as well as cleverness. In *Bobby Otter and the Blue Boat,* by Margaret Burdick, Bobby Otter longs for the blue boat in the window of Mr. Badger's Trading Post. Mr. Beaver carved the boat and wants to make a trade. But what could Bobby Otter trade that would be just as valuable? He gathers a bouquet of colorful autumn leaves. Unfortunately, Mr. Badger decides that the leaves would not be a fair exchange. Bobby Otter then gathers a bundle of delicious elm twigs. Mr. Badger rejects this offer, too.

"These twigs will make a fine meal for Mr. Beaver. But he can enjoy them for only one night. You will enjoy the boat for many days and nights. It is not a fair trade. Here is a fresh fish for your twigs. That is a fair trade."

Bobby's family appreciates the fish, but he still longs for the blue boat. He finds some bright and colorful pebbles in the riverbed, but they turn dull when taken out of the water. That night Bobby dreams of the blue boat, and when he wakes up the next morning he has the solution to his problem—the perfect trade. He will create something for Mr. Beaver that is as bright and long-lasting as his blue boat, a painting that is an equal work of beauty.

Some problems may seem especially formidable. Take, for example, the wind. How can you stop it from blowing so hard? In *Jack and the Whoopee Wind,* by Mary Calhoun, an old geezer named Jack is determined to do just that.

Jack liked a breeze now and then, but where he lived in Whoopee, Wyoming, people had to tie down their cats so they didn't blow away. He lived on a farm, except that most of it had blown away. The chickens were bald, and the wind had scooped up the fence posts and sprinkled them on the prairie.

When the wind torments his dog Mose, Jack decides he has had enough. He will tame the wind.

But one clever scheme after another fails to ease the wind's relentless fury. Jack and his friends try blowing the wind back with a fan, catching it in a huge bundle or curtain, blocking it, and capturing it in a tunnel. But all their efforts fail. Despite these setbacks Jack never waivers in his determination to master the wind. Then an offhand remark by one of his cowboy friends gives him an idea. Instead of fighting the wind, why not use its power? So Jack's final alternative is the best solution—a field of windmills. Dick Gackenbach's bright and energetic illustrations add the right touch of humor to this story of persistence and creativity.

These stories promote problem-solving by encouraging children to respond thoughtfully to challenges. If they can keep thinking of different alternatives and persevere despite setback, they might be able to resolve the problem. "Do not give in to discouragement," these stories seem to say. "You have a creative mind. You will come up with a solution."

Young children are impulsive. One of their toys is taken from them and SMACK! They hit the offender. They may know other ways to respond to the conflict but cannot mentally stand back and analyze what is going on. During the later preschool years children gradually become more capable of putting more effective alternatives into action.

In addition to presenting ideas for solving problems, stories can provide opportunities to engage children in a social problem-solving discussion. When the story is completed, a parent might ask children, for example, to think of other kinds of houses the little pig could have built to keep the wolf out. Or they could consider other ways the tomten could have protected his hens from the fox, or other objects Bobby could have traded with Mr. Beaver for the blue boat.

Consider the Consequences of What You Do

Most of us can remember those dire warnings our parents gave us when we misbehaved. "You're going to break your neck if you keep jumping off that bed!" or "If I've told you once, I've told you a million times: No jumping on the bed! One day it'll crash right through the floor. Now lie down and go to sleep." Tedd Arnold shows how a child reacts to such a prediction in *No Jumping on the Bed!* After falling asleep Walter resumes his jumping. With a shock he and his bed actually do go crashing through the floor, right into Miss Hattie's spaghetti and meatballs. Now Miss Hattie is falling with him as they both crash into Mr. Matty's TV room. Mr. Matty joins them as they plummet through the apartment building. Soon a crowd of people, animals and objects are cascading from one floor to the next. But then Walter opens his eyes and realizes he was only dreaming. Tedd Arnold's amusing illustrations provide a wonderful sense of motion as his characters descend through spaghetti, wooden blocks and paint. *No Jumping on the Bed!* emphasizes consequences with hilarious exaggeration.

Stories provide wonderful opportunities for showing the consequences of violence, misbehavior, greed, and dishonor. Becoming aware of these consequences makes it possible for children to choose more wisely between several alternatives when trying to solve a problem.

Consequences of Violence

Our children live in a world that often romanticizes violence and idealizes those who have become proficient with force. They witness senseless violence on television and in the movies. War toys abound in most toy stores. Some children's stories counteract this emphasis on force by showing the consequences of violence.

In *Tiger Watch,* by Jan Wahl, a hunter's son learns what it really means to kill. Azad wants to be a mighty hunter like his father and do more than stalk toy animals with a toy rifle. He craves to prove himself a man by hunting a real tiger. Azad finally has his chance when his father is asked to hunt down a rogue tiger that has terrorized a nearby village. Despite his mother's protests, his father agrees to take him on the hunt. Azad will even have his own gun to carry.

The villagers build a platform high in a wide oak and provide a bull calf for bait. Father and son wait silently and patiently, into the day and then into the night. The calf whimpers, a pair of jackals come to drink at the water hole, and a clumsy warthog waddles into view. Azad remains quiet and still for hours despite feeling cramped.

Then, suddenly, he sees it. The tiger appears at the water hole as if by magic. Did his father see it? Azad dares not turn his head. He is amazed by the tiger's great beauty—his coat glowing a deep orange-black by the light of the moon. How could his father shoot such a thing? Then Azad takes a breath, the tiger hears and leaps, and shots ring out, ". . . the most terrible sound Azad had ever heard." The tiger is dead.

The next morning Azad and Mustapha climb down from the safety of their platform. Azad is introduced to the reality of hunting, to the real consequences of violence:

> Azad dared to touch the tiger. It was real and still warm, as warm as his own body.
>
> "Oh, how the shot must have hurt!" he said. "How fine he looks!"
>
> "Yes," agreed Mustapha. "Such dignity! See those porcupine quills stuck in his left foreleg and chest?"
>
> The boy saw the wounds—tough, deep and swollen. They counted thirty-two quills.
>
> "Since he could not run as he once did," said Mustapha, "he became a killer of humans and defenseless animals."
>
> Azad hung his head. Again he touched the moist warm fur, stroking it.

Later, as they walked in silence, the tiger swinging on a carrier held by villagers, Azad turns to his father and says, "I do not choose to become a hunter, Father." His father takes his arm and says, "It is well, son."

The story is over, and we are left feeling . . . what? Maybe sadness over the death of the great tiger who was trying to survive. Possibly admiration for an understanding father who respects the animals he hunts and has no real love for killing. We might also be happy that a young boy has made a momentous discovery about himself. He makes a choice, beginning with the voice inside his mind that shouts, "DON'T SHOOT!" We see his decision more clearly when he tells his father, "I do not choose to become a hunter, Father." That choice will have a long-lasting effect on his life. This poignant story of the death of a magnificent animal and a boy taking his first step across the threshold of manhood is brought to life by Charles Mikolaycak's colorful and energetic illustrations.

A deeply touching story of the tragic consequences of war is provided in *Faithful Elephants,* a true story by Yukio Tsuchiya about a trainer and his elephants in Japan during World War II. Bombs are dropping on Tokyo. By command of the army all zoo animals are to be killed to prevent their possible escape and threat to the populace. The keepers of three performing elephants—John, Tonky, and Wanly—respond to the order by giving them lethal injections. But the elephants' skin is too thick for the injection to be effective. So the keepers decide to starve them to death.

The story of the keepers' anguish and the elephants' bewilderment and pitiful attempts to regain grace are heartbreaking. Parents should be ready to take as much time as they need to talk to their children about the tragedy after they read the story. But the value of *Faithful Elephants* is not just in its capacity to provoke tears. It reminds us how the consequences of war can devastate us all. And we can all identify with the keepers and their agonizing conflict between doing their duty and remaining faithful to the animals who trust them. The story has been reprinted in Japan seventy times and is read aloud on Japanese radio every year to mark the anniversary of Japan's surrender in World War II. *Faithful Elephants* is a cautionary tale illustrating in a simple, uncluttered manner the horrors of war.

The Man Who Could Call Down Owls, by Eve Bunting, is a haunting and lyrical tale that shows the consequences of the misuse of power. Every night, the man who could call down owls' walks in the woods, his cape drifting about him like marsh mist and a willow wand pointing to the starry sky. And every night the owls come, beckoned by the wand, to sit on his arms and shoulders and perch on nearby branches. A young village boy named Con takes a special interest in the old man who shows him how to mend the owls' wings and splint their legs.

But then one night, a stranger watches the mysterious ceremony. He lusts to have the Owl Man's power for his own. "A man who can command the birds of the air has power indeed!" he whispers to himself. The following night the stranger appears in the forest, wearing the Owl Man's hat and cloak and carrying his willow wand. At that moment, we realize that he has murdered the old man in an effort to assume the mantle of his power.

But when the stranger holds the willow wand to the night sky and beckons the owls, the results are dramatically different. The owls descend on him with all their fury, violently driving him away, the white cloak falling from him to lie in a drift of snow. The owls then return, ". . . swooping on noiseless wings" to perch on the boy's head and shoulders. Con assumes authority and will now be the one to call down the owls.

In an age of potential nuclear catastrophe and genetic manipulation our children should be informed of the consequences of the misuse of power. In *The Man Who Could Call Down Owls* the stranger wanted the power without having the heart, the respect, the love for the creatures he wanted to control. His arrogance and cruelty create a furious backlash. Only the young boy, whose heart was filled with love and compassion for the owls, could be the rightful inheritor of the Owl Man's authority. Charles Mikolaycak's black-and-white illustrations contrast the dark tones of the forest at night with the shimmering brilliance of the snow and moon. His vivid portrayal of the violent retribution of the owls demonstrates the terrible consequences of the misuse of power.

In his most recently illustrated book, *The Rumor of Pavel and Paali,* a Ukrainian folktale adapted by Carole Kismaric, Charles Mikolaycak has continued to focus on the tragic results of violence and cruelty. Pavel and Paali are two twin brothers who disagree about good and evil. Paali is kind and generous. He insists that, "Though life can be cruel and hard, it is certainly better to do good than evil." The cruel and selfish Pavel claims differently: "It is through cunning and deception that things get done." To settle their differences the two brothers agree on a wager. If the first three people they meet agree with one of their positions the winner could claim everything the loser owns.

Paali loses the wager. His brother takes all he and his wife own and everything they need to make a living. Hunger and desperation later force Paali to plead with his brother for a measure of grain. Pavel agrees, but at a cruel price—his brother's sight. Now Paali is blind and is forced to beg at the crossroads.

This final indignity sets into motion a strange turn of events. On his return home one evening Paali becomes lost in the Great Forest. While he rests in the limbs of a thick tree he overhears the spirits whispering their secrets as they rush through the branches near his hiding place. This knowledge enables him to cure his blindness, discover water for the village, and heal the tsar's crippled daughter.

Pavel learns about the reasons for his kind brother's success. So one night he enters the Great Forest to climb the thickest tree and eavesdrop on the evil spirits. But they are angered by Pavel's discoveries and seek revenge. This time they are waiting for the intruder when he returns. Pavel pays a horrible price for both his cruelty and his greed.

Instead of admonishing children to "Be nice!" these books show the pain, grief, and self-destruction that are the results of violence and cruelty. They make strong emotional appeals for kindness and respect, showing the tragic consequences of doing harm to others. Depending on their maturity and their experience with books, some four- and five-year-olds and most kindergarten children will love these high-protein stories of Tough Magic.

Consequences of Misbehavior

Showing the consequences of misbehavior is a common theme in many children's books. Characters may be innocently involved in a misadventure and carried away by their enthusiasm and excitement for some new experience. *Kitten in Trouble,* by Maria Polushkin, is a humorous look at what happens when a kitten wakes early and decides to explore the house. Listeners can laugh at the poor kitty's predicament when she leaps on a boy's foot, plays with yarn and ball, pounces on breakfast and chases a butterfly. The repetitive, "Oh, oh. Kitten's in trouble!" will bring a smile to any young child who knows what it means to be carried away by enthusiasm.

Children can also empathize with the three careless kittens in the popular Mother Goose rhyme *Three Little Kittens,* retold and illustrated by Paul Galdone. When their mother tells them they cannot have any pie for losing their mittens, their mournful chorus of "Meow, meow, meow" is sure to touch any child's heart. The threesome win back their mother's good graces when they find their mittens. But then they get into trouble once again when they wear the mittens to eat their pie. They have to make up for their carelessness by cleaning the soiled mittens.

Sarah Hayes expands on another familiar nursery rhyme in her book, *Bad Egg: The True Story of Humpty Dumpty.* We know that "Humpty Dumpty sat on a wall, Humpty Dumpty had a great fall. . . ." But what happened in between? As we soon discover, Humpty Dumpty was not entirely blameless in his misfortune. His downfall is brought about by his arrogance and foolishness. Fortunately for Humpty Dumpty, all the king's horses and all the king's men are able to put him back together again.

Kitten in Trouble, Three Little Kittens, and *Bad Egg* humorously portray for young children the consequences of misadventure. They have simple plots built entirely around the problem created by character action.

Stories with more sophisticated plots can also emphasize consequences. *The Season Clock,* by Valerie Littlewood, is inspired by the "Sorcerer's Apprentice" dilemma in which an apprentice attempts to use the authority of his master only to lose control of the power it unleashes. Sam is an apprentice to Father Time. He controls the Season Clock, a complicated mechanism that ensures that Spring, Summer, Fall, and Winter will all arrive at their proper time. But Sam grows impatient and bored during Father Time's absence. So he tampers with the Clock and causes the great mechanism to spin out of control. Unfortunately, the Season Catcher and his demons capture Spring and Summer when they flee the clock in confusion.

Sam finds Father Time and admits his role in the chaos that results from his tampering. Father Time and Fall pursue the Season Catcher and his captives. Sam follows and eventually rescues Spring and Summer from the dungeons of the Season Catcher. Father Time scolds him for his lack of foresight.

"I should be angry with you," he said. "You cannot meddle with the Seasons. But I will forgive you this time for you were brave in the end. Now let us go on with your lessons."

The Season Clock is similar to *The Man Who Could Call Down Owls* because they both examine the consequences of the misuse of power. Sam's mistake is an innocent act of foolishness. In contrast, the stranger uses force to wrench control of the power to call down owls from its rightful master. Both have to suffer the consequences of their misdeeds. But Sam redeems himself, while the stranger faces a more violent retribution.

Consequences of Greed

Some stories examine the consequences of selfishness. The Greek myth of King Midas is a classic example of the consequences of greed. When King Midas is given one wish by the gods, he asks that everything he touches be changed into gold. The king soon discovers that there can be too much of a good thing after he unintentionally changes his pet, his food, and his daughter into gold. But the gods hear his plea to restore them to their original form and return the king to normal.

Margot Zemach's reinterpretation of *The Little Red Hen* is another familiar example of the consequences of selfishness. The industrious red hen wants to make some bread, but the goose, the cat, and the pig refuse to help. They won't plant the seeds, or harvest and thresh the wheat, or take it to the mill. They won't even help her bake it. "Then I'll do it myself," she says each time they turn down her request for help. Of course, when the bread is finished, the goose, the cat, and the pig want to eat some. The little red hen tells her friends that no, since she did all the work, "I'm going to eat it myself." And she does!

The Little Red Hen is a simple story that emphasizes the importance of making a contribution and the consequences of being selfish for even the youngest child. The goose, the cat, and the pig should not expect to benefit from someone else's labor when they failed to contribute assistance.

Greed may also take the form of possessiveness. *The Selkie Girl* is Susan Cooper's retelling of an ancient legend from the coasts and islands of Scotland and Ireland. This bittersweet story tells of the futile selfishness of a man blinded by love. Donallan has fallen in love with a selkie, a seal that is capable of shedding her skin and taking human form. When the selkie and her sisters sun themselves on a rock, Donallan creeps up to where they lie and steals her skin. Now she has no choice but to follow him if she ever hopes to rejoin her family of the sea. Donallan hides her skin and faithfully moistens it to keep her alive. They marry and eventually have five children.

But the selkie eventually learns from one of her children where the skin is hidden. She is faced with a difficult decision—now that she has the freedom to leave, where should her loyalty reside? She sadly decides to return . . . to the seal family she was forced to leave behind. Donallan discovers to his dismay that selfish possession is no basis for a lasting love.

Fairy tales like *Snow White* and *Cinderella* are filled with examples of characters whose selfish actions bring about their own ruin. In *The Water of Life,* a Brothers Grimm tale retold by Barbara Rogasky, three brothers seek the Water of Life to save their ailing father. One by one, they set out to find the magic potion. The oldest and middle sons seek the water only to win their father's favor. As they begin their journey, each is cursed by a dwarf for their selfishness and then trapped in a narrow ravine. The youngest son, though, desires only to restore his father's health. In return for his kindness the dwarf assists him in his quest.

Again and again the two selfish brothers plot against their younger brother. Eventually a beautiful princess is freed from imprisonment, a magic sword brings victory, and love is redeemed through trial. The younger brother's pure devotion ultimately wins his father's heart and the hand of the princess. The two older brothers' treachery is repaid with banishment.

Consequences of Dishonor

Some stories show the consequences of breaking one's word. This type of story begins with a problem. Those affected by the problem then make a contract with someone who promises to resolve the issue . . . for a price. The "expert" solves the problem, but those who asked for help refuse to fulfill their part of the bargain. This dishonor has terrible consequences.

The Pied Piper of Hamelin, retold and illustrated by Mercer Mayer, is a perfect example of such retribution. Hamelin is overrun by rats. The town fathers appeal to the Pied Piper, a mysterious stranger who can lure any living creature with his enchanted music.

> "We will pay you whatever you wish to rid us of these rats. One thousand. No, ten. No, fifty thousand, in royal silver."
> "One thousand will do fine," said the piper, with a

twinkle in his eye. Stepping from the hall, he raised his pipe to his lips and blew a note so sweet that it made one believe that all creatures in heaven and on earth were finally well and at peace. As he walked he played on, and all that heard him were transfixed. . . .

In this manner the rats left Hamelin and were lured to their death in a nearby river. But when the Piper asks for his money, the mayor refuses to give what was promised:

> The piper's face grew grim and tense. "I do not bargain with sultans, kings, or the likes of you. Settle your debt with me as agreed, or you might find me piping in a way you do not like."

But the mayor stubbornly refuses to pay what he promised. So the Piper plays another tune. Now it is the children who are enchanted by his music, and they leave Hamelin . . . for good. A promise is a promise, after all, and the piper must be paid.

The consequences of another broken promise are portrayed in Margaret Leaf's *Eyes of the Dragon*. The magistrate of a Chinese village builds a magnificent wall to protect his people from wild creatures and evil spirits. He summons Ch'en Jung, the greatest of all dragon painters, to create the final decorative touch—a portrait of the Dragon King. The old painter insists, and the magistrate agrees, that the work will be done under two conditions:

> ". . . that I may paint your dragon in my own manner and that you will accept it. You must also give me forty silver coins, which I will donate to the followers of the Tao. . . ."

The great painter creates a magnificent dragon on the wall surrounding the town. The dragon's body is covered with fiery red scales, his great head shaped like a camel's, with shaggy eyebrows and a pointed beard. And under his chin a large pearl glistens with all the colors of the rainbow. But the magistrate refuses to pay the forty silver coins because the dragon has no eyes. "It would be dangerous to paint eyes on this dragon," replies Ch'en Jung. "And you promised to accept the dragon as I painted him." The magistrate continues to demand that the dragon be given eyes. The painter complies and then quietly leaves. To their dismay, the magistrate and villagers discover the reason for Ch'en Jung's warning. The dragon comes to life.

Summary

Children learn about consequences from experience. They throw a glass jar and it breaks. They hit someone who then hits them back. They pound on the living room wall with a hammer and their parents become upset. Gradually they begin to make connections between what they do and the reactions of others.

Learning about consequences does not mean that children can use this knowledge to modify their actions. A parent may read his four-year-old all sorts of stories emphasizing the nonviolent resolution of conflict. But he may still hit when another child intrudes into his play and grabs his toys. Under these conditions he is too young to set aside his anger to respond thoughtfully to a conflict.

Using stories to nurture a personal story based on a sound ethical and moral foundation is a long process. Success cannot be fully measured by immediate results. The child's moral framework is like a cathedral, and ideas found in stories are like its stones. The cathedral is built gradually over a period of time. Once completed it is both magnificent and strong, able to withstand mighty forces.

We can see a cathedral beginning to take shape in its early stages of construction. We can also observe signs of our children's capacity to solve problems nonviolently. Self-control and knowledge of alternatives should begin to work in greater concert as children begin school. The results of our efforts are even more apparent as our children struggle with the challenges of adolescence. But the foundation of decency and good sense we provide them through our words and deeds during their early years will continue long after our direct influence passes.

Our children can learn from us that they are able to make choices and take action to solve problems. No problem is so great that it cannot be faced courageously. Children are not marionettes whose strings are pulled by forces completely outside of their control. They have magnificent minds capable of responding to a challenge with solutions that show respect for themselves and others.

CHAPTER TEN

From The Ugly Duckling to Knots on a Counting Rope:

Forming a Positive Self-Image

Children's discovery of their own existence is a powerful moment in which they go beyond experiencing themselves as objects to experiencing the person that resides within. This recognition of one's personhood begins during the preschool years as children first learn to recognize themselves and then gradually become aware of their underlying selves, the actors behind the action. They also begin to draw conclusions about the self, the package in which their identity resides. They may come to believe they are smart or stupid, that they are competent or that they cannot hope to have any control over their lives, that they are lovable or unworthy of another's affection.

Children also have feelings about these beliefs. They may become angry about a failure or pleased with what they have accomplished. Some of these feelings endure and comprise a child's self-esteem. Self-esteem is the value we place on what we believe to be true about ourselves. For example, a child may believe he is unlovable because his parents never spend any enjoyable time with him. "I must be awful," he thinks. "I'm just a nobody; how could anybody love somebody like me?" Although some of this anger may be directed toward his parents, most of his hostility is likely to be reserved for himself. Self-hate lies at the core of low self-worth. Children with low self-esteem believe that there is something intrinsically wrong with them. They believe they are faulty merchandise.

Self-esteem is important for two reasons. First, children act consistently with their beliefs about themselves. If a child *believes* something is true, that belief affects her actions as much as anything that is objectively true. So a child who believes she is unattractive, stupid, or unpleasant may withdraw or draw attention to herself in socially unacceptable ways.

Second, children's perceptions of the world around them are filtered through their self-esteem. Their beliefs about themselves act a screen that may distort their view of what really happens to them. The child with low self-worth focuses on failure instead of success, problems instead of challenges, difficulties instead of possibilities. A child with low self-worth experiences the world as a dark and gloomy place, filled with danger and threat. A child with high self-esteem may see the world, with all its assets and liabilities, more realistically.

Each of the seven major children's-story themes in Chapters Three through Nine relate to self-esteem. Children who have positive self-worth will begin to sense a purpose that gives meaning to their lives. They respond to life courageously. They are capable of giving and receiving love. Significant loss can disrupt but not destroy their self-esteem—they can express grief in a way that helps them restore their sense of well-being. They are open to the world and aware of what goes on around them. They also tend to view challenges as problems rather than as barriers.

These seven themes are like segments in a chain. Self-esteem is the linchpin that connects them to form a circle, a circle representing a unified framework of beliefs that provides the foundation for a child's sense of character. In this chapter we will examine books that focus even more clearly and specifically on children's attitudes toward themselves.

How Stories Contribute to a Child's Self-Esteem

Many of the stories we heard as children were like mirrors in which we could see our own reflections. We could feel our muscles strain as the Little Engine That Could struggled up the hill with his load of toys. "I think I can, too!" we might have thought. We might have felt ourselves soaring through the clouds with Peter Pan. Or we may have been amused by the kiss that transformed a frog into a prince (*The Frog King*) or concerned about the spell that changed seven brothers into ravens (*The Seven Ravens*). We were fascinated by these dramatic physical changes and talents. We too could feel ourselves growing, changing, becoming stronger and more capable with the passage of time.

Although we were fascinated with our newfound capabilities, we could also be alarmed about change. New responsibilities accompanied each stage of maturation. And occasionally we felt out of sorts, out of sync with ourselves, with our bodies. At times we may have drifted between pride and panic. One moment we felt at home with ourselves, as though we had grown closer to a wonderful friend. At other times we might have found the stranger who greeted us from the mirror quite disconcerting.

Hans Christian Andersen's *The Ugly Duckling,* as retold by Marianna Mayer and magnificently illustrated by Thomas Locker, is a powerful story of self-doubt and discovery. Who among us could not identify with the odd-looking Ugly Duckling, out of place, mocked by the other farm animals, and then banished from the farm for his unusual appearance? The forlorn duckling wanders through marshes and lakes, manages to escape harm at the hands of a group of hunters, and, with the help of a kind family, survives a harsh winter. He yearns to belong, to be accepted. Because of his terrible rejection and isolation, the duckling feels only contempt for himself. But a subtle transformation is slowly taking place, both in nature around him and in himself.

The change begins when spring arrives and the duckling discovers he can fly. Then three beautiful swans appear. He desperately wants to be near them but he fears another rejection. To his surprise, the visitors arch their long necks and swim toward him in greeting when they see him.

> Humbly he cast down his eyes. He could already hear their harsh words, though they had not uttered a sound. At that moment he spied his own reflection in the water. Confused, he could not quite understand what he saw. There, mirrored in the water, was a splendid swan. He was no longer an overgrown, gangly, gray bird, but a swan.

The three swans who swim to his side make a circle around him and greet him by gently touching him with their beaks. The ugly duckling has finally found himself and friends who will accept him.

With its theme of injustice, self-hate, and transformation, *The Ugly Duckling* helps to direct children's attention to several important issues related to self-esteem. Much of our self-image is derived from what others tell us is true about ourselves. Sometimes these comments are unfair and incorrect. The barnyard animals who ridiculed the duckling were misinformed as well as cruel. They failed to recognize the duckling's true nature. Unfortunately, the duckling came to believe their misconceptions. He translated their rejection into self-disgust.

Children sometimes doubt themselves, especially when they pass through adolescence. *The Ugly Duckling* reminds all of us that appearances can be deceiving, that cruelty can result in self-hate, and that change takes time. We are all growing, changing, becoming richer in experience and wisdom.

Like the Ugly Duckling, we all yearn to be accepted. At the very core of every child's self-esteem is the realization that he or she really matters to someone else. All children yearn for affirmation and recognition from a parent or special teacher. They want to be appreciated not for their color, intelligence, physical appearance, or capabilities, but for the very fact that they exist. This theme of unconditional acceptance is given special emphasis in *Knots on a Counting Rope,* by Bill Martin, Jr., and John Archambault, with illustrations by Ted Rand.

On a cool, dark night an Indian boy and his grandfather sit close together around a campfire. Stars shimmer overhead, and the moon casts a warm glow over the rust-colored mesas surrounding their camp. The young boy asks,

> "Tell me the story once again, Grandfather. Tell me who I am."
> "I have told you many times, Boy. You know the story by heart."
> "But it sounds better when you tell it, Grandfather."
> "Then listen very carefully. This may be the last telling."

Grandfather tells him about the night of his birth and the fear, the excitement, the love that his family felt as he made his entry into the world. But he was weak and close to death. Two great blue horses came galloping by, an omen of the strength he would need to live.

Knots on a counting rope . . . one, two, three. . . . Each one a memory, each one a hope, each one a dream of what a boy was and what he could be. Each one is special, you see, for this young boy was born blind.

> Will I always have to live in the dark?
> Yes, Boy. You were born with a dark curtain in front of your eyes.
> But there are many ways to see, Grandfather.
> Yes, Boy, you are learning to see through your darkness because you have the strength of blue horses.

Grandfather describes the events of his first horse race. He didn't come in first, but he raced the darkness and won. As he completes the telling, Grandfather finishes another knot on the rope.

Now, Boy . . . now that the story has been told again, I will tie another knot in the counting rope. When the rope is filled with knots, you will know the story by heart and can tell it to yourself.

So that I will grow stronger, Grandfather?

Yes . . . stronger . . . strong enough to cross the dark mountains.

There is no pity or sentimentality in Grandfather's message. His account of the significant events in his grandson's life emphasizes strength, hope, and an enduring love. He believes in his grandson—that's what really matters. Like the young Indian boy, all children need to hear, again and again, that they are special to parents or grandparents. This comforting message lingers in the mind long after those who conveyed their affection have passed from their lives.

Stories promote children's self-esteem in at least three ways. First, they show characters engaging in self-reflection. Second, stories may show how ridicule and other forms of cruelty can diminish self-worth and aggravate a person's self-doubt and shame. And third, stories may show how self-doubt and low self-esteem are overcome when characters become aware of their personal strengths.

Many stories encourage children to reflect on their attitudes toward themselves and their treatment of others. Stories can provide a foundation for self-esteem by expanding a child's personal story to include these concepts:

- You are a special person with a body that is just right for you.
- You are filled with life and energy.
- You have a unique way of relating to the world that makes you special.
- You are an individual with your own likes and dislikes.
- You are growing and changing in many ways.
- We all have natural limitations on what we can do.
- You are a worthwhile person regardless of mistakes.

You Are a Special Person with a Body That Is Just Right for You

The moment they learn to recognize themselves in a mirror at about fifteen months, children begin to form attitudes about what they see in themselves. For some children, the words, "ugly," "stupid," or "naughty" begin to take on meaning relative to their sense of self. Certain parts of their bodies may, unfortunately, become taboo, and certain activities—many of them involuntary—may become labeled as disgusting.

Stories can help us convey to our children that they are some-body special. No matter what the sex or race, no matter what their appearance or how disabled they may be, they are beautiful, wonderful, magnificent human beings.

Body Integrity

Body integrity refers to a child's sense of physical unity and connectedness, the degree they feel "at home" with themselves. Physical self-awareness is brought into sharper focus in stories that contrast the child's body with something else.

In *Dad's Car Wash,* Harry Sutherland compares a child's bath with a car wash.

> "Dad scrubbed John's wheels to remove all of the road dust and dirt. He washed the hub caps thoroughly. He soaped up the drive shafts, to be sure the rear wheels had good traction . . . and degreased the front axle from shoulder to fingertips."

Illustrations by Maxie Chambliss show John's toy dinosaur washing his model car as a counterpoint to John's bath.

In *Birdsong Lullabye,* by Diane Stanley, a young girl shares a special bedtime fantasy with her mother. If she were a bird she would be capable of doing many wonderful things. She could fly to windows and watch children having a party or glide above their backyards and look down and watch them play. She could catch lost balloons and return them to the children who lost them. "If I were a bird, I could soar through the air, then land gently and not hurt myself at all. I could float on the wind and touch the clouds!" By imagining what she might be, the little girl is also reflecting on the person she really is.

Body integrity means that a child views him or herself as a whole person. In *It's Just Me, Emily,* by Anna Grossnickle Hines, a young girl proudly proclaims her sense of self in a delightful game of make-believe with her mother. "What is that under Mother's covers, down by her feet wiggling and twitching and tickling her toes?" Mother asks if it's a cat, a weasel, or mole down in his hole. Emily peeks out from the covers. "No! It's just me . . . Emily." The delightful game continues throughout the day. Emily growls from behind a door. Could it be a lion, a tiger, or a bear? She thumps and bumps under the table. Could that be an elephant, rhino, or even a medium-sized dino? How about that splashing in the tub? Maybe it's a porpoise, a hippopotamus, or a fat old walrus? To each of these and other inquiries Emily announces, "No, Mama, no. It's just me . . . Emily." Emily is proud to announce that she is a special person. By contrasting herself with these other creatures she makes a claim about herself and her capabilities. She knows she is somebody, but she also needs an audience.

Some stories portray a sudden loss of body integrity through a dramatic transformation. Deprived of her true identity, a character may struggle to maintain a sense of self and continue to hold out hope for personal restoration. The prince-turned-frog will have a long wait to be restored to his former self by the kiss of a princess.

A child discovers that the life of a dog is not as easy as he expected in *Dog for a Day,* by Dick Gackenbach. Sidney is in second grade and is good at inventing things. His greatest invention is a Changing Box that can change anything he places inside it. He changes a football into a toaster and the cat into a canary. He even changes his sister into a lamp but then has to change her back again. One morning he decides to change himself. "I am tired of being Sidney," he says. Being a dog sounds like fun, so he takes Wally, his pet dog, into the changing box with him. When they emerge their identities are exchanged—Sidney has Wally's body and Wally has Sidney's. Sidney is pleased with the change—that is, until the problems start.

When he tries to attend school, Sidney is thrown out because dogs are not allowed. The boys won't let him play on their baseball team, and he cannot buy a ticket to go to the movie. The owner of the ice cream store gives him some ice cream, but Sidney has to eat it out of a dish on the floor. "It's no fun being a dog," Sidney complains. "I'm going home and change back to being a boy again." On the way home, a gang of bully dogs attack him and five stray cats chase him up a light pole. Even the dog catcher tries to capture him. Sidney is definitely ready to be himself once again. He returns to the Changing Box and, much to his relief, switches his and Wally's identities back to their former selves.

This dramatic alteration of physical identity and well-being is a familiar theme in three of William Steig's books, beginning with *Sylvester and the Magic Pebble,* winner of the Caldecott Award for illustration in 1977. Sylvester Duncan finds a magic pebble one rainy day. Quite by accident he discovers that he can make anything come true as long as he touches the rock as he makes his wish. What a discovery! But on the way home to show his parents, Sylvester panics when he meets a lion. To save himself he wishes he was a rock.

Poor Sylvester—now he's a large rock. But rocks cannot reach out to touch a pebble, so a rock he must remain. His unfortunate wish is the beginning of a year of misery. His parents and friends search for him everywhere, but to no avail. The seasons change. The leaves fall from the surrounding trees. Snow begins to fall. That spring his still-grieving parents go on a picnic to lighten their sorrow. When his mother sits on the Sylvester-rock she wakes him up from his deep winter sleep.

"Mother! Father! It's me, Sylvester, I'm right here!" But he couldn't talk. He had no voice. He was stone-dumb.

STORYBREAK

Penelope Wants to Fly

Once upon a time, in the wonderful town of Butterberry Hill . . .

Penelope Pig hated being a pig. "Pigs are dirty and sloppy," she would say to herself. "Pigs have to waddle on the ground, not soar in the sky." Penelope dreamed about flying every day. If she could fly . . . well, then she would really be special, no ordinary pig. Everyone in Butterberry Hill would take notice of her then.

One day Penelope decided that she would make her dreams come true. She made a pair of wings out of sticks and paper and glued them to her shoulders. She waddled up to a hill overlooking Butterberry Hill. "Won't everyone be surprised when I fly over the town," she thought. She took a deep breath and leaped into the air. But what do you think happened? Did she fly? Poor Penelope! She fell with a thud into a pile of damp leaves.

In addition to everything else, though, Penelope was stubborn. She decided to build a better pair of wings, this time out of cardboard. As soon as she made these new wings she strapped them on and waddled back to that hill. "This time I will fly!" she thought. "No more piggy-walking for me!" When Penelope leaped from the hill she flapped her cardboard wings as hard as she could. For a moment she thought maybe she would really fly. But then she crashed again to the ground. Penelope was so sad! She cried and cried. She wanted to fly! But she realized now that wings on a pig are useless.

Aristotle the mouse came walking by and asked her what was wrong. "I want to fly!" said Penelope. "No problem," said Aristotle. "You can fly with me. I just learned to fly . . . an airplane!" In just a short while Penelope and Aristotle were soaring through the clouds in his airplane. People waved when they passed over Butterberry Hill. Even though she needed a airplane to do it, Penelope was happy to be flying. She did not have to be different to do something she wanted. With Aristotle's help she could be a high-flying piggy.

His father notices the magic pebble, though, and places it on the rock as Sylvester's mother sets out the food. Sylvester has no idea the pebble is sitting on him now. Fortunately, he does make his wish, "I wish I were myself again, I wish I were my real self again!" Instantly he is restored to his old self, much to his parent's joy.

In 1977 Steig wrote *Caleb and Kate,* the story of a carpenter turned into a dog by the mischievous Yedida the witch. Caleb wakes up from his nap in the forest to discover his plight.

> He was on his feet in an instant, all four of them. Terrified, he spun around to see what he could see of himself. He couldn't believe what he saw. Of course not! Such things don't happen. Oh no? "This is clearly me," he realized. "I'm not dreaming. I'm a dog!"

Caleb's stable sense of self is completely overturned. He returns home to his wife, Kate, and tries to tell her, "Katie, it's me!" But only a plaintive growl escapes his throat. Kate leaves to search the forest that night and the following day. She has no idea the dog that follows her is her husband.

As time passes, Katie grows to love her dog, but she longs for her missing husband. Then one night a pair of robbers sneak into their home. Caleb hears them and goes to his dear wife's defense. A fierce fight ensues, pitting dangerous fangs against a deadly knife. The terrified thief slashes crazily at Caleb, slicing a bit of skin off a toe on his front paw. Caleb is instantly transformed back into his old self, terrifying the robbers who escape out the open window. Apparently, the thief had undone the spell by cutting the toe through which Yedida had worked her magic. Caleb and Kate are finally reunited.

In 1985 Steig returned to the same theme of magical transformation in *Solomon the Rusty Nail.* Young Solomon is an ordinary rabbit except for a unique talent. Every time he scratches his nose and wiggles his toes at exactly the same time he changes into a rusty nail. To turn back to a rabbit, all he has to do is think "I'm no nail, I'm a rabbit!"

Solomon enjoys tricking his friends with his disappearances. But then a nasty one-eyed cat named Ambrose discovers his secret and captures him. The cat knows the nail is really Solomon, but Solomon refuses to change back into a rabbit. So the hungry cat locks the nail in a cage. After three long weeks of waiting, Ambrose loses his patience and hammers the nail into the side of his house. After Ambrose leaves, Solomon tries to change back into himself, but the pressure of the wood prevents him from changing his shape. Solomon finally manages to escape when Ambrose accidentally starts a fire that burns down his house and frees the nail from its prison in the wood. When no one is around, Solomon changes back into himself and returns to his family.

In each of these stories the main character's physical identity is profoundly changed. As a result, the characters find themselves alone, separated from family and friends. After enduring the change over an extended period of time, fate gives them another chance to be restored to their true identity and to be reunited with their families.

Children are drawn to this contrast between me and not-me because they are just beginning to acquire a sense of their own identity. "Sylvester is not a rock—he's a young donkey. I'm somebody too," a child may think to herself. Children also like to act out these transformations in their play when they pretend to be animals, trees or anything else that attracts their attention. There are times, though, when children feel anything but themselves. Like Sylvester, Caleb, Solomon, and the rest, they may begin to wonder who they really are. But each story concludes with a restoration of self, offering hope that there is a real person beneath the confusion.

Sex Education

An important part of body awareness involves reflecting on one's origins. Most books that focus on conception, pregnancy, and birth tend to emphasize body parts and functions. They may approach the topic seriously, like *Making Babies,* by Sara Bonnet Stein, or more humorously, like *Where Did I Come From?,* by Peter Mayle. These books take a "fixtures and plumbing" approach to sex education.

Books offering worthwhile stories to help children better understand the orgins of human life are much rarer. *Mouskin's Woodland Birthday* is part of a series featuring Mouskin, a character created by Edna Miller. This particular story introduces children to the events preceding and following Mouskin's birth.

A more direct and powerful statement relating the issue to a child's self-worth is provided by *Wind Rose,* Crescent Dragonwagon's touching portrayal of parental love.

"Wind Rose, we had too much love for two and that was the night we thought of you."

Mother recalls the conception, her pregnancy, and finally the birth of her daughter, Wind Rose. In a story within a story, she describes the affection and hope that surrounded the beginning of her daughter's life. Crescent Dragonwagon provides factual information about conception, pregnancy, and birth. But she is much more interested in telling a story about the parents' relationship and how they felt about the prospect of having a child. With soft illustrations and poetic verse, *Wind Rose* links sexuality, conception, and birth with parental love and commitment.

Fewer topics can trigger a parent's anxieties and self-doubts as much as questions about sexuality. Parents may be comfortable talking about such sensitive issues as death and nuclear war but feel like hiding when their children inquire about sex. We may respond this way because of the personal nature of the topic, or we may have learned to distrust our feelings and ideas about human sexuality.

Regardless of our apprehensions, however, children continue to have unexpressed questions about sexuality. Faced with uncertainties about the changes in their bodies and frightened of unfamiliar feelings, children will look to their parents for guidance. Sexuality can be an enigma, an issue

STORYBREAK

```
┌─────────────────┐
└─────────────────┘
```

No Animals Allowed

Once upon a time, in the wonderful town of Butterberry Hill . . .

Wealthy Mrs. Winterbones's nephew Rodney decided to start a club. His club would be a special club with only special people. So he put up a sign "SPECIAL PEOPLE ONLY. NO ANIMALS ALLOWED!" by the door of the tree house that was in Mrs. Winterbones's backyard. He sent letters to Amy and Casey, inviting them to join his club. Amy and Casey did not want to be left out of something so special, so they agreed to be in Rodney's club. They had a wonderful time, eating chocolate eclairs and cream sodas from France that Mrs. Winterbones brought back from one of her trips.

Briarbutton Rabbit and Penelope Pig passed by the clubhouse and asked if they could join too. Rodney pointed to the sign and said, "Can't you read? NO ANIMALS ALLOWED!" Briarbutton and Penelope were so sad! They wanted to eat some yummies too. So they started their own club. Outside of Penelope's playhouse they put their own sign. "SPECIAL ANIMALS ONLY. NO CREATURES ALLOWED!" They prepared their own feast of spinach sandwiches and corn pudding.

Seymour Creature saw them having a good time and asked if he could join their club. Briarbutton pointed to the sign and said, "Hey silly! Can't you read? NO CREATURES ALLOWED." Poor Seymour, he was so sad. "I am yucky," he thought. "No one wants to play with me."

Grandpa Jake was sitting in the big rocking chair on his front porch and saw Seymour walking by with his head down. He walked over to Seymour and asked him what was wrong. Seymour told him that he could not be in any of the fancy food clubs that Rodney and Briarbutton started. "Then we will start one too," said Grandpa Jake. In just a little while, Grandpa Jake put out a sign on his front porch. "EVERYONE IS SPECIAL, GOOD EATING CLUB. EVERYONE WELCOME."

Meanwhile, Amy and Casey were tired of Rodney being the

boss of everything. They also missed their animal friends. So they left Rodney's tree house. Briarbutton and Penelope decided their club was no fun either. What fun was a two-person club? So they left their playhouse. All four passed by Grandpa Jake's house and saw the sign on his porch.

"Will Grandpa Jake let us join?" Amy wondered. "I'll bet he has some of his special, premium popcorn," Casey said. "Yea, the kind from his own farm," offered Briarbutton. "I bet his club even has those delicious taffy apples," Penelope wished out loud. All four walked up to his house. When they knocked on the front door, who should open it but Seymour Creature. "Oh, oh," they all thought. "Seymour will never let us join."

"Ah, Seymour. We were wondering," said Casey. "Could we be a part of your and Grandpa Jake's club?" In his scratchy voice Seymour said, "Read the sign. See—EVERYRONE IS SPECIAL . . . EVERYONE WELCOME. Come on in!" And they did. Everyone had a good time, with Grandpa Jake's most wonderful and delicious food. Everyone joined . . . except Rodney. He stayed home and ate all the chocolate eclairs by himself . . . and got a big belly ache.

---

of universal concern that few are willing to acknowledge, a secret known to everyone. How can parents be open with what is hidden; how can they be clear about what is confusing; and how can they convey pleasure about something so fraught with risk? Stories, whether read from a book or recalled from our own personal experiences, can help us put into words what we know and feel about this important aspect of human life.

Sex Role and Race

Children's self-esteem is also affected by their attitudes toward their sex and race. Sex role refers to those expectations and obligations children believe are associated with being either male or female. If children have a low opinion about their sex or their race they may feel trapped in a body they do not want. This personal rejection slowly erodes

whatever self-belief they may have, giving self-hate space
to grow.

Stories can promote self-esteem by showing males and
females and characters of all races engaging in a wide
range of competent and productive behavior.

Critics of fairy tales may complain that females are too
often portrayed as dependent, indecisive, and weak. But
some fairy tales show females acting courageously in overcoming obstacles to a goal. The young girl who rescues her
brothers in *The Seven Ravens,* by the Brothers Grimm, and
the young girl who journeys far and wide to rescue her
young friend in *The Snow Queen,* by Hans Christian Andersen, are just a few examples. Even a casual glance
through Andrew Lang's classic collection of fairy tales com-
piled at the turn of the century (for example, *The Red
Fairy Tale Book, The Green Fairy Tale Book*) reveals a
large number of stories with heroic female characters. Fairy
tale heroines typically reach their goals through quick
thinking and intelligence rather than force. In many stories their courageous and determined action reveals inner
qualities of strength and compassion.

Recent books have also been showing tenderness and
caring in male characters. Good examples include *I'll Always Love You,* by Hans Wilhelm, and *Ben's Baby,* by
Michael Foreman. Books like *Juma and the Magic Jinn,*
by Joy Anderson, *The Patchwork Quilt,* by Valerie Flournoy,
The Girl Who Loved Wild Horses, by Paul Goble, and *The
Weaving of a Dream,* by Marilee Heyer, show characters of
different races engaging in compassionate, assertive, and
heroic action. The tales in Andrew Lang's collections come
from around the world and retain the racial and cultural
identities of the original characters.

We should be aware of the potential stereotypes conveyed in the stories we read to our children. The key is to
read a wide variety of good stories, some showing females
and males as active and independent, others showing them
as nurturing and compassionate. The same can be said for
stories with characters of different races. If the only story
we read to our children is *Cinderella* then we can expect

them to form a distorted, limited view of female experience and ambition. But there is nothing wrong with *Cinderella* if it is balanced by stories like *The Snow Queen.*

Inequities still exist in the field of children's literature. We need more books featuring females as primary characters in the stories. Although a large number of wonderful books have nonstereotyped female characters, the majority of books still tend to focus on male characters. The same is true for racial and ethnic backgrounds. Handicapped children are noticeably absent from children's literature, although there are notable exceptions (e.g., *Knots on a Counting Rope,* by Bill Martin, Jr., and John Archambault, and *The Seeing Stick,* by Jane Yolen).

You Are Filled with Life and Energy

Young children's sense of self-worth is closely related to their capacity for action. Between three and eight months they can engage in purposeful behavior by deliberately trying to make something move. By twenty-four months they are aware of what they can and cannot do. At about two years of age there is an increase in the number of "I play . . ." "I do . . ." declarations they make to others. "Look at me!" they mean to say. "Watch what I can *do!*"

When asked to describe themselves, three- to five-year olds will refer to actions more than physical descriptions. They are more likely to say, "I walk to school," or "I jump rope," than "I am tall," or "I have brown hair." Older children, however, describe themselves in terms of how their abilities compare to those of others. To describe themselves, these older children may say something like, "I can ride a bike better than Jamie." For all children, the ideas of engaging in action, of accomplishing something, of having some control over one's life are critical for self-esteem.

Stories contribute to this sense of competence when they emphasize the spark of life, the exuberant greeting of the world that is the trademark of a child in love with existence. The books of Nancy White Carlstrom emphasize this overflowing sense of life and energy. Her lovable and curious Jesse Bear typifies this playful attitude. In *Jesse Bear, What Will You Wear?* we follow Jesse Bear's adventures throughout the day. His morning begins with his mother's question:

> Jesse Bear, what will you wear?
> What will you wear in the morning?
> My shirt of red
> Pulled over my head
> Over my head in the morning.
> I'll wear my pants
> My pants that dance
> My pants that dance in the morning.

Jesse Bear wears everything that day—a rose between his toes, sand on his hands, rice in his hair, and pj's with feet and a face on the seat. Why not? The day is filled with sunny, warm weather and fun things to do, whether playing in his sandbox, chasing a butterfly, or having lunch. If you like the world so much why not wear it? By the end of the day, Jesse is ready for bed and something else special to wear.

> Sleep in my eyes
> And stars in the skies
> Moon on my bed
> And dreams in my head
> That's what I'll wear tonight.

We continue to follow Jesse's adventures in *Better Not Get Wet, Jesse Bear.* Like a lot of other children, Jesse loves to play with water. Despite repeated warnings, he just cannot resist getting wet. Whether helping his mother with the dishes or his father water the flowers, Jesse Bear manages to drench himself and everything around him. When his parents find an acceptable outlet for his interest, they can relax, and Jesse can do what he wants to do. Bruce Degan's charming illustrations of Jesse and his patient and understanding parents perfectly complement Nancy White Carlstrom's whimsical verse.

In *Wild, Wild Sunflower Child Anna* we meet an energetic young girl in a bright yellow dress. Anna drifts and glides, runs and jumps her way through a brilliantly colored field of wild flowers. She smells and touches and floats on a sea of lush green grass. Shoes left behind, she tiptoes across a stream and climbs a tree. She stops to watch the ants ". . . in their dance pulling softly pulling," and the spiders ". . . spinning silent webs around the silver winking." Like the dialogue in the Jesse Bear books, Nancy White Carlstrom's text is a joy to read, filled with words that sparkle with color and energy. Jerry Pinkney's splashes of yellow, purple, green, and red spill across the page, reminding us of the warm summer days of our past.

Wild, Wild Sunflower Child Anna beckons us to hear nature's call, to rediscover our childlike capacity for wonder. Take off your shoes, feel the soft, cool earth, and take time to smell the flowers. These books put into words and pictures the feelings that children have about participating in the ebb and flow of life that flows around them. "There is a spark of life in you that is wonderful," they seem to say. "Greet the world; never lose the capacity for delight."

You Have a Unique Way of Relating to the World That Makes You Special

Every child has a unique way of relating to the world, an evolving style based on their physical abilities, temperament, and personal values. Self-esteem depends on recognizing and "coming to terms" with this style. Feeling at home with oneself means more than accepting physical characteristics. It also means being comfortable with one's choices and the consequences that result. A temperamentally shy child and her parents, for example, have to learn to adjust and build on this part of her personality. A boy who prefers painting and dancing rather than playing

STORYBREAK
┌─────────────────┐
└─────────────────┘

Pigs Stink

Once upon a time, in the wonderful town of Butterberry Hill . . .

Penelope Pig made a terrible discovery one day. Someone had written on a big sign just outside of Butterberry Hill, "PIGS STINK!" You could read it from a long way off because the words were splashed across the sign in bright red paint. Now, when Penelope the Pig read that sign she became mighty upset. Penelope hated being a pig. She thought everything associated with pigs, including herself, was awful. Now you know, and I know, that Penelope did not stink. She was the cleanest pig in Butterberry Hill. But when she saw that sign she thought, "I am a pig . . . so I stink. I'm just a good-for-nothing, stinky pig. Woe is me. . . ." Penelope started to cry. And she cried and cried.

Then she had an idea. She could just sweeten herself up a little. So she went to the store and bought a huge bottle of cheap perfume. She ran home and sprayed it all over her body. Then she put on even more to be sure. Wow! Penelope thought she smelled great. But now no one could stand to be around Penelope because that perfume really smelled disgusting. It smelled like old fish ground up with rotten flowers.

Poor Penelope. She stopped to talk to Casey, but he hurried away. Briarbutton the Rabbit stopped to ask her about a recipe. But he ran away before she could finish. "I must not have put on enough of that perfume," she thought. So she went back home and put on even more. She even took a shower in it. But now no one would even come near her. "Poor me," she thought. "I'm just a stinky pig."

Now there was one person who would stop and talk to her. Grandpa Jake saw Penelope and how sad she looked. He walked up to her but stopped when he noticed the terrible odor. "What smells so bad, Penelope?" he asked. "It's just me, Grandpa Jake. I'm a stinky pig." "I never noticed that smell before!" Grandpa Jake responded. "Is that perfume you are wearing?"

Penelope told Grandpa Jake all about the sign and how she tried to cover up her piggy smell with the perfume. When she was finished Grandpa Jake told her, "Penelope, you are the cleanest, sweetest-smelling creature in Butterberry Hill. You do not stink at all. That sign is wrong, because it is not true for you." Just to make sure Penelope was listening he told her the same thing again. Penelope knew that Grandpa Jake never, ever told a lie. So she went home right away and took another shower . . . this time with soap and water.

They never did find out who made the nasty sign. Some say, though, that Rodney was seen not long afterward with a little red paint on his nose.

football has to learn to accept his talents in a world that emphasizes sports.

Some stories give children permission to be different from others, to be faithful to themselves by finding and then following their own way. They acknowledge that friends and authority figures may pressure them to change, to become something that makes them uncomfortable, and that being different can bring them into conflict with others.

The Story of Ferdinand, by Munro Leaf, about the lovable bull who prefers smelling flowers to being aggressive, is still popular today even though it was written in 1936. Ever since he was a calf, Ferdinand loved to sit in the shade all day among the flowers. During a visit by a group of dignitaries looking for a mighty bull to fight in the ring, Ferdinand is stung by a bee. The startled Ferdinand goes berserk with pain and begins leaping into the air and pawing the ground. Of course, the visitors see him and choose him for the ring for what they think is his ferocious nature.

But when he later finds himself in the middle of the ring, Ferdinand notices the flowers in all the women's hair. Instead of pawing and snorting, he just sits quietly and smells. The banderilleros, the picadores, and the matador can do nothing to make Ferdinand fight. So he is returned to his home and the hill with the sweet-smelling flowers. Ferdinand is not a coward. He is a peaceful creature by nature who has no desire to be aggressive and violent.

Denys Cazet introduces us to a child who has a difficult time being successful at school in *Frosted Glass*. Gregory would rather draw a city than do his math. While the other children play at recess, he would much rather watch big machines working across the street. During art class his drawing of a vase and flowers becomes a rocket ship blasting through space. Gregory likes mechanical things. Instead of criticizing his work, though, Gregory's teacher recognizes his talent and gives his drawing a central location in the collection of finished art work.

Being different can be lonely. Oliver Button doesn't like to do the things that boys usually do. In *Oliver Button is a Sissy* Tomie dePaola gives us a glimpse of the isolation children may feel when they refuse to live up to other people's expectations. Oliver is a lot like Gregory and Ferdinand the bull. He prefers walking in the woods or drawing and reading to playing ball. But what he really likes to do is dance. And, almost every day, the boys tease him. Someone even writes "Oliver Button is a Sissy!" on the school wall. But Oliver continues to attend dancing school because that's what he wants to do.

Oliver signs up for a talent show at the movie theater. His teacher encourages the class to attend and cheer him on. Oliver dances his best in the competition but loses to the baton twirler. When the award is handed out he tries not to cry. His parents and dance teacher try to console him. His father tells him, "Never mind . . . we are taking our great dancer out for a great pizza. I'm so proud of you." But Oliver does not want to go to school the next day. Fortunately, when he arrives at school his fear of further ridicule vanishes when he sees another message written on the school wall: "Oliver Button is a Star!"

In *Shy Charles*, Rosemary Wells introduces us to a special young boy who is painfully shy. His parents are concerned about his timidity. So his mother enrolls him in a ballet class. But Charles spends all his time pretending to be asleep. His father involves him in football. But the coach says Charles looks sick. That evening, Charles shows everyone that he can take action when a genuine emergency exists as he rescues his baby sitter after she falls down the stairs. Maybe now his parents will accept his shyness.

Ferdinand, Gregory, Oliver Button, and Charles are all trying to come to terms with personal qualities that set them apart from others. Their stories show both the problems and advantages of being a nonconformist. They are simply trying to live up to their own nature. This theme provides encouragement to all children who have to make a choice between acting according to what feels right or trying to live up to someone else's image of who they should be.

You Are an Individual with Your Own Likes and Dislikes

In addition to having a unique personal style, children also form opinions about what they like and dislike. These preferences contribute to their uniqueness. All children, for example, have favorite foods, games, clothes, or places to visit. Feeling comfortable with their choices contributes to self-esteem.

Many children's stories contrast likes and dislikes of characters. Aesop's fable, *The Town Mouse and the Country Mouse,* retold and illustrated by Janet Stevens, compares two different lifestyles. "The country mouse lived in a barn. He got up at sunrise and worked hard all day. The town mouse lived in a fancy apartment building. She ate breakfast in bed and was very lazy." When town mouse visits her country cousin, she soon realizes she is not suited to the casual pace of rural life.

> "This life is too slow for me . . . I'm going home. Why don't you come with me? I'll show you how *I* live. Then you will see what the good life is like."

So country mouse visits the city. Near disasters with traffic, a mousetrap, rich food, and snarling dogs show him that the city is no place for him. His town cousin might like the fast life, but he prefers a calm and easy-going lifestyle.

When the country mouse got back to his barn, he breathed a sigh of relief. "I've learned an important lesson," he thought to himself. "IT'S BETTER TO HAVE BEANS AND BACON IN PEACE THAN CAKES AND PIES IN FEAR."

Joan W. Blos makes a plea for tolerance of individual differences in *Old Henry,* illustrated by Stephen Gammell. Old Henry moves into a dilapidated old house on a hill overlooking his neighbors. He is content with the way he lives, though others wish he would clean his place up. But Henry never does. The neighbors try being friendly, but Henry refuses to accept either their food or their offers to help shovel his snow.

Now Henry, too, had his fill. That night he grumbled, "I never *will* live like the rest of them, neat and the same. I am sorry I came."

So Henry leaves, and the old house lies abandoned, dark and empty. The neighbors soon begin to miss the eccentric old man. Where has he gone and will he ever come back? Many of the neighbors reflect on his absence.

"Having him gone doesn't make us more right."
"Maybe some other time, we'd get along not thinking that somebody *has* to be wrong."
"And we don't have to make such a terrible fuss because everyone isn't exactly like us."

Henry misses his old home and his neighbors, too. He writes a letter to the mayor, telling him that he would like to return.

"If I mended the gate, and I shoveled the snow, would they not scold my birds? Could I let my grass grow?"

We see both sides willing to make a compromise, to respect each other's likes and dislikes in order to get along.

Each person, with his or her own individual likes and dislikes, is part of the patchwork quilt of humanity. Our uniqueness contributes to the overall pattern of the social fabric. Alison Lester introduces us to seven wonderfully diverse children in *Clive Eats Alligators*. We meet each of them as they begin their day with breakfast.

Frank eats granola. Celeste has tea and toast in bed. Nicky has a banana. Rosie likes eggs and bacon. Tessa eats a sausage. Ernie has porridge. But Clive eats alligators.

Alligator Pops cereal, that is. Each child differs in terms of their clothes, play, pets, favorite treats, where they shop, and what they do to get ready for bed.

Young children will enjoy comparing Alison Lester's characters to each other, as well as contrasting themselves with each of the characters. *Clive Eats Alligators* is likely to prompt considerable discussion between parents and their children about what they like to do. Older preschoolers, though, may follow each child's choices throughout the day and form conclusions about each of their unique styles. For example, Rosie is a country girl who loves the outdoors, while Ernie is drawn to natural science. During the early years of grade school children gradually become more capable of realizing that they differ from others not simply because they look different or have different material possessions but because they have different thoughts and feelings.

You Are Growing and Changing in Many Ways

Another important aspect of children's self-awareness is the realization that they are growing and changing, acquiring new capabilities with the passage of time. Some stories focus on the eagerness children feel about growing older.

The Growing Story, by Ruth Krauss, is a classic example of stories with this theme. A young boy notices the growth of living things around his house and asks his mother, "Will I grow too?" "Of course you'll grow too," his mother replies. Time passes and each seasonal change is followed by another. The boy can see the growth around him, in the plants and animals around his home. But he is not so sure about himself. "Am I growing too?" he asks uncertainly. Again, his mother reassures him, "Oh yes, of course." Again and again he asks the same question. But no answer is satisfying until he tries to put on last year's winter clothes. Now he has a visible sign of his own growth—his clothes are too small!

Because change occurs so gradually, young children are not likely to be conscious of growing up. Like Ruth Krauss's young boy, children might find evidence of their growth from old clothes or a height chart on a closet door. We can also show pride in their new capabilities, pointing them out as signs of their increasing maturity.

Leo the Late Bloomer is another delightful book for young children about the uncertainties of growing up. Robert Kraus tells us, "Leo couldn't do anything right." He knew he couldn't do some of the things his friends could. His father fretted, and his mother waited patiently until ". . . one day in his own good time, Leo bloomed!" Leo masters some of his problems only after his parents come to accept his own unique timetable for development.

Children are drawn to *The Growing Story* and *Leo the Late Bloomer* because they know what it means to become frustrated with their limitations. But growth cannot be hurried. Attempts to hurry development or force learning are not only futile but damaging to self-esteem. What children need is gentle encouragement and patient acceptance.

In *Crazy Clothes* Niki Yektai has created another delightful child excited about the prospect of growing up. Patrick insists on putting on his own clothes.

"Mommy, come here! Sit down!" said Patrick. "I want you to watch me. I'm going to get dressed all by myself." "Good," said Mommy. "I'd love to watch. You're very grown up."

Patrick puts his pants on his head, wears his sweater as his pants, and can't quite get his shirt over his head. He puts his socks on his hands and puts his shoes on different feet. Patrick has a great time with his little joke. But by now his mother is becoming impatient. So Patrick tells her to close her eyes and count to a hundred. By the time she is finished he promises to have all his clothes on correctly.

Children love to have an audience to show off their new capabilities. "Watch *me* climb the stairs, Daddy!" or "See *me* ride my bike!" They need a sympathetic audience to confirm what they hope is true about themselves. Listeners will also appreciate Patrick's sense of humor in his performance and the silly way he wears his clothes.

Changes that accompany growing up can sometimes be confusing and aggravating. During a time of rapid change, children are constantly forming and then expanding their identities. Parents are challenged to keep pace and provide support for their children's efforts. *Nata,* by Helen Griffith, with illustrations by Nancy Tafuri, introduces us to a tiny fairy who does not act like her usual self. Nata teases the bees, spoils the spider's web, ties the cricket's feelers in a knot, and makes faces at the deer mice babies—not at all like her usual friendly self. Then she realizes that she is unable to fly. No one knows what is wrong, except for toad. He knows that each spring Nata sheds her wings and grows a new pair. But everyone, including Nata, forgets. As soon as the transformation takes place all the swamp creatures gather around to admire her new wings.

They were damp and heavy at first, but as she shook them out and spread them in the sun, they began to brighten and flash with colors.
"Like a rainbow!" exclaimed the spider.

STORYBREAK

Penelope Gets Her Wish

Once upon a time, in the wonderful town of Butterberry Hill . . .

Penelope Pig continued to be unhappy about being a pig. "I don't like pigs," she would say. "They stink, they are dirty, and they are fat. I am no pig. I am a *lady*!" Yes, poor Penelope did not like what she was. And no matter how hard she wished, Penelope could never stop being a pig. There was only one person who could help her, and that was Witch Wart. Now Witch Wart had magic for everything. But sometimes her magic didn't work quite right, and she always demanded something special as a price for her help.

"I want the little ballerina statue next to your bed," Witch Wart said when Penelope asked for her help. "You know, the one with the bright red dress and the golden tinsel crown." "Oh, no," Penelope thought. "That is my favorite thing." She thought for a moment and then announced, "Yes, you can have my ballerina. But you have to change me into something special, something that is not Penelope Pig."

Penelope went home and returned with her most favorite thing. As soon as the ballerina was placed on her shelf, Witch Wart went to work right away. She sat Penelope in the changing chair and began waving her magic wand over her head while she threw magic sparkly dust over her head. Suddenly, there was a POOF! There on the chair sat Penelope Bird. "I'm a bird!" Penelope chirped. And off she flew.

Now, it was very hot that day in Butterberry Hill. Pretty soon, Penelope Bird became very hot. "Oh, for a cool mud bath," she told herself. But bird bodies are not good for mud baths. So she returned to Witch Wart. "I want to be something different, something that can take a mud bath," she said. So Witch Wart put her back on the chair, said the words, tossed the magic sparkly dust, and POOF! there was Penelope Snake. "Oh, a snake," she hissed. "Snakes can slither through the cold mud." And off she went to cool off in the mud.

But pretty soon she became awful hungry. "Oh, for a taste of delicious corn," she told herself. But snakes cannot eat corn. So Penelope returned to Witch Wart once again. "I want to be something different, something that can eat corn." Now Witch Wart was becoming quite angry because of all the extra work she was doing. So when she said the magic words and threw the magic sparkly dust, the magic didn't work quite right. POOF! There was Penelope Tiger. "Oh, a tiger," she growled. "See how strong and swift I am!" And off she went to show everyone her new body. She was so excited she even forgot she was hungry.

But everyone in Butterberry Hill ran away from Penelope Tiger. To a lot of people, tigers are pretty fierce- and scary-looking creatures. No one would even get close to her. Pretty soon, Penelope started to feel lonely. She went back to Witch Wart once more. "I want to be something that likes the mud, eats corn, and does not scare anyone," she said. In just a few moments . . . POOF! There sat Penelope Pig. "What you really want to be is what you are, Penelope—a pig. You would not be happy as anything else." Penelope thought for a moment and decided maybe there were a few nice things about being a pig, after all. "Can I have my ballerina back?" she asked. "No, certainly not!" said Witch Wart. "Think of all the work I did!"

That night Penelope Pig went to bed a little happier about being a pig. But she was also sad about the little ballerina girl that used to sit next to her bed. But when she woke up next morning, there it was, just where it should be. Next to the little statue was a note. "Dear Penelope. If you are a pig, be the best pig you can be. Your friend, Witch Wart."

Once the change is completed, Nata returns to being her friendly old self.

These stories show that growth and development is part of nature's plan. Growing up involves a series of transformations, each characterized by a new level of skill and responsibility.

We All Have Natural Limitations on What We Can Do

Acceptance of physical limitations is another common theme in children's stories. Characters may want to be something contrary to their nature. As a result of some experience they may learn to value what they are capable of doing. They might also learn other ways to reach a goal. This issue is particularly important for children who have handicaps. Somehow we have to help all children learn to come to terms with their limitations while continuing to strive for worthwhile goals.

A turtle has his heart set on being something he is not in *I Wish I Could Fly* by Ron Maris. He wishes he could fly like a bird, jump like a frog, climb like a squirrel, or run like a rabbit. He sees no value in himself. But when it rains and the other animals get wet, he decides it's not so bad to be a turtle after all.

Michael Foreman introduces us to a cat who wishes he could fly in *Cat and Canary*. Cat is unusual because his best friend is a canary. Together they like to visit the rooftop of their apartment building. Cat's wish to fly finally comes true when he becomes entangled in the string of a runaway kite that lifts him into the air, high above the city.

Cat's initial ecstasy turns to fear as storm clouds cover the sun and gusty winds carry him over the icy river. Now he just wants to go back home. Just as he is about to give up, Canary appears with a large flock of birds to pull him back to their apartment building. " 'Oh, to be a cat,' he thought, 'to stay home where it's cozy and do nothing.' " With help from his friends he just might be able to fly again. Cat learns that ingenuity and cooperation can make some dreams come true.

Hot Hippo, by Mwenye Hadithi, tells the story of how the Hippo came to live in water. Hippo gazes at the "little fishes" that live in the river. "If I could live in the water," he thought, "how wonderful life would be." So Hippo humbly petitions Ngai, the god of Everything and Everywhere, to give him the capacity to live in water. Ngai agrees, with the condition that Hippo not eat his little fishes. Hippo runs all the way home and jumps in the water . . . only to sink like a stone. But wait! He can hold his breath while walking along the bottom. "And now and then he floats to the top and opens his huge mouth ever so wide and says, 'Look, Ngai! No fishes!' "

Turtle learns to recognize his own strengths. Cat learns to compensate for his capabilities. Hippo is given the opportunity to find his special place in the scheme of nature. Each responds in his own way to his limitations. In a similar way, children can learn to accept those limitations they cannot change. But they can also use their ingenuity or seek the assistance of someone who can help them overcome some of these limitations.

You Are a Worthwhile Person Regardless of Mistakes

Children can become quite impatient with themselves. They may find it difficult to accept their limitations or imperfections. Some stories emphasize that people are not perfect, that they make mistakes. Children may find these stories reassuring as they contemplate their own shortcomings.

Self-worth is an important theme in *Basil of Bywater Hollow,* by Jill Baker. Basil recognizes his bungling mistakes. First he tears his pants. Then he spills raspberries all over the kitchen floor. *"Now I've really made a mess of things!"* he thinks as he headed for his favorite spot down by the stream. *"I'm nothing but a big, clumsy bear!"* He tries to help the beaver family build a dam but succeeds only in sending their last log downstream. He breaks Holly the raccoon's clothesline and soils her clean clothes, then damages Nelson squirrel's kite. Poor Basil. With every misfortune he mutters to himself, "I can't do anything right. I'm just a big, clumsy bear."

Basil is apprehensive when he arrives at the Bywater

Hollow Fair to compete in the pie-eating contest. A fierce storm erupts during the contest, and the tent collapses on the contestants. Basil jumps on the table and lifts the tent high overhead, allowing his friends to escape. "Thank goodness Basil was here!" one of the animals shouts as they run for the shelter of the forest. Later, while sitting on the side of a hill with his friends and listening to music drifting up from the fair, Basil realizes he can do something right after all. Lynn Bywaters Ferris's accurately detailed illustrations of the forest animals are delightful to behold while giving a touch of realism to this story of a bear who finally saves the day.

Bungling is not the only problem children have. Forgetting can be a frustration, too. Dyan Sheldon introduces listeners to a child who has trouble remembering in *I Forgot*. Jake is always in a hurry. When he leaves the house he forgets to put on his shoes. He leaves his bike at the store. He overlooks the cat getting into mischief. After running out to the garden he forgets about the mud on his shoes. Then we find out why Jake was in such a hurry. He went to the store and picked a flower for his mother's birthday. He didn't forget the most important thing after all.

A young boy learns about self-worth in Beatrice Schenk de Regniers's book, *Everyone is Good for Something*, illustrated by Margot Tomes. The story begins on a sad note:

> There was this boy. His mother said he was good for nothing. And so the boy, too, thought he was good for nothing.

Jack and his poor widowed mother are close to starvation, so he leaves home to find work. Of course, who would hire a good-for-nothing? Despite a terrible opinion about himself, the boy has a kind heart. When a stranger hires him for a penny to throw a cat into the river, his merciful nature finally pays off. He removes the hungry cat from her prison and uses the penny to purchase a fish for her to eat. The cat leads Jack to a little sailboat. Jack falls asleep as the wind drifts them out to sea. When he awakes the cat is steering for a nearby island. In gratitude for his kindness she promises to help him make his fortune on the island. Apparently, the islanders were once known for their great cheese but have fallen on hard times because of the mice that have infested their home. Jack becomes a hero when he and the cat rid the island of its pests. In exchange for his help the islanders fill his boat with cheese. When he arrives at the mainland he sells the cheese and then returns triumphantly home.

Basil and Jack are very conscious of their bungling mistakes. Like many children they define themselves as failures. "I'm nothing but a big, clumsy bear," Basil tells himself. When he is asked about what he can do when he looks for work, Jack responds, "Nothing. I'm good for nothing." Jake will certainly arrive at the same conclusion if his mother continues to criticize him for his mistakes. In each story, though, something happens to make the characters realize that their low opinion about themselves is incorrect. Basil rescues his friends, Jack remembers his mother's birthday, and Jake helps the islanders. The tenderness children feel toward these characters as they learn of their misfortunes is likely to be translated into self-acceptance when they encounter problems of their own.

Summary

The people and things that surround us are ephemeral parts of our lives. Ultimately, each of us is alone. What we have is what stands before us in the mirror. Our life is measured not by the material things we gain or the number of friends that surround us, but by the character that resides within. Happiness begins with coming to terms with our nature, from learning to recognize what really counts. The stories we tell and the books we read to the children we love provide us with that opportunity to convey these and other important principles for living.

Afterword

The eight themes described in *From Wonder to Wisdom* summarize the major issues that affect adults' as well as children's sense of well-being in the world.

Each of us yearns to reach goals worthy of our lives. Like Scuffy the Tugboat seeking a greater world down river, children may dream about becoming policemen, doctors, ballerinas, nurses, or soldiers when they grow up. They long for a future filled with potential, one that can inspire their best efforts. Stories that show characters acting with fidelity toward their dreams can encourage children to form worthwhile goals and have hope in their future.

The pursuit of dreams requires both decisiveness and perseverance. We all struggle to overcome fears that heighten self-doubt and delay action. We look for courage to overcome obstacles that would interfere with progress toward our goals. Like the Little Engine That Could, children also want to believe in themselves. They too want the fortitude or inner strength to say no to a bully, confront the monsters in their closet, or risk falling as they learn to ride a bicycle. Stories that show characters overcoming

266

obstacles, escaping danger, and performing deeds of bravery can nurture courageous conviction.

Inner strength is nurtured by love and kinship. Each of us aches to be close to someone, to find companions on our journey. Children also need the support of friends. Like Hansel and Gretel, they want someone they can depend on to play with and share their difficult times. The love of a parent provides a safe haven, a place where courage can be slowly nurtured. The affection of friends is a special confirmation of children's self-worth. Love and devotion is a common theme in stories.

Loss and separation are also a part of forming attachments. We feel sad when separated from someone we love. We feel ourselves torn apart when faced with a tragic loss. Children experience grief too. Just as the Emperor mourned the loss of the precious Nightingale, children may cry after losing a favorite toy. In such stories as *Christmas Moon* and *Goodbye Rune*, they can also find sympathy for such tragic losses as the death of a grandparent or dear friend.

The experience of loss is a reminder of the preciousness of life. Regardless of how empty the world around us may seem, each of us has probably experienced a moment when we felt the distance between us and others reduced by an act of simple, unselfish kindness. St. George rescued the kingdom from the ravages of a fierce dragon; children may comfort a crying classmate, help a younger child get a drink of water, or share a cookie with a hungry friend. Stories that show characters giving, sharing, helping, or performing a rescue reinforce the importance of reaching out and using one's abilities to benefit others.

Making contact can be hindered by misconceptions we have about ourselves and others. To overcome these illusions we seek insight about ourselves and the realities that surround us. Yet we may also avoid that reality by pretending something is true when it is not or insisting something is not true when it is. Like the little boy in *The Emperor's New Clothes,* children prefer to face the world honestly. They have not learned how to hide behind masks or weave a web of pretense. Stories can encourage children to maintain this sense of honesty in their exploration of the world. They may also caution them about the dangers of deception.

Justice is an integral part of the world. Every act has its consequences. We know that restraint and thoughtfulness are necessary for success. Goldilocks's foolishness led to unfortunate consequences for the Three Bears. Children make mistakes too—they misuse a toy and it breaks; they hit someone and are hit in return. Stories can show the dramatic results of violence, misbehavior, greed, and dishonor.

Finally, regardless of the prosperity we achieve or the hard times that descend upon us, we know that what really counts is the true value we have for ourselves. We have nothing if we have no worth for the one who returns our mirrored gaze. Like the Ugly Duckling, children may sometimes feel overlooked and unlovable. Stories can affirm their dignity and worth.

Quality literature reflects children's experiences. But story concepts and themes are important for all of us, regardless of our age. The child of our youth is never really left behind. We never truly outgrow *Sleeping Beauty, The Little Engine that Could,* or *Where the Wild Things Are.* The literature described in this book can touch the fibre of *our* memories as well as the lives of our children. Storytime provides us with a powerful opportunity to talk to children about the important things in life while drawing us closer to the young people we love. We can use wonder to nurture wisdom.

If you would like information about WonderWise workshops and materials, contact:

Charles A. Smith, Ph.D.
Department of Human Development and
  Family Studies
Kansas State University
Manhattan, Kansas 66506

Bibliography of Children's Books

Age guidelines for these books are approximations only. In some cases children may be able to appreciate a book listed for younger or older children. Books that might appeal to children one year younger than the age category where it is listed are marked with a (-). Books that are likely to have special appeal to children in the next older age-range category are indicated with a plus sign (+). Books that would appeal to both older and younger children are marked with both signs.

So if you are looking for a good book for a five-year-old, examine the books in the section "Books Appropriate for Older Preschoolers." Then look through the previous section, "Books Appropriate for Young Preschoolers," for those titles with a plus (+). Then examine books listed in "Books Appropriate for Kindergartners and Early Grade-Schoolers," for those titles with a minus (–).

Books Appropriate for Young Preschoolers
(Two and Three Years Old)

The Adventures of Simple Simon, written and illustrated by Chris Conover. Farrar, Straus, Giroux, 1987. +

Albert's Toothache, by Barbara Williams; illustrated by Kay Charao. E. P. Dutton, 1974. +

Ben's Baby, written and illustrated by Michael Foreman, Harper and Row, 1987. +

Better Not Get Wet, Jesse Bear, by Nancy White Carlstrom; illustrated by Bruce Degen. Macmillan, 1988. +

Birdsong Lullabye, written and illustrated by Diane Stanley. William Morrow, 1985. +

Bobby Otter and the Blue Boat, written and illustrated by Margaret Burdick. Little, Brown, 1986. +

Chicken Little, retold and illustrated by Steven Kellogg. William Morrow, 1985. +

Clive Eats Alligators, written and illustrated by Alison Lester. Houghton Mifflin, 1986. +

Cock-a-doodle-doo, by Franz Bradenberg; illustrated by Aliki. Greenwillow Books, 1986.

Country Bear's Good Neighbor, by Larry Dane Brimner; illustrated by Ruth Tietjen Councell. Orchard Books, 1988. +

Crazy Clothes, by Niki Yektai; illustrated by Sucie Stevenson. Bradbury Press, 1988. +

Dad's Car Wash, by Harry Sutherland; illustrated by Maxie Chambliss. Atheneum, 1988. +

The Dead Bird, by Margaret Wise Brown; illustrated by Remy Charlip. Young Scott Books, 1965. +

December 24, written and illustrated by Denys Cazet. Bradbury Press, 1986. +

Do You Know What I'll Do?, by Charlotte Zolotow; illustrated by Garth Williams. Harper and Row, 1958. +

The Dream Child, written and illustrated by David McPhail. E. P. Dutton, 1985. +

A Fairy Went A-Marketing, by Rose Fyleman; illustrated by Jamichael Henterly. E. P. Dutton, 1986. +

Farm Morning, written and illustrated by David McPhail. Harcourt Brace Jovanovich, 1985. +

First Flight, written and illustrated by David McPhail. Little, Brown, 1987. +

Franklin in the Dark, by Paulette Bourgeois; illustrated by Brenda Clark. Scholastic, 1986. +

Furlie Cat, by Berniece Freschet; illustrated by Betsy Lewin. Lothrop, Lee and Shepard, 1986. +

George Told Kate, written and illustrated by Kay Chorao. E. P. Dutton, 1987. +

The Growing Story, by Ruth Krauss; illustrated by Phyllis Rowand. Harper and Row, 1947. +

Half Moon and One Whole Star, by Crescent Dragonwagon; illustrated by Jerry Pinkney. Macmillan, 1986. +

Hattie and the Fox, by Mem Fox; illustrated by Patricia Mullins. Bradbury Press, 1986. +

I Hear, written and illustrated by Rachel Isadora. Greenwillow Books, 1985.

I See, written and illustrated by Rachel Isadora. Greenwillow Books, 1985.

I Touch, written and illustrated by Rachel Isadora. Greenwillow Books, 1985.

I Spy at the Zoo, written and illustrated by Maureen Roffey. Four Winds Press, 1988.

I Spy on Vacation, written and illustrated by Maureen Roffey. Four Winds Press, 1988.

I Wish I Could Fly, written and illustrated by Ron Maris. Greenwillow Books, 1986.

I Forgot, by Dyan Sheldon; illustrated by John Rogan. Four Winds Press, 1988. +

I'm Going on a Dragon Hunt, retold by Maurice Jones; illustrated by Charlotte Firmin. Four Winds Press, 1987. +

In Our House, written and illustrated by Anne Rockwell. Crowell, 1985. +

Is Anyone Home?, written and illustrated by Ron Maris. Greenwillow Books, 1985. +

It's Just Me, Emily, written and illustrated by Anna Grossnickle Hines. Clarion Books, 1987. +

Jesse Bear, What Will You Wear?, by Nancy White Carlstrom; illustrated by Bruce Degan. Macmillan, 1986. +

Kitten in Trouble, by Maria Polushkin; illustrated by Betsy Lewin. Bradbury Press, 1988. +

Leo the Late Bloomer, by Robert Kraus; illustrated by Jose Aruego. E. P. Dutton, 1973. +

The Little Engine That Could, by Watty Piper; illustrated by George and Doris Hauman. Platt and Monk, 1954. +

The Little Red Hen, written and illustrated by Margot Zemach. Farrar, Straus and Giroux, 1983. +

Mouskin's Woodland Birthday, written and illustrated by Edna Miller. Prentice-Hall, 1974. +

Mushroom in the Rain, by Mirra Ginsburg; illustrated by Jose Aruego and Ariane Dewey. Macmillan, 1988. +

Night in the Country, by Cynthia Rylant; illustrated by Mary Szilagyi. Bradbury Press, 1986. +

No Jumping on the Bed!, written and illustrated by Tedd Arnold. Dial Books for Young Readers, 1987. +

Oliver Button Is a Sissy, written and illustrated by Tomie dePaola. Harcourt Brace Jovanovich, 1979. +

Once: A Lullabye, by bp Nichol; illustrated by Anita Lobel. Greenwillow Books, 1983. +

Play with Me, written and illustrated by Marie Hall Ets. Viking, 1955. +

Rebecca's Nap, by Fred Burstein; illustrated by Helen Cogancherry. Bradbury Press, 1988. +

Sam at the Seaside, by Keith Faulkner; illustrated by Jonathan Lambert. Macmillan, 1987. +

Sarah's Questions, by Harriet Ziefert; illustrated by Susan Bonners. Lothrop, Lee and Shephard, 1986. +

Scuffy the Tugboat, by Gertrude Crampton; illustrated by Tibor Gergely. Western, 1955. +

Shy Charles, written and illustrated by Rosemary Wells. Dial Books for Young Readers, 1988. +

Some Things Go Together, by Charlotte Zolotow; illustrated by Karen Gundersheimer. Thomas Y. Crowell, 1969. +

The Sun's Asleep Behind the Hill, by Mirra Ginsburg; illustrated by Paul O. Zelinsky. Greenwillow Books, 1982. +

That Olive, by Alice Schertle; illustrated by Cindy Wheeler. Lothrop, Lee and Shepard, 1986. +

Three Little Kittens, retold and illustrated by Paul Galdone. Clarion Books, 1986. +

Three Little Pigs, retold and illustrated by Paul Galdone. Clarion Books, 1970. +

The Tomten and The Fox, written and illustrated by Astrid Lindgren. Coward-McCann, 1966. +

Ton and Pon: Big and Little, written and illustrated by Kazuo Iwamura. Bradbury, 1984. +

Trilby's Trumpet, written and illustrated by Sarah Stapler. Harper and Row, 1988. +

The Two Giants, written and illustrated by Michael Foreman. Random House, 1967. +

Up and Down the Merry-Go-Round, by Bill Martin, Jr., and John Archambault; illustrated by Ted Rand. Henry Holt, 1988.

The Very Hungry Caterpillar, written and illustrated by Eric Carle. World, 1970.

Waiting, written and illustrated by Nicki Weiss. Greenwillow Books, 1981. +

Welcome, Little Baby, written and illustrated by Aliki. Greenwillow, 1987.

What is Beyond the Hill?, by Ernst Ekker; illustrated by Hilde Heyduck-Huth. J. B. Lippincott, 1985. +

When I'm Sleepy, by Jane R. Howard; illustrated by Lynne Cherry. E. P. Dutton, 1985. +

Books Appropriate for Older Preschoolers
(Four and Five Years Old)

The Accident, by Carol Carrick; illustrated by Donald Carrick. Clarion Books, 1976. +

Alexander and the Terrible, Horrible, No Good, Very Bad Day, by Judith Viorst; illustrated by Ray Cruz. Macmillan, 1972. +

Always, Always, by Crescent Dragonwagon; illustrated by Arieh Zeldich. Macmillan, 1984. +

The Amazing Voyage of Jackie Grace, written and illustrated by Matt Faulkner. Scholastic Hardcover, 1987. +

Amifika, by Lucille Clifton; illustrated by Thomas DiGrazia. E. P. Dutton, 1977. +

Angelina on Stage, by Katherine Holabird; illustrated by Helen Craig; Clarkson N. Potter, 1986. − +

Annie and the Wild Animals, written and illustrated by Jan Brett. Houghton Mifflin, 1985. − +

Apple Tree, written and illustrated by Peter Parnall. Macmillan, 1987. +

Baby Brother Blues, by Maria Polushkin; illustrated by Ellen Weiss. Bradbury Press, 1987. −

Baby Hugs, written and illustrated by Dave Ross. Thomas Y. Crowell, 1987. − +

Bad Egg: The True Story of Humpty Dumpty, by Sarah Hayes; illustrated by Charlotte Voake. Little, Brown, 1987.

Badger's Parting Gifts, written and illustrated by Susan Varley. Lothrop, Lee and Shepard, 1984. − +

Basil of Bywater Hollow, by Jill Baker; illustrated by Lynn Bywaters Ferris. Henry Holt, 1987. +

Ben and the Porcupine, by Carol Carrick; illustrated by Donald Carrick. Clarion Books, 1981. +

The Black Dog Who Went into the Woods, written by Edith Thacher Hurd; illustrated by Emily Arnold McCully. Harper and Row, 1980. +

A Book of Scary Things, by Paul Showers; illustrated by Susan Perl. Doubleday, 1977. +

The Boy Who Cried Wolf, written and illustrated by Tony Ross. Dial Books for Young Readers, 1985. +

Brave Irene, written and illustrated by William Steig. Farrar, Straus and Giroux, 1986. +

Caleb and Kate, written and illustrated by William Steig. Farrar, Straus and Giroux, 1977. +

The Castle Builder, written and illustrated by Dennis Nolan. Macmillan, 1987. +

Cat and Canary, written and illustrated by Michael Foreman. Dial Books for Young Readers, 1985. −

Chester and Uncle Willoughby, by Patricia Kier Edwards; illustrated by Diane Worfolk Allison. Little, Brown, 1987. +

Christmas Moon, written and illustrated by Denys Cazet. Bradbury Press, 1984. +

Cinderella, retold by Amy Ehrlich; illustrated by Susan Jeffers. Dial Books for Young Readers, 1985. +

Come Out and Play, Little Mousie, by Robert Kraus; illustrated by Jose Aruego and Ariane Dewey. Greenwillow Books, 1987. –

Crow Boy, written and illustrated by Taro Yashima. Viking, 1983. +

Cully Cully and the Bear, by Wilson Gage; illustrated by James Stevenson. Greenwillow Books, 1983.

Darkness and the Butterfly, written and illustrated by Ann Grifalconi. Little, Brown, 1987. +

The Dead Tree, by Alvin Tresselt; illustrated by Charles Robinson. Parent's Magazine Press, 1972. +

Doctor Rabbit's Foundling, by Jan Wahl; illustrated by Cyndy Szekeres. Pantheon Press, 1977. +

Dog for a Day, written and illustrated by Dick Gackenbach. Clarion Books, 1987. –

Donna O'Neeshuck Was Chased by Some Cows, by Bill Grossman; illustrated by Sue Truesdell. Harper and Row, 1988. – +

Don't Touch My Room, by Patricia Lakin; illustrated by Patience Brewster. Little, Brown, 1985. – +

The Emperor's New Clothes, by Hans Christian Andersen; retold by Anthea Bell; illustrated by Dorothee Duntze. North-South Books, 1986. +

Everyone Knows What a Dragon Looks Like, by Jay Williams; illustrated by Mercer Mayer. Four Winds Press, 1976. +

Everyone Is Good for Something, by Beatrice Schenk de Regniers; illustrated by Margot Tomes. Clarion Books, 1980. +

Eyes of the Dragon, written by Margaret Leaf; illustrated by Ed Young. Lothrop, Lee and Shepard, 1987. +

Family Under the Moon, by Nancy Jewell; illustrated by Leonard Kessler. Harper and Row, 1976. – +

Fang, by Barbara Shook Hazen; illustrated by Leslie Holt Morrill. Atheneum, 1987. –

A Father Like That, by Charlotte Zolotow; illustrated by Ben Schecter. Harper and Row, 1971. +

A Fish in His Pocket, written and illustrated by Denys Cazet. Orchard Books, 1987. +

Follow the Drinking Gourd, written and illustrated by Jeanette Winter. Alfred A. Knopf, 1988. +

The Foundling, by Carol Carrick; illustrated by Donald Carrick. Clarion Books, 1977. +

Freckles and Willie, by Margery Cuyler; illustrated by Marsha Winborn. Holt, Rinehart and Winston, 1986. – +

Frosted Glass, written and illustrated by Denys Cazet. Bradbury Press, 1987.

George and Martha, written and illustrated by James Marshall. Houghton Mifflin, 1972. – +

Georgia Music, by Helen V. Griffith; illustrated by James Stevenson. Greenwillow Books, 1986. +

Ghost's Hour, Spook's Hour, by Eve Bunting; illustrated by Donald Carrick. Clarion Books, 1987. +

The Gift, a wordless picture book illustrated by John Prater. Viking Kestrel, 1985. – +

Go and Hush the Baby, by Betsy Byars; illustrated by Emily A. McCully. Viking, 1971. – +

Goldilocks and the Three Bears, retold and illustrated by Lorinda Bryan Cauley. G. P. Putnam's Sons, 1981. –

Goldilocks and the Three Bears, retold and illustrated by Janet Stevens. Holiday House, 1986. –

Goldilocks and the Three Bears, retold by Armand Eisen; illustrated by Lynn Bywaters Ferris. Alfred A. Knopf, 1987. –

Good Night, Pippin, written and illustrated by Joan Elizabeth Goodman. Western, 1986. +

Goodbye Max, written and illustrated by Holly Keller. Greenwillow Books, 1987. – +

The Great Escape, a wordless picture book illustrated by Philippe Dupasquier. Houghton Mifflin, 1988. – +

The Green Lion of Zion Street, by Julia Fields; illustrated by Jerry Pinkney. Macmillan, 1988. +

Hansel and Gretel, retold by Rika Lesser; illustrated by Paul O. Zelinsky. Dodd, Mead, 1984. +

Happy Birthday, Grampie, by Susan Pearson; illustrated by Ronald Himler. Dial Books for Young Readers, 1987. +

Harald and the Giant Knight, written and illustrated by Donald Carrick. Clarion Books, 1982. +

Harald and the Great Stag, written and illustrated by Donald Carrick. Clarion Books, 1988. +

The Hare and the Tortoise, retold by Caroline Castle; illustrated by Peter Weevers. Dial Books for Young Readers, 1985.

Harry and the Terrible Whatzit, written and illustrated by Dick Gackenbach. Houghton Mifflin, 1978. −

Harry (The Monster), by Ann Cameron; illustrated by Jeanette Winter. Pantheon Books, 1980. −

Hiawatha, by Henry Wadsworth Longfellow; illustrated by Susan Jeffers. Dial Books for Young Readers, 1983. − + (all ages)

Hiawatha's Childhood, by Henry Wadsworth Longfellow; illustrated by Errol Le Cain. Farrar Straus and Giroux, 1984. − + (all ages)

Hot Hippo, by Mwenye Hadithi; illustrated by Adrienne Kennaway. Little, Brown, 1986. +

The House on Maple Street, by Bonnie Pryor; illustrated by Beth Peck. William C. Morrow, 1987. +

How Many Days to America, by Eve Bunting; illustrated by Beth Peck. Clarion Books, 1988. +

I Don't Care, by Marjorie Sharmat; illustrated by Lillian Hoban. Macmillan, 1977. − +

I Want Mama, by Marjorie Sharmat; illustrated by Emily Arnold McCully. Harper and Row, 1974. +

I Loved Rose Ann, by Lee Bennett Hopkins; illustrated by Ingrid Fetz. Alfred A. Knopf, 1976. +

I'll Always Love You, written and illustrated by Hans Wilhelm. Crown, 1985. − +

Ira Sleeps Over, written and illustrated by Bernard Waber. Houghton Mifflin, 1972. +

Island Rescue, written and illustrated by Charles E. Martin. Greenwillow Books, 1985. +

It's Perfectly True, adapted from Hans Christian Andersen; illustrated by Janet Stevens. Holiday House, 1988. +

Jack and the Whoopee Wind, by Mary Calhoun; illustrated by Dick Gackenbach. William Morrow, 1987.

A Kiss for Little Bear, by Else Holmelund Minarik; illustrated by Maurice Sendak. Harper and Row, 1968. – +

Knots on a Counting Rope, by Bill Martin, Jr., and John Archambault; illustrated by Ted Rand. Henry Holt, 1987. +

The Lady and the Spider, by Faith McNulty; illustrated by Bob Marshall. Harper and Row, 1986. – +

Liar, Liar, Pants on Fire, by Miriam Cohen; illustrated by Lillian Hoban. Greenwillow Books, 1985.

Lilly of the Forest, by Brian McConnachie; illustrated by Jack Ziegler. Crown, 1987.

Little Fox Goes to the End of the World, by Ann Tompert; illustrated by John Wallner. Crown, 1976. –

The Little Old Lady Who Was Not Afraid of Anything, by Linda Williams; illustrated by Megan Lloyd. Thomas Y. Crowell, 1986. +

Lizzie and Harold, by Elizabeth Winthrop; illustrated by Martha Weston. Lothrop, Lee and Shepard, 1986. +

The Loathsome Dragon, retold by David Wiesner and Kim Kahng; illustrated by David Wiesner. G. P. Putnam's Sons, 1987. +

The Lonely Prince, by Max Bolliger; illustrated by Jurg Obrist. Atheneum, 1982. – +

The Maggie B., written and illustrated by Irene Haas. Atheneum, 1975. – +

Making Babies, by Sara Bonnet Stein; photographed by Doris Pinney. Walker, 1974. +

The Mare on the Hill, written and illustrated by Thomas Locker. Dial, 1985. +

Michael, written and illustrated by Liesel M. Skorpen; illustrated by Joan Sandin. Harper and Row, 1975.

The Midnight Farm, by Reeve Lindbergh; illustrated by Susan Jeffers. Dial Books for Young Readers, 1987. – +

Miss Maggie, by Cynthia Rylant; illustrated by Thomas DiGrazia. E. P. Dutton, 1983. +

Miss Rumphius, written and illustrated by Barbara Cooney. Viking, 1982. +

The Monster Bed, by Jeanne Willis; illustrated by Susan Varley. Lothrop, Lee and Shepard, 1987. –

Monster Mary, Mischief Maker, written and illustrated by Kazuko Taniguchi. McGraw-Hill, 1976. – +

The Mother's Day Mice, by Eve Bunting; illustrated by Jan Brett. Clarion, 1986. – +

Mrs. Huggins and Her Hen Hanna, written and illustrated by Lydia Dabcovich. E. P. Dutton, 1985. – +

The Mud Pony, retold by Caron Lee Cohen; illustrated by Shonto Begay. Scholastic Hardcover, 1988. +

My Friend John, by Charlotte Zolotow; illustrated by Ben Shecter. Harper and Row, 1968. – +

The Mysteries of Harris Burdick, a wordless picture book illustrated by Chris Van Allsburg. Houghton Mifflin, 1984. +

Nadia the Willful, by Sue Alexander; illustrated by Lloyd Bloom. Pantheon Books, 1983. +

Nata, by Helen V. Griffith; illustrated by Nancy Tafuri. Greenwillow Books, 1985. +

Nathan's Fishing Trip, written and illustrated by Lulu Delacre. Scholastic Hardcover, 1988. –

No Friends, written and illustrated by James Stevenson. Greenwillow Books, 1986. +

Old Henry, by Joan W. Blos; illustrated by Stephen Gammell. William Morrow, 1987.

Once There Was a Tree, by Natalia Romanova; illustrated by Gennady Spirin. Dial Books for Young Readers, 1985. – +

Once Around the Block, by Kevin Henkes; illustrated by Victoria Chess. Greenwillow Books, 1987. –

One More Time, by Louis Baum; illustrated by Paddy Bouma. William Morrow, 1986. – +

One Frog Too Many, a wordless picturebook illustrated by Mercer Mayer and Marianna Mayer. Dial, 1985. – +

One Summer Night, written and illustrated by Eleanor Schick. Greenwillow Books, 1976. – +

Owl in the Garden, by Berniece Freschet; illustrated by Carol Newsom. Lothrop, Lee and Shepard, 1985. +

The Paper Crane, written and illustrated by Molly Bang. Greenwillow Books, 1985. +

The Patchwork Quilt, by Valerie Flournoy; illustrated by Jerry Pinkney. Dial Books for Young Readers, 1985. +

Patrick and Ted, written and illustrated by Geoffrey Hayes. Four Winds Press, 1984. – +

The Pied Piper of Hamelin, retold and illustrated by Mercer Mayer. Macmillan, 1987. +

The Polar Express, written and illustrated by Chris Van Allsburg. Houghton Mifflin, 1985. +

The Porcelain Cat, by Michael Patrick Hearn; illustrated by Leo and Diane Dillon. Little, Brown, 1987. +

Porcupine's Christmas Blues, written and illustrated by Jane Breskin Zalben. Philomel Books, 1982. – +

The Real Hole, by Beverly Cleary; illustrated by DyAnne DiSalvo-Ryan. William Morrow, 1986.

The Relatives Came, by Cynthia Rylant; illustrated by Stephen Gammell. Bradbury Press, 1985. +

The Ringdoves, retold and illustrated by Gloria Kamen. Atheneum, 1988. +

Rosalie, by Joan Hewett; illustrated by Donald Carrick. Lothrop, Lee and Shepard, 1987. +

Rosie and Michael, by Judith Viorst; illustrated by Lorna Tomei. Atheneum, 1974. +

Rumpelstiltskin, retold and illustrated by Paul Galdone. Clarion Books, 1985. +

Scary, Scary Halloween, by Eve Bunting; illustrated by Jan Brett. Clarion Books, 1986. +

The Season Clock, written and illustrated by Valerie Littlewood. Viking Kestrel, 1986. +

Seeing Stick, by Jane Yolen; illustrated by Remy Charlip and Demetri Maraslis. Thomas Y. Crowell, 1977. +

The Selkie Girl, retold by Susan Cooper; illustrated by Warwick Hutton. Macmillan, 1986. +

The Seven Ravens, retold and illustrated by Donna Diamond. Viking Press, 1979. +

Shadows, written and illustrated by John Canty. Harper and Row, 1987.

The Sign in Mendel's Window, by Mildred Phillips; illustrated by Margot Zemach. Macmillan, 1985. +

The Snowman Who Went for a Walk, by Mira Lobe; illustrated by Winfried Opgenoorth. William Morrow, 1984. −

Solomon the Rusty Nail, written and illustrated by William Steig. Farrar, Straus and Giroux, 1985. +

Song and Dance Man, by Karen Ackerman; illustrated by Stephen Gammell. Alfred A. Knopf, 1988. +

Soup for Supper, by Phyllis Root; illustrated by Sue Truesdell. Harper and Row, 1986. +

Star Mother's Youngest Child, by Louise Moeri; illustrated by Trina Schart Hyman. Houghton Mifflin, 1975. +

The Steadfast Tin Soldier, by Hans Christian Andersen; illustrated by David Jorgensen. Alfred A. Knopf, 1986. +

Stopping By Woods on a Snowy Evening, by Robert Frost; illustrated by Susan Jeffers. E. P. Dutton, 1978. − +

The Story of Ferdinand, by Munro Leaf; illustrated by Robert Lawson. Puffin Books, 1936.

Sylvester and the Magic Pebble, written and illustrated by William Steig. Prentice-Hall, 1969. +

That Dreadful Day, written and illustrated by James Stevenson. Greenwillow Books, 1985. +

The Tenth Good Thing about Barney, by Judith Viorst; illustrated by Erik Blegvad. Atheneum, 1971. +

There's a Nightmare in My Closet, written and illustrated by Mercer Mayer. Dial Books for Young Readers, 1968.

There's Nothing To Do!, written and illustrated by James Stevenson. Greenwillow Books, 1986. +

There's Something in My Attic, written and illustrated by Mercer Mayer. Dial Books for Young Readers, 1988.

Tiger Watch, by Jan Wahl; illustrated by Charles Mikolaycak. Harcourt Brace Jovanovich, 1982. +

Time for Uncle Joe, by Nancy Jewell; illustrated by Joan Sandin. Harper and Row, 1981. +

Toby's Toe, by Jane Goodsell; illustrated by Gioia Fiammenghi. William Morrow, 1986.

The Town Mouse and the Country Mouse, adapted and illustrated by Janet Stevens. Holiday House, 1987.

The Twelve Days of Christmas, illustrated by Jan Brett. Dodd, Mead, 1986. All ages.

Two Bad Ants, written and illustrated by Chris Van Allsburg. Houghton Mifflin, 1988. +

Two Monsters, written and illustrated by David McKee. Bradbury Press, 1985.

The Two of Them, written and illustrated by Aliki. Greenwillow Books, 1979. − +

The Unicorn and the Lake, by Marianna Mayer; illustrated by Michael Hague. Dial Books for Young Readers, 1982.

A Walk in the Rain, by Ursel Scheffler; illustrated by Ulises Wensell, G. P. Putnam's Sons, 1986. − +

Walls Are To Be Walked, by Nathan Zimelman; illustrated by Donald Carrick. E. P. Dutton, 1977.

What's the Matter Sylvie, Can't You Ride?, written and illustrated by Karen Born Andersen. Dial Books for Young Readers, 1981. +

Wheels, by Jane Resh Thomas; illustrated by Emily Arnold McCully. Clarion Books, 1986. −

When I Was Young in the Mountains, by Cynthia Rylant; illustrated by Diane Goode. E. P. Dutton, 1982. +

Where the River Begins, written and illustrated by Thomas Locker. Dial Books, 1984. +

Where the Wild Things Are, written and illustrated by Maurice Sendak. Harper and Row, 1963. +

Why Mosquitos Buzz in People's Ears, by Verna Aardema; illustrated by Leo and Diane Dillon. Dial Books for Young Readers, 1975. +

Wild, Wild Sunflower Child Anna, by Nancy White Carlstrom; illustrated by Jerry Pinkney. Macmillan, 1987.

Wilfrid Gordon McDonald Partridge, by Mem Fox; illustrated by Julie Vivas. Kane/Miller, 1985. +

Will It Be Okay?, by Crescent Dragonwagon; illustrated by Ben Shecter. Harper and Row, 1977. − +

Wings: A Tale of Two Chickens, written and illustrated by James Marshall. Viking Kestrel, 1986. – +

A Wolf Story, written and illustrated by David McPhail. Charles Scribner's Sons, 1981. – +

The Wreck of the Zephyr, written and illustrated by Chris Van Allsburg. Houghton Mifflin, 1983. +

The Zabajaba Jungle, written and illustrated by William Steig. Farrar, Straus and Giroux, 1987. +

Books Appropriate for Kindergarten and Early Grade-School Children
(Six and Seven Years Old)

Amy's Goose, by Efner Tudor Holmes; illustrated by Tasha Tudor. Thomas Y. Crowell, 1977. – +

Annie and the Old One, by Miska Miles; illustrated by Peter Parnall. Little, Brown, 1971. +

Beauty and the Beast, retold by Deborah Apy; illustrated by Michael Hague. Holt, Rinehart and Winston, 1983. +

The Boy Who Held Back the Sea, retold by Lenny Hort; illustrated by Thomas Locker. Dial Books, 1988. – +

The Changing Maze, by Zilpha Keatley Snyder; illustrated by Charles Mikolaycak. Macmillan, 1985. – +

East of the Sun and West of the Moon, written and illustrated by Mercer Mayer. Four Winds Press, 1980. – +

Faithful Elephants: A True Story of Animals, People and War, by Yukio Tsuchiya, translated by Tomoko Tsuchiya Dykes; illustrated by Ted Lewin. Houghton Mifflin, 1988. +

The Girl Who Loved Wild Horses, written and illustrated by Paul Goble. Bradbury Press, 1978. –

Goodbye Rune, written by Marit Kaldhol; illustrated by Wenche Oyen. Kane/Miller, 1987. +

The Happy Funeral, by Eve Bunting; illustrated by Vo-Dinh Mai, Harper and Row, 1982. – +

Juma and the Magic Jinn, by Joy Anderson; illustrated by Charles Mikolaycak. Lothrop, Lee and Shepard, 1986. – +

The Lie, by Ann Helena; photographed by Ellen Pizer. Raintree Publishers, 1977.

Little Red Riding Hood, retold by Armand Eisen; illustrated by Lynn Bywaters Ferris. Alfred A. Knopf, 1988.

Little Red Riding Hood, written and illustrated by James Marshall. Dial Books for Young Readers, 1987. –

The Man Who Could Call Down Owls, by Eve Bunting; illustrated by Charles Mikolaycak. Macmillan, 1984. +

The Mountains of Tibet, written and illustrated by Mordicai Gerstein. Harper and Row, 1987. +

Mufaro's Beautiful Daughters, written and illustrated by John Steptoe. Lothrop, Lee and Shepard, 1987. +

The Nightingale, by Hans Christian Andersen; illustrated by Nancy Ekholm Burkert. Harper and Row, 1965. – +

The Old Man and the Bear, written and illustrated by Janosch. Bradbury Press, 1985. +

Once There Were No Pandas, by Margaret Greaves; illustrated by Beverly Gooding. E. P. Dutton, 1985. – +

Peter and the Wolf, by Sergei Prokofiev, translated by Maria Carlson; illustrated by Charles Mikolaycak. Puffin Books, 1986. +

Red Riding Hood, retold and illustrated by Trina Schart Hyman. Holiday House, 1983. –

The Rumor of Pavel and Paali, retold by Carole Kismaric; illustrated by Charles Mikolaycak. Harper and Row, 1988. +

Saint George and the Dragon, retold by Margaret Hodges; illustrated by Trina Schart Hyman. Little, Brown, 1984. – +

Sir Gawain and the Loathly Lady, retold by Selina Hastings; illustrated by Juan Wijngaard. Lothrop, Lee & Shepard, 1985. +

The Sleeping Beauty, retold and illustrated by Trina Schart Hyman. Little, Brown, 1977. – +

Sleeping Beauty, retold and illustrated by Mercer Mayer. Macmillan, 1984. – +

The Snow Queen, by Hans Christian Andersen, translated by Naomi Lewis; illustrated by Angela Barrett. Henry Holt, 1988. +

Snow White and the Seven Dwarfs, retold by Randall Jarrell; illustrated by Nancy Ekholm Burkert. Farrar, Straus and Giroux, 1972. − +

That Is That, by Jeanne Whitehouse Peterson; illustrated by Deborah Ray. Harper and Row, 1979. − +

The Ugly Duckling, by Hans Christian Andersen; retold by Marianna Mayer; illustrated by Thomas Locker. Macmillan, 1987. − +

The War Party, by William O. Steele; illustrated by Lorinda Bryan Cauley. Harcourt Brace Jovanovich, 1978. +

The Water of Life, retold by Barbara Rogasky; illustrated by Trina Schart Hyman. Holiday House, 1986. − +

The Weaving of a Dream, retold and illustrated by Marilee Heyer. Viking Kestrel, 1986. +

Wind Rose, by Crescent Dragonwagon; illustrated by Ronald Himler. Harper and Row, 1976. − +

Yonder, by Tony Johnston; illustrated by Lloyd Bloom. Dial Books for Young Readers, 1988. +

Books Appropriate for Older Grade Schoolers
(Eight Years and older)

The Green Fairy Tale Book, edited by Andrew Lang, Dover, 1976.

The Red Fairy Tale Book, edited by Andrew Lang, Dover, 1976.

Where Did I Come From?, by Peter Mayle; illustrated by Arthur Robbins. Lyle Stuart, 1973.

Wizard of Oz, by L. Frank Baum; illustrated by Michael Hague. Holt, Rinehart and Winston, 1982. +

References and
Suggested Reading

CHAPTER ONE

Applebee, Arthur N. *The Child's Concept of Story*. Chicago: University of Chicago Press, 1978. See pp. 74–76.

Bettelheim, Bruno. *The Uses of Enchantment: The Meaning and Importance of Fairy Tales*. New York: Alfred A. Knopf, 1976.

Bernstein, J. E. *Books to Help Children Cope With Separation and Loss*. New York: R. R. Bowker, 1983.

Bruner, Jerome. *Actual Minds, Possible Worlds*. Cambridge, Mass.: Harvard University Press, 1986. See pp. 11–43.

Campbell, Joseph, and Bill Moyers. *The Power of Myth*. New York: Doubleday, 1988.

Coles, Robert. *The Call of Stories: Teaching and the Moral Imagination*. Boston: Houghton Mifflin, 1989.

Favat, Andre. *Child and Tale: The Origins of Interest*. Urbana, Ill.: National Council of Teachers of English, 1977. See pp. 1–6.

Feinstein, David and Stanley Krippner. *Personal Mythology: The Psychology of Your Evolving Self*. Los Angeles: Jeremy P. Tarcher, 1988.

Gardner, Howard. "The Making of a Storyteller," *Psychology Today,* March (1982): 49–63.

Gardner, Richard. *Therapeutic Communication with Children: The Mutual Storytelling Technique.* New York: Science House, 1971.

Jalongo, Mary Renck. *Young Children and Picture Books: Literature from Infancy to Six.* Washington, D.C.: National Association for the Education of Young Children, 1988.

Lewis, C. S. *An Experiment in Criticism.* Cambridge: University Press, 1961.

Luthi, Max. *Once Upon a Time.* Bloomington, Ind.: Indiana University Press, 1976. See pp. 14, 70, and 138.

Moody, M. T. and H. K. Limper. *Bibliotherapy: Methods and Materials.* Chicago: American Library Association, 1971.

Murray, John P. and Barbara Lonnborg. *Children and Television: A Primer for Parents.* Boys Town, Neb.: The Boy's Town Center, 1988.

Piaget, Jean. *The Child's Conception of the World.* Totowa, N. J.: Littlefield, Adams and Co., 1975.

Rosen, Sidney. *My Words Will Go With You: The Teaching Tales of Milton H. Erickson.* New York: W. W. Norton, 1982.

Trelease, Jim. *The Read-Aloud Handbook.* New York: Viking Penguin, 1985.

Van Dongen, Richard. "Children's Narrative Thought, at Home and at School," *Language Arts* 641(1987): 79–87.

Vandergrift, Kay. *Child and Story: The Literary Connection.* New York: Neal-Schuman Publishers, 1980.

Yolen, Jane. "How Basic is SHAZAM?" *Childhood Education* February (1977): 186–191.

Yolen, Jane. *Touch Magic: Fantasy, Faerie, and Folklore in the Literature of Childhood.* New York: Philomel Books, 1981. See pp. 18–19, 72–73.

CHAPTER TWO

Baker, Augusta. *Storytelling: Art and Technique.* New York: Bowker, 1977.

Children's Book Council. *Choosing a Child's Book.* A pamphlet available from The Council at 67 Irving Place, New York, NY 10003.

Lamme, Linda Leanord, and Athol B. Packer. "Bookreading Behaviors of Infants." *The Reading Teacher* February (1986): 504–509.

Lent, Blair. "There's Much More to the Picture than Meets the Eye." In Robert Bator, ed., *Signposts to Criticism of Children's Literature.* Chicago: American Library Association, 1983, pp. 156–161.

Lewis, C. S. *An Experiment in Criticism.* Cambridge: Cambridge University Press, 1961.

Livo, Norma J., and Sandra A. Rietz. *Storytelling: Process and Practice.* Littleton, Colo.: Libraries Unlimited, 1986.

Lukens, Rebecca. *A Critical Handbook of Children's Literature.* Glenview, Ill.: Scott, Foresman, 1986.

Magee, Mary Ann, and Brian Sutton-Smith. "The Art of Storytelling: How Do Children Learn It?" *Young Children* May (1983): 4–12.

Maguire, Jack. *Creative Storytelling: Choosing, Inventing, and Sharing Tales for Children.* New York: McGraw-Hill, 1985.

Sawyer, Ruth. *The Way of the Storyteller.* New York: Viking, 1962.

Shulevitz, Uri. *Writing With Pictures.* New York: Watson-Guptill, 1985.

CHAPTER THREE

Buhler, Charlotte, and Fred Massarick. *The Course of Human Life.* New York: Springer, 1968.

Frank, Victor E. *Man's Search for Meaning.* New York: Harper and Row, 1977.

Singer, Dorothy and Jerome Singer. *Partners in Play: A Step-by-Step Guide to Imaginative Play in Children.* New York: Harper and Row, 1977.

Sutton-Smith, Brian, and Shirley Sutton-Smith. *How to Play With Your Children (and When Not To)*. New York: Hawthorn Books, 1974.

CHAPTER FOUR

Joseph, Steven M. *Children in Fear*. New York: Holt, Rinehart and Winston, 1974.

Kellerman, Jonathan. *Helping the Fearful Child*. New York: W. W. Norton, 1981.

May, Rollo. *Power and Innocence*. New York: W. W. Norton, 1972.

Sarafino, Edward P. *The Fears of Childhood: A Guide to Recognizing and Reducing Fearful States in Children*. New York: Human Sciences Press, 1986.

Wolman, Benjamin. *Children's Fears*. New York: Grosset and Dunlap, 1978.

CHAPTER FIVE

Corsaro, William. *Friendship and Peer Culture in the Early Years*. Norwood, N. J.: Ablex, 1985.

Dodge, Kenneth, David Schlundt, Iris Schocken, and Judy Delugach. "Social Competence and Children's Sociometric Status: The Role of the Peer Group Entry Strategies." *Merrill-Palmer Quarterly* 29(1983): 309–336.

Kaye, Kenneth. "Organism, Apprentice, and Person." In Edward Z. Tronick, ed., *Social Interchange in Infancy*. Baltimore: University Park Press, 1982, pp. 183–196.

Ladd, Gary W., and Elizabeth Emerson. "Shared Knowledge in Children's Friendships." *Developmental Psychology* 20(1984): 932–940.

Montagu, Ashley. *Touching*. New York: Columbia University Press, 1971, pp. 81–160.

Piaget, Jean. *The Moral Judgement of the Child*. New York: The Free Press, 1965.

CHAPTER SIX

Bluebond-Langner, Myra. "Meanings of Death to Children." In Herman Feifel, ed., *New Meanings of Death*. New York: McGraw-Hill, 1977, pp. 48–56.

Bowlby, John. *Attachment and Loss*. New York: Basic Books, 1969–1981.

Bowlby, John. "Grief and Mourning in Infancy and Early Childhood." *The Psychoanalytic Study of the Child* 15(1960): 9–52.

Childers, P., and M. Wimmer. "The Concept of Death in Early Childhood." *Child Development* 42(1971): 1299–1301.

Frey, William H. *Crying: The Mystery of Tears*. Minneapolis: Winston Press, 1985.

Grollman, E. A., ed. *Explaining Divorce to Children*. Boston: Beacon Press, 1969.

Jewett, Claudia. *Helping Children Cope With Separation and Loss*. Harvard, Mass.: Harvard Common Press, 1982.

Kubler-Ross, Elizabeth. *On Death and Dying*. New York: Macmillan, 1979.

Melear, J. D. "Children's Conceptions of Death." *Journal of Genetic Psychology* 123(1973): 359–360.

Nagy, Maria. "The Child's Theories Concerning Death." *Journal of Genetic Psychology* 73(1948): 3–27.

Ordal, Carol C. "Death as Seen in Books Suitable for Young Children." *Omega* 14(1983–84): 249–277.

Piaget, Jean. *The Child's Conception of the World*. New York: Harcourt Brace, 1929.

Salk, Lee. *What Every Child Would Like Parents to Know About Divorce*. New York: Harper and Row, 1978.

Schaefer, Dan and Christine Lyons. *How Do We Tell the Children?* New York: Newmarket Press, 1986.

Speece, Mark W., and Sandor Brent. "Children's Understanding of Death: A Review of Three Components of a Death Concept." *Child Development* 55(1984): 1671–1686.

Veninga, Robert. *A Gift of Hope*. Boston: Little, Brown, 1985.

Wass, Hannelore, and Charles Corr. *Childhood and Death*. New York: Hemisphere, 1984.

CHAPTER SEVEN

Berman, Phyllis W. "Children Caring for Babies: Age and Sex Differences in Response to Infant Signals and to the Social Context." In Nancy Eisenberg, ed., *Contemporary Topics in Developmental Psychology*. New York: John Wiley, 1987, pp. 141–164.

Hoffman, Martin L. "Developmental Synthesis of Affect and Cognition and its Implications for Altruistic Motivation." *Developmental Psychology* 11(1975): 607–622.

Johnson, Daniel B. "Altruistic Behavior and the Development of the Self in Infants." *Merrill-Palmer Quarterly* 28(1982): 379–388.

Mussen, Paul, and Nancy Eisenberg-Berg. *Roots of Caring, Sharing, and Helping*. San Francisco: W. H. Freeman, 1977.

Radke-Yarrow, Marion, and Carolyn Zahn-Waxler. "Roots, Motives, and Patterns in Children's Prosocial Behavior." In Ervin Staub, Daniel Bar-Tal, Jerzy Karylowski, and Janusz Reykowski, eds., *Development and Maintenance of Prosocial Behavior*. New York: Plenum Press, 1984, pp. 81–100.

Rheingold, Harriet L. "Little Children's Participation in the Work of Adults, a Nascent Prosocial Behavior." *Child Development* 53(1982): 114–125; Rheingold, Harriet L., Dale F. Hay, and Meredith West. "Sharing in the Second Year of Life." *Child Development* 47(1976): 1148–1158.

Schulman, Michael, and Eva Mekler. *Bringing Up a Moral Child*. Reading, Mass.: Addison-Wesley, 1985.

Smith, Charles A. *Promoting the Social Development of Young Children*. Palo Alto, Calif.: Mayfield, 1982.

Staub, Ervin. "The Influence of Age and Number of Witnesses on Children's Attempts to Help." *Journal of Personality and Social Psychology* 14(1970): 130–140.

———. "Helping a Person in Distress: The Influence of Implicit and Explicit 'Rules' of Conduct on Children and Adults." *Journal of Personality and Social Psychology* 17(1971): 137–144.

CHAPTER EIGHT

Jensen, Larry C. *That's Not Fair*. Provo, Utah: Brigham Young University Press, 1977.

Goleman, Daniel. *Vital Lies, Simple Truths: The Psychology of Self-Deception*. New York: Simon and Schuster, 1985.

Snyder, Martha, Ross Snyder, and Ross Snyder, Jr. *The Young Child as a Person*. New York: Human Sciences Press, 1980.

CHAPTER NINE

Crum, Thomas F. *The Magic of Conflict*. New York: Simon and Schuster, 1987.

Schmookler, Andrew B. *Out of Weakness: Healing the Wounds that Drive Us to War*. New York: Bantam, 1988.

Shure, Myrna B., and George Spivak. *Problem-Solving Techniques in Childrearing*. San Francisco: Jossey-Bass, 1978.

Smith, Charles A. "Puppetry and Problem-Solving Skills." *Young Children* March(1979): 4–11.

Spivak, George, Jerome Platt, and Myrna B. Shure. *The Problem-Solving Approach to Adjustment*. San Francisco: Jossey-Bass, 1976.

CHAPTER TEN

Briggs, Dorothy Corkville. *Your Child's Self-Esteem*. Garden City, N.Y.: Doubleday, 1970.

Clarke, Jean Illsley. *Self-Esteem: A Family Affair*. Minneapolis: Winston Press, 1978.

Coopersmith, Stanley. *The Antecedents of Self-Esteem*. San Francisco: W. H. Freeman, 1967.

Damon, William, and Daniel Hart. "The Development of Self-Understanding from Infancy through Adolescence." *Child Development* 53(1982): 841–864.

Glenn, Stephen, and Jane Nelson. *Raising Children for Success*. Fair Oaks, Calif.: Sunrise Press, 1987.

Leahy, Robert L. *The Development of the Self*. New York: Academic Press, 1985.

Singer, Dorothy, and Jerome Singer. *Partners in Play: A Step-by-Step Guide to Imaginative Play in Children.* New York: Harper and Row, 1977.

Smith, Charles A. *I'm Positive: Growing Up With Self-Esteem.* Manhattan, Kans.: Kansas State University Extension Service, 1988.

Subject Index

Goal seeking, how stories
contribute to, 43–45
Goals,
commitment to, 51–55
nutured by the imagina-
tion, 48–51
ownership of, 51–52
persevering toward, 55,
58–60
as a personal journey,
45–48
provide a purpose, 42–43
Greed, consequences of,
227–29
Grief, *see* death, loss;
sadness
Growing up and change,
257–59, 261

Handicaps, 249, 262–63
Helping, 160–64. *See also*
kindness
as an expression of love,
99
as a way of overcoming
fear, 75–80
by young children, 163–64
Home, as a place of security,
95–97
Honesty, 175–76

Illustrations, evaluating the
quality of, 30
Imagination
compliments rational thinking, 51
as a foundation for one's
personal dream, 48–51

confronting fears in the,
71–72, 74
Innocence, loss of, 173–76

Justice, as a common theme
in stories, 158–59

Kindness, forms of
caretaking, 104–05, 151–53
comforting, 145–51
generosity, 98–99, 156–60
helping, 75–80, 99, 160–64
as promoted in stories,
144–45
protection, 164–67
rescuing, 167–71
sharing, 153–56

Life cycle, 123–25
Life and energy, 249–51
Limitations, natural, 262–63
Linkage of actions, 211–16
Loss. *See also* death; sadness
funerals and, 137–38
happy memories and, 134–37
and separation, 118–22
how stories help children
come to terms with,
113–15
Love, 91–93, 97–101. *See
also* friends
Lying, *see* deception

Misbehavior, consequences
of, 226–27

Author Index

Aardema, Verna, 212
Ackerman, Karen, 50
Aesop, 7, 58, 197, 255
Alexander, Sue, 136
Aliki, 91, 99
Andersen, Hans C., 7, 19, 55,
    113, 146, 177, 193,
    235, 248
Andersen, Karen B., 43, 82
Anderson, Joy, 248
Archambault, John, 179, 237
Arnold, Tedd, 220, 221
Baker, Jill, 263
Bang, Molly, 158
Baum, Louis, 121
Berman, Phyllis, 148
Bettelheim, Bruno, 14
Bloom, Lloyd, 96
Blos, Joan W., 256
Bluebond-Langner, Myra,
    126
Bolliger, Max, 117
Bonners, Susan, 183
Bourgeois, Paulette, 69
Bowlby, John, 130
Brandenburg, Franz, 179
Brett, Jan, 108, 156
Brewster, Patricia, 154

Brimner, Larry D., 159
Brown, Margaret Wise, 137
Buhler, Charlotte, 42
Bunting, Eve, 17, 29, 74,
    96, 98, 137, 223
Burdick, Margaret, 218
Burkert, Nancy Ekholm, 194
Burstein, Fred, 100
Byars, Betsy, 148
Calhoun, Mary, 219
Cameron, Ann, 77
Canty, John, 72
Carlstrom, Nancy White,
    249, 251
Carrick, Carol, 70, 133, 152
Carrick, Donald, 70, 123,
    166, 208
Cauley, Lorinda Byran, 208
Cazet, Denys, 29, 33, 35,
    114, 137, 199, 254
Chambliss, Maxie, 239
Cherry, Lynne, 30, 85
Chesterton, C. K., 60
Chorao, Kay, 195
Cleary, Beverly, 53
Clifton, Lucille, 75
Cohen, Caron Lee, 161
Cohen, Miriam, 198